The Meaning of
Marriage Payments

STUDIES IN ANTHROPOLOGY

Under the Consulting Editorship of E. A. Hammel,
UNIVERSITY OF CALIFORNIA, BERKELEY

Andrei Simić, THE PEASANT URBANITES: A Study of Rural-Urban Mobility in Serbia

John U. Ogbu, THE NEXT GENERATION: An Ethnography of Education in an Urban Neighborhood

Bennett Dyke and Jean Walters MacCluer (Eds.), COMPUTER SIMULATION IN HUMAN POPULATION STUDIES

Robbins Burling, THE PASSAGE OF POWER: Studies in Political Succession

Piotr Sztompka, SYSTEM AND FUNCTION: Toward a Theory of Society

William G. Lockwood, EUROPEAN MOSLEMS: Economy and Ethnicity in Western Bosnia

Günter Golde, CATHOLICS AND PROTESTANTS: Agricultural Modernization in Two German Villages

Peggy Reeves Sanday (Ed.), ANTHROPOLOGY AND THE PUBLIC INTEREST: Fieldwork and Theory

Carol A. Smith (Ed.), REGIONAL ANALYSIS, Volume I: Economic Systems, and Volume II: Social Systems

Raymond D. Fogelson and Richard N. Adams (Eds.), THE ANTHROPOLOGY OF POWER: Ethnographic Studies from Asia, Oceania, and the New World

Frank Henderson Stewart, FUNDAMENTALS OF AGE-GROUP SYSTEMS

Larissa Adler Lomnitz, NETWORKS AND MARGINALITY: Life in a Mexican Shantytown

Benjamin S. Orlove, ALPACAS, SHEEP, AND MEN: The Wool Export Economy and Regional Society in Southern Peru

Harriet Ngubane, BODY AND MIND IN ZULU MEDICINE: An Ethnography of Health and Disease in Nyuswa-Zulu Thought and Practice

George M. Foster, Thayer Scudder, Elizabeth Colson, and Robert Van Kemper (Eds.), LONG-TERM FIELD RESEARCH IN SOCIAL ANTHROPOLOGY

R. H. Hook (Ed.), FANTASY AND SYMBOL: Studies in Anthropological Interpretation

Richard Tapper, PASTURE AND POLITICS: Economics, Conflict and Ritual Among Shahsevan Nomads of Northwestern Iran

George Bond, Walton Johnson, and Sheila S. Walker (Eds.), AFRICAN CHRISTIANITY: Patterns of Religious Continuity

John Comaroff (Ed.), THE MEETING OF MARRIAGE PAYMENTS

in preparation

Michael H. Agar, THE PROFESSIONAL STRANGER: An Informal Introduction to Ethnography

Eric B. Ross (Ed.), BEYOND THE MYTHS OF CULTURE: A Reader in Cultural Materialism

The Meaning of Marriage Payments

Edited by
J. L. COMAROFF
Department of Anthropology
University of Chicago
Chicago, Illinois, USA

1980

ACADEMIC PRESS
London · New York · Toronto · Sydney · San Francisco
A Subsidiary of Harcourt Brace Jovanovich, Publishers

Academic Press Inc. (London) Ltd
24—28 Oval Road
London NW1

US edition published by
Academic Press Inc.
111 Fifth Avenue,
New York, New York 10003, U.S.A.

British Library Cataloguing in Publication Data

The meaning of marriage payments. — (Studies
in anthropology; 7).
1. Bride price — Congresses
2. Dowry — Congresses
I. Comaroff, J   II. Series
392′.5   GN484.45   79-42827

ISBN 0-12-183450-6

Printed in Great Britain by Galliard (Printers) Ltd, Great Yarmouth

List of Contributors

R. H. Barnes, *Institute of Social Anthropology, University of Oxford, 51 Banbury Road, Oxford, OX2 6FF, England*

J. L. Comaroff, *Department of Anthropology, University of Chicago, 1126 East 59th Street, Chicago, Illinois 60637, U.S.A.*

D. Parkin, *Department of Anthropology, School of Oriental and African Studies, University of London, Malet Street, London WC1 7HP, England*

E. L. Peters, *Department of Social Anthropology, University of Manchester, Oxford Road, Manchester MI3 9PL, England*

D. B. Rheubottom, *Department of Social Anthropology, University of Manchester, Oxford Road, Manchester MI3 9PL, England*

A. J. Strathern, *Department of Anthropology, University College, University of London, Gower Street, London WC1E 6BT, England*

D. Turton, *Department of Social Anthropology, University of Manchester, Oxford Road, Manchester MI3 9PL, England*

Preface

For the uninitiated, making sense of what anthropologists have had to say about marriage, and, therefore, about marriage payments, cannot be easy. On the one hand, Meyer Fortes's celebrated opening statement in "Marriage in Tribal Societies" suggests that we know so much about the subject that "it might seem doubtful if anything new can be added" (p. 1); and, while Fortes later concedes the possibility of continuing theoretical innovation, he appears never to question the security of our ontological foundations in this field. Yet, not ten years later, Peter Rivière observes, with equal certitude, that "marriage as an isolable phenomenon of study is a misleading illusion".[1] How is it that, over a decade, comfortable certainty in some professional quarters has given way, in others, to such thorough-going scepticism? The answer clearly does not lie solely with evidence. There has been no sudden discovery of new data to startle us from our complacency; indeed, it is rarely by means of such empirical revelation that anthropological enquiry gains its momentum.

Perhaps the solution is to be found in the implications of the question itself. Some years ago, Geertz remarked that anthropological work on religion had made no theoretical advances since the 1940s; the "dead hand of competence" had ensured stagnation, a parasitic dependence upon the conceptual capital of our scholarly ancestors.[2] It would seem that a similar observation might be made in respect of the study of marriage. Within given orthodoxies, we have continued to debate and

---

[1] Marriage: A Reassessment, p. 57. In "Rethinking Kinship and Marriage", (ed.) R. Needham. London: Tavistock, 1971.

[2] Religion as a Cultural System, pp. 1-2. In "Anthropological Approaches to the Study of Religion", (ed.) M. Banton. London: Tavistock, 1960.

solve a host of ethnographic puzzles, to compound analytical examples, and to confirm our assumptions; in short, to account for the data which have steadily become available to us. But that is precisely the point: if we can account for everything so comfortably, the danger exists that the foundations of our assumptions might have been tautological and unchallengable in the first place. Thus, for example, Rivière's scepticism derives from the fact that anthropological approaches to the study of marriage have been almost exclusively functionalist in orientation: in essence, they assume that "marriage is what marriage does", a position which leads inexorably towards circular explanation.

The way out of the predicament, as Geertz, Leach and others have asserted for the discipline at large, clearly lies in the reconsideration of basic theoretical and methodological assumptions, and it was for this purpose that the symposium upon which the present volume is based was organized. Such collective efforts to 'rethink' well established themes are hardly novel, of course, but this makes them no less valuable. Quite the contrary, they are the intellectual life-blood of any scholarly tradition. Held at the University of Manchester in the winter of 1976-7, the symposium originally grew out of informal discussions among a few colleagues whose interests and anxieties had begun to converge. In our early deliberations concerning marriage and its associate prestations, some expressed the view, already manifest in other branches of anthropology, that we might allow ourselves more scope for analytical creativity if we substituted the orthodox concern for function with a focus on meaning and message; that is, if we sought to re-analyse familiar marriage transactions with particular reference to their semantic and symbolic properties. At the same time, an effort was made to avoid placing excessive constraints upon contributors. For, while thematic unity is important, its value is never absolute. Moreover, in recruiting participants, who included both members of the Manchester department and invited outsiders, some attention was given to geographical spread: East and Southern Africa, the Middle East, Melanesia, Indonesia and Yugoslavia are all represented. However, no attempt at full 'coverage', either regional or thematic, was made; given the diversity of the subject matter, such an ideal is in any case chimerical. As a result of these considerations, the essays included here are relatively diverse in their content, although they do display an underlying unity which is spelled out in the Introduction.

Obviously not all the contributors shared opinions on the central issues in question. The point of talking around a theme is not to arrive at consensus; it is, rather, to open or expand a universe of discourse. This, we would like to believe, is what our discussions set out to achieve. It is to be hoped that we succeeded, if nothing else, in giving impetus to an ongoing debate over fundamental concepts.

I should like to record our collective thanks to those of my former colleagues at Manchester who either gave actively of their support, or at least did not complain when, for several weeks, departmental corridors reverberated with single-minded conversation. I owe my personal gratitude to Jean Comaroff, whose affinal relationship to this volume cannot have been an easy one; not only has she tolerated its presence in our domestic lives, but has helped throughout with creative suggestions.

Chicago   JOHN COMAROFF
1980

Contents

List of Contributors   v

Preface   vii

Chapter 1
Introduction. J. L. COMAROFF   1

Chapter 2
The Central and the Contingent: bridewealth among the
   Melpa and the Wiru. A. J. STRATHERN   49

Chapter 3
The Economics of Mursi Bridewealth: a comparative
   perspective. D. TURTON   67

Chapter 4
Marriage, Exchange and the Meaning of Corporations
   in Eastern Indonesia. R. H. BARNES   93

Chapter 5
Aspects of Bedouin Bridewealth among
    Camel Herders in Cyrenaica. E. L. PETERS   125

Chapter 6
Bridewealth and the Control of Ambiguity in
    a Tswana Chiefdom. J. L. COMAROFF   161

Chapter 7
Kind Bridewealth and Hard Cash: eventing
    a structure. D. PARKIN   197

Chapter 8
Dowry and Wedding Celebrations in
    Yugoslav Macedonia. D. B. RHEUBOTTOM   221

Index   251

1 Introduction

JOHN COMAROFF

"There is only one method in social anthropology, the comparative method — and that's impossible."

E.E. Evans-Pritchard[1]

I

During the last twenty years or so, intermittent efforts have been made to evaluate the epistemological foundations and basic categories of anthropological discourse. These efforts, however, have had a limited impact upon the mainstream. Indeed, in many quarters, invocations to "re-think" fundamental concepts have been stoically ignored, notwithstanding the persuasiveness of some of the arguments involved; in others, the very notion of epistemological self-consciousness has been seen as ill-advised and even dangerous.[2] That such has been the case is due to a number of paradigmatic considerations (cf. e.g. Jarvie, 1964, 1965; Crick, 1976), as well as the fact that much polemical writing of this type has been predominantly negative. Nonetheless, having been given impetus some time ago by Leach (1961), the self-critical tendency appears to have gained identifiable momentum; enough, at

[1] This aphorism, apparently never published, is quoted by Needham (1975, p. 365).
[2] Fortes (1961, p. 211; quoted by Barnes, 1971, p. 179) for example, has remarked that his "instinct is to shy away from methodological discussion." Barnes, noting this, also points out that " . . . Fortes's dislike of discussion of analytical procedures and conceptual schemes is shared by many of his colleagues . . ." More explicitly, Loudon (1976, p. 38) has argued that "A supposedly empirical discipline which gets unduly concerned about epistemological worries is in danger of losing its way." (For discussion on this question, see also Jean Comaroff, 1978, p. 248, Needham, 1971a, p. xvii and Crick, 1976, p. 1 ff.)

least, to warrant Ardener's observation (1971, p. 450) that there has
been an "epistemological break" in anthropology.[1]

While it is not my intention to discuss such general issues here, their
more specific implications touch upon present concerns. For, as is by
now well-known, "marriage" is one of those analytic categories whose
constitutive validity has been questioned, most vigorously perhaps, by
Needham (1971b, p. 5 ff) and Rivière (1971, p. 57 ff). The former
suggests that this term, while a useful "odd-job" word, refers to a
polythetic class of phenomena (1975, pp. 362-3). Consequently, cross-
cultural comparisons and classifications of manifest conjugal forms —
at least those based upon (pseudo-) technical definitions derived from
Western concepts — do not yield explanations or generalizations. They
lead, at worst, to scientistic distortion; at best they are merely a waste
of effort (cf. Leach, 1955, 1961, p. 27).[2] Similar statements have also
occasionally been made of marriage prestations: given the patent
diversity in their content and timing, their structural contexts and
their symbolic ramifications, is it valid to reduce them to a single
analytical class? Both Turton and Peters raise the question below, but
do not pursue it, preferring rather to adopt heuristic solutions for their
immediate purposes. Nevertheless, it is obviously fundamental to this
symposium as a whole. The point of such an exercise, after all, is to
contribute to a universe of discourse. If, however, there is no intrinsic
unity in the phenomena under study, what is to be achieved by that
discourse?

Of course, in phrasing the conundrum in this fashion, it is implicitly
assumed that the cross-cultural diversity of marriage payments is
indeed too great to be subsumed within a single analytical domain —
and that such diversity precludes meaningful comparison. This, it

---

[1] As Crick (1976, p. 1) suggests, "We have left behind the certainty that the old functionalist
position conferred, but without as yet securing any new definite identity . . . Currently there is
little agreement as to what the academic locus of social anthropology is or should be . . ." These
remarks are, of course, addressed primarily to British social anthropology, whose predicament in
this respect has clearly been affected by the confrontation with French structuralism. (It seems no
coincidence that Leach, Crick and Ardener all found their critiques at least partly upon aspects
of structuralist logic.)

[2] See also Chaney (1978, p. 40) who observes that "Polythetic classification is actuarial data
summary, not explanatory theory."

seems to me, cannot be conceded without careful reflection. For the issue is more complex than the assumption suggests. In order to address it, I shall examine, in some detail, the implications of the present studies for received wisdom on the subject. These studies, taken together, cast doubt not only upon many existing explanations, but also upon the manner of their production. In so doing, though, they do not merely lead back to the epistemological issues raised by Leach and Needham. Rather, the commentary which they provide may also be seen to illuminate *constructively* the problem of comparison and generalization in socio-cultural anthropology at large, and its relevance to the comprehension of marriage payments in particular.

It is self-evident that explanations of the form and content of these payments vary with the theoretical paradigms from which they derive; and that, within each paradigm, emergent generalizations are entailed in, and express, ontological and taxonomic assumptions. Consequently, I shall consider, in turn, the way in which the symposium informs the structural functionalist, Marxist and structuralist approaches to the question. This is not intended as a review of the literature, however. In each case, I seek to identify some major analytic themes, expose them to critical evaluation, and extract from them constructive theoretical insights. Thereafter, in the final section, I attempt to draw the latter together and to consider how a comparative discourse on the meaning of marriage payments may be constituted without either creating a conceptual artifice or dissolving the category entirely.

Of the three approaches, structural functionalism has unquestionably been the major source of both descriptions and explanations of marriage payments, and many of the generalizations which have flowed from them have gained the status of received wisdom (cf. Comaroff, Chapter 6). This, therefore, is the appropriate place to begin. Admittedly, some commentators have predicted, and even declared, the demise of structural functionalism, implying that its concerns need no longer detain us. But if it is in practice that orthodoxies are found, this approach undeniably continues to represent a dominant one. In short, to portray it as a "straw man" is to liken much of anthropology to hay-making.

Structural functionalist perspectives

A. *Overarching Schemes*

Within this paradigmatic context, the most ambitious analytical efforts have sought to comprehend the full range of marriage payments in a single explanatory scheme. Thus, for example, Spiro (1975, pp. 89-90) distinguishes four possible types of prestations: *dowry* and *dower* involve property which is brought to a union, the former being provided by the bride's family and the latter by that of the groom; *bridewealth* is tendered by the husband's grouping to the kin of his wife, while *groomwealth* moves in the opposite direction. These four types, he argues, have generally been conflated into two. Since groomwealth has no clearly recorded empirical instances (p. 114)[1], it has been ignored for analytical purposes, and dower has regularly been mistaken for bridewealth, primarily because its source is the same. This reduction has not merely obscured the "differential determinants" of payments of the various kinds. It has also vitiated the solution of the prior problem; namely, why marriage prestations occur — or do not — in the first place. Spiro's own explanation (p. 98) suggests that they are found in those systems where:

> . . . the cost-benefit ratio of marriage to its principals is unbalanced . . . the type of payment is determined by which of these principals — bride, groom, bride's family, groom's family — is the most disadvantaged.

When the cost-benefit ratio is balanced, so that no party stands to gain or lose either materially or socially, prestations are unlikely to be transferred. The absence of institutionalized groomwealth, then, reflects the fact that there are no regular situations in which a man's grouping suffers disadvantage by the alienation of his productive and reproductive powers.[2]

At first sight, Spiro's scheme might appear to account for the associations frequently made between dowry and the negotiation of

---

[1] This point is also made by Goody (1973, p. 6). In contrast, Tambiah (1973, pp. 63-5) discusses the emergence of transactions akin to groomwealth in South Asia. See also Nash (1978, pp. 106-108) for an account of an instance of groomprice in Papua New Guinea.

[2] For summary purposes, I do not include ethnographic typifications of the cost-benefit calculations involved in the other three modes of transaction. However, it is to be noted that Spiro characterises these calculations in carefully considered terms: they may involve (i) gains enjoyed by the wealth giver(s); (ii) protection against potential loss; and (iii) compensations for actual loss.

status on the one hand, and bridewealth and the alienation of rights in women on the other (see below). Several of the ethnographies below offer instances which do not fit into it, however, and in so doing, call its logic into question. Thus, Rheubottom demonstrates that dowry in Macedonia may have little to do with gains in prestige or affluence on the part of the bride or her family; in most unions, moreover, there is no loss, either actual or potential, incurred by the groom. The villagers of Skopska Crna Gora are organized into tightly bounded, patrilineally linked corporate households which, while they differ in wealth and standing, are not incorporated into an elaborate status hierarchy. Some women, it is true, seek husbands from units of higher standing than their own, and the union of one sibling may influence the prospects of the others. But hypergamy — or, more generally, "status placement" — does not give systematic form to the flow of payments. On the contrary, families strive to ensure that their womenfolk are endowed in equal measure, whomsoever they marry. Hence Rheubottom (Chapter 8) poses the question:

> Why, in a patrilineal, virilocal society would the wife-givers endow the groom with rights over the bride's labour, her sexuality, her reproductive capacity, and then give the couple a substantial amount of clothing, cash and furniture as well?

His answer makes a significant comment upon Spiro's approach, and has wider implications for the comparative analysis of dowry:

> The bride's family does *not* endow the groom or his household; they endow the bride.

The manner in which this is done, moreover, encodes a series of transformations of female roles, and their relationship to the constitution of households. Equations of cost and benefit, as Rheubottom's analysis demonstrates, simply do not comprehend the order of values which give meaning to Macedonian dowry.

Objections to Spiro's model may equally be raised in regard to its explanations of bridewealth. Such prestations are held to occur where marriage alienates a woman's "productivity and/or reproductivity" to the husband's grouping (p. 112); in matrilineal societies with a virilocal residence rule, only her productivity is transferred, but it is sufficient to warrant some payment. In terms of this logic, of course, the patrilineal, virilocal Macedonian villagers should offer bridewealth: they do not. But there are also problematic cases in which it *is* transferred. The

Buna of Eastern Indonesia, for instance, have two forms of marriage (Barnes, Chapter 4). The first involves complementary prestations, patrilocal residence and the affiliation of children to the husband's descent group. Significantly, though, counter gifts *include* dowry (cf. also Strathern, Chapter 2), a possibility which Spiro's model does not readily comprehend. The second type, moreover, brings about uxorilocal residence and the matrifiliation of children. If anything, this would represent a *prima facie* case in which the model should predict groomprice; yet some bridewealth is still tendered under conditions in which the bride's unit does not incur the loss of her productivity or reproductivity. As Barnes shows, the logic of prestations here is inscribed in the relationship between the structure of (non-unilineal) descent groups, an entailed pattern of asymmetrical alliance, and alternative modes of affiliation — a complex equation which, again, does not reduce to the economics of compensation. Nor is it only in Eastern Indonesia that the model runs into difficulties. Its application in the classical African systems is also dubious, albeit in different ways.

If it were the economistic logic of loss and gain entailed in marriage which gave form to prestations, it follows that there ought to be some relationship between their value and the extent of the costs and benefits involved. But in East Africa the size of bridewealth varies widely (Turton, Chapter 3), while the values alienated by the bride's kin may not differ appreciably. Furthermore, where such payments have more than one component — as among the Mijikenda peoples (Parkin, Chapter 7) — their signifcance in mediating the exchanges and status transformations embodied in the conjugal process becomes much too complex to assimilate to the calculus which underlies Spiro's scheme.

More generally, even if it *could* be shown that different types of prestation co-exist with the appropriate cost-benefit ratios, this would merely represent a second order datum — a correlation concerning the directionalities of exchange, not an explanation of their form, value or meaning. The co-existence of two phenomena does not itself establish that the one motivates the other. Spiro does not demonstrate such motivation, and the Mursi ethnography below provides cogent counter-evidence for his causal assumptions. Among them, as in some Eastern Indonesian systems, it is precisely the mobilisation and distribution of bridewealth, and the rules which govern them, that effectively constitute wife-giving and wife-taking groups. As Turton remarks:

> It would . . . be circular to interpret the payment of bridewealth as compensating a group of agnates for the loss of a sister or daughter, when bridewealth is such an important factor in making them such a group in the first place.

These examples, taken together, indicate why this economistic model cannot illuminate the meaning of marriage payments. Apart from the fact that it assimilates all prestations of a "kind" into an undifferentiated category, and disregards the implications of flows of exchange, it takes for granted exactly what it is that we are trying to explain; namely, the constitutive relationship between the payments and the other elements of the socio-cultural system in which they occur.

The other notable recent attempt to elaborate an overarching scheme, that of Goody (1973), concentrates primarily upon bridewealth and dowry (cf. Spiro, op. cit., f.n.2) — which are associated respectively with Africa and Eurasia, where their practice is seen to be functionally related to contrasting organisational tendencies. For Goody, it is the nature of enduring social and economic structures, not the commercial logic of conjugal transactions, which gives form and meaning to these payments. His argument is straightforward: bridewealth and dowry involve the redistribution of property at marriage, and must consequently be analysed in the wider context of property relations (p. 1 ff). But such relations are themselves entailed in an encompassing social order. Thus dowry, which is a form of diverging devolution, is associated with bilateral systems, since heritable wealth is not retained within the bounds of a corporate unit (p. 17 ff, 26); bridewealth, on the other hand, typically involves a transfer between corporations (minimally defined), and is linked to lineal devolution and descent structures.

Moreover, the contrasting ecological situations in which these prestations occur are given causal significance. In Africa, hoe agriculture precludes marked wealth differences, so that hierarchization is limited (Goody, 1973, pp. 28-30) and one union is much like another in its status implications. In Eurasia, however, intensive plough agriculture admits major differentiation and, therefore, social stratification is well-developed (p. 23 ff). Under these conditions, the endowment of the bride is a corollary of "upward nubility": it serves to maintain or improve her standing and mediate inequalities between affines. In short, Eurasian dowry is associated with hierarchy and hypergamy, African bridewealth with their absence. This, in turn, has further social correlates. Diverging devolution places a stress upon both the marital bond and strong affinal ties. For the couple, who are beneficiaries of a conjugal fund at the expense of the interest of sibling group and descent corporation, become central in a set of social and material relations. In contrast, bridewealth does not differentiate or attach privilege to the couple, who are not endowed at the cost of sibling unity or corporate interest: the establishment of a conjugal fund is patently antithetical to property relations in descent systems with lineal inheritance arrangements. Here, as a result, affinity takes second place to descent as a principle of social organization. Taking this a step further, it is those societies where dowry is endemic which, in their emphasis upon the primacy of affinity, have been the regional source of "alliance theory", while those characterised by bridewealth and lineal devolution have yielded "descent theory". These theories, argues Goody, reflect objective structural differences. The observation is not new (Leach, 1961; Dumont, 1971, p. 119; Lewis, 1973), but the causal attribution of these differences to contrasting patterns of stratification and property relations (p. 46) does represent a somewhat novel perspective.[1]

Goody ends with a caveat to the effect that he is concerned primarily with a generalised contrast between types; the full range of variations within and between these types, while given careful recognition, are ultimately reduced to two polarities. Honest as this is, it does not obscure the fact that, in order to sustain his scheme, he has relied upon gross, and often misleading, analytical categories. This is especiallly evident in his treatment of social differentiation. While it is asserted in passing that some African societies are hierarchically ordered (p. 23), Africa is characterized as egalitarian by contrast with Eurasia (pp. 28-30). Thereafter, its ostensible homogeneity and socio-economic equality are analytically opposed to Eurasian hierarchy. Not only is it logically dubious to constitute a category of "*un*stratified systems" purely on these

---

[1] I have not explicitly considered the question of causality in Goody's approach, since I believe that the objections raised above and below come logically prior to it. Briefly, his procedure involves the identification of two contrasting socio-economic complexes, within which two elements (property arrangements, of which marriage payments are part, and stratification) are held to be "causal" (p. 46). While there have been defences of this notion of causality (cf. Barth, 1973, p. 4 ff), which attributes to select elements in a functionally inter-related set the capacity to generate and/or motivate the set as a whole, it has also been subjected to criticism in the literature on the methodology of structural functionalism. I see little point in covering this ground yet again.

grounds,[1] but a concept of stratification which incorporates the Mursi and Ganda or the Nuer and Swazi into a single class, even for ideal-typical purposes, is unhelpful (cf. Fallers, 1973). Where it becomes the causal basis of an explanatory model, problems inevitably follow. Take the example of bridewealth: once it is typologically associated with broadly egalitarian systems, the point is missed that under certain conditions — the Swazi providing a notable instance (H. Kuper, 1949, pp. 98, 152; A. Kuper, 1978, pp. 568, 576) — it may be precisely the instrument by means of which inequalities are generated and power relationships contrived.

The essays below confirm the difficulty of sustaining a correlation between differentiation and particular modes of marriage transaction, even if the exact conceptual terms of the former could be discerned. Again, Rheubottom's Macedonian case is instructive, for it occurs in a socio-economic situation which Goody would typify as African: a patrilineal system with a rigid patriviri-local residence rule, in which descent and corporate unity are stressed and affinity largely denied; where substantial surpluses are unlikely and inequalities marginal. Yet dowry is a necessary condition for most marriages. In Eastern Indonesia, furthermore, there is wide variability in the nature of hierarchization, but it appears impossible to relate these patterns to contrasting forms of marriage payment. Although Goody does not consider the Middle-East, it also provides cases which cannot be accommodated with his binary scheme. For here there "are many communities which practise some form of bridewealth, and where the plough has long been used" (Peters, Chapter 5). This, in turn, raises another dimension of the model which is too gross for comfort: the reduction of Africa and Eurasia to two ecological orders. As Turton shows, it may be the very contrasts *within* African regional areas which underlie variations in the function and meaning of marriage transactions.

Finally, Goody has founded his scheme upon the taxonomic opposition between bridewealth and dowry, an opposition which is held to comprehend differences in group structure, marriage systems, kinship relations, property arrangements and stratification (p. 46).

---

[1] The criteria of equality and hierarchization are in themselves never satisfactorily typified; rather, they are described, in relative terms, as a corollary of two dominant modes of production (p. 23 ff).

But this assumes *a priori* that these modes of transfer may in fact be validly treated as undifferentiated and meaningful "types" for explanatory purposes. Following Leach (1961, *passim*) and Sahlins (1976, p. 14 ff) on the dangers of abstracting principles from arbitrarily derived typologies, it is apposite to ask why these particular categories, familiar though they might be, are given unquestioning analytical priority. Strathern (Chapter 2) and Barnes (Chapter 4), for example, demonstrate the importance of two-way flows of prestations in some societies. Why not, therefore, allow that the contrast between "undirectional" and "complementary" alienations of wealth, or for that matter the immediacy or deferral of payment, may be equally fundamental for comparative purposes? After all, the labels "bride-wealth" and "dowry" select, as analytical significata, only the source and destination of transfers, leaving as residual the dimensions of content, context and meaning. If this reduction nonetheless yielded theoretical insight, well and good; but it requires demonstration. However, given the logic of generating explanation from taxonomic procedures, this would not be easy. As Sahlins (1976, pp. 14-15) notes, discussing Radcliffe-Brown's methodology (1950), where a principle or generalization derives from

> . . . a taxonomic class, the wider it is the fewer and more general must be the criteria for inclusion within it. Therefore, the greater the "generalization" or "law", the less it says about anything in particular. In the course of grouping more and more diverse forms under wider and wider principles, Radcliffe-Brown explained less and less about any one of them. The "principles" cannot hope to account for particularity, because they destroy it.

While neither of the overarching schemes developed by Spiro and Goody respectively yields a satisfactory explanation of marriage payments, and both are mired in methodological problems, two constructive observations flow from their consideration. First, Goody is correct in insisting that these payments be analyzed in the context of total systems, although it does not follow that such a system need be constituted of functionally related institutions (see below). Secondly, both schemes stress the economic implications of marriage payments, and rightly so. Evans-Pritchard (1934, p. 172), as Barnes points out, long ago noted that bridewealth everywhere has economic value. But economy and commerce are not coterminous, and the fact that exchanges have economic *implications* does not necessarily mean that they are commercially or economically *motivated*. Moreover, the way in which actors experience and construe transactions does not itself explain why those transactions occur,[1] or how they relate to an ordered set of values in any socio-cultural system. There is, quite patently, a difference between the manner in which exchanges are *constituted* in a society and the way in which they are *experienced* by its members.[2] But I shall return to these distinctions.

Structural functionalist discourse on marriage payments, however, has been addressed less to the elaboration of overarching models than to the analysis of bridewealth and dowry respectively. I consider the latter first, since some of the issues have already been introduced.

B. *Dowry*

Although dowry occurs in a limited number of culture areas, its manifest form varies widely (e.g. Tambiah, 1973, *passim*; Mair, 1971, p. 65 ff). Nevertheless, it is frequently reduced, in general descriptions, to a "paradigmatic conception" (Tambiah, ibid., 61 ff); a typification, that is, of its dominant characteristics and social correlates. Such general typifications differ remarkably little in the literature. First, dowry is usually held not merely to entail female property rights, but also to be inseparable from pre-mortem inheritance (e.g. Tambiah, ibid., p. 64) and "diverging devolution" (Goody, op. cit., p. 17), since it is tranferred from common familial holdings to a daughter at marriage. There are a few dissenters from this view:

---

[1] This point makes reference to the criticisms directed at utilitarian positions in general (cf. e.g. Sahlins, 1976) and transactional analysis, especially as developed by Barth (1966), in particular (cf. Kapferer (ed) 1976, *passim*; Comaroff and Roberts, forthcoming). Briefly, it is all very well to assume, *for heuristic purposes*, that actors may enter transactions because they are rationally motivated by pragmatic considerations, and that they experience social interaction in these terms. Leaving aside the patent fact of cross-cultural variation in this respect, however, we are still left with the prior analytical problem of how the ideology of pragmatism is itself culturally constituted; why it is, and also when it is, that transactions are experienced in this fashion. In the absence of such an explanation (and, in most utilitarian methodologies, it is absent), pragmatic individualism is transformed from a heuristic assumption to a first order theoretical principle capable of accounting for everything, and, therefore, nothing. Indeed, Blau (1964, p. 1 ff), himself an influential exchange theorist, has pointed out that this leads directly to tautology.

[2] These comments (see also below) have obvious implications for "economistic" explanations of bridewealth (e.g. Gray 1960; Goldschmidt, 1969, 1974; Laughlin, 1973). I do not subject the latter to evaluation in their own right here, partly because it would require lengthy re-analyses of ethnographic data. More importantly, however, my later discussion of bridewealth and the circulation of value points out why it is that explanations of these payments in largely commercial terms have little general application.

Madan (1965, p. 156 ff), describing a Kashmiri village, specifically does not make the connection; and Yalman (1967, pp. 174-5) says of the Kandyan Sinhalese that female inheritance is "merely a reflection of the general descent ideology", while dowry is the "result of a bargain" struck in the negotiation of status relations. But these reservations have not substantially affected dominant orthodoxies (cf. Goody, op. cit., p. 17). Secondly, dowry is generally viewed as implying a stress upon bilateral kinship, since it mitigates the exclusive retention of property within a corporate (unilineal) descent group. The corollary is that the conjugal bond and affinal linkages — predicated upon a shared interest in the marriage — acquire social primacy, notwithstanding the existence of descent ideologies. The reasoning behind this typification is so well rehearsed as not to require reiteration. But it is to be added that positive marriage rules are frequently attributed to the material logic of systems of this kind (e.g. Yalman, 1967; Goody, op. cit.). For cousin marriage arrangements of various kinds may have the effect — or be conceived indigenously to have it — of either retaining property within (as in FBD unions), or returning it to (as in cross-cousin unions), a grouping which, at least notionally, holds or once held it.[1]

Thirdly, as already emphasized, dowry is generally seen to be related to hypergamy. Even where it is the dominant type of prestation, it may not be transferred in unions between equals or children of the poor, for whose marriages bridewealth is more usually tendered. As Tambiah puts it, dowry may, in this aspect, be conceived of as a direct exchange of status for wealth (op. cit., 64); in India, "It is a superb pawn to use in the formation of marriage alliance and in pursuing the game of

---

[1] The logic of this, as concerns FBD unions, is clear: in such unions, any value circulated is retained within the wider boundaries of an agnatic grouping, since wife-givers and takers are all members of it. Hence, under these conditions, dowry or diverging devolution ostensibly would not involve the outward flow of property from that group. In the case of cross-cousin marriage, as emerges clearly from Yalman's description (1967, Ch. 16) of the Kandyan Sinhalese, the family property divided between brother and sister in one generation is, at least notionally, united again in the marriage of their offspring. In a more general discussion of related questions, Leach (1955, 1961, pp. 109-110) has pointed out that a patent contradiction is entailed in the coexistence of (i) the ideal that patrimonial inheritance remains intact and (ii) a recognition of female property rights. This contradiction is widely manifest in South Asia, where different communities show contrasting "solutions". Of these, he mentions patrilineage endogamy, reciprocal or patrilateral cross-cousin marriage and adelphic polyandry as variations on the same theme (a view criticized, in part, by Berreman, 1962). While these considerations may go some way in explaining the ideology of marriage preference, it is important to stress that such conjugal arrangements are never sufficient, in practical terms, to sustain all property within descent corporations.

hypergamy" (p. 72). Its association with an emphasis upon affinity and the negotiation of prestige and status, moreover, is often taken to explain a tendency towards monogamy, the careful arrangement of unions, and the co-existence of alternative patterns of residence and affiliation. None of these characteristics is universal, but each may be present to a greater or lesser extent in any one community.

This, then, represents a descriptive typification of the manifest social characteristics which are generally associated with dowry. In the classical terms of the comparative method, such a typification is usually treated, implicitly or explicitly, as the first step towards explanation and generalization. It is, however, a logically dubious step. In order to underline this, I return briefly to some of the ethnographic cases below.

Bridewealth occurs in most Tswana chiefdoms, of which the Tshidi is one. But only among the Kgatla is dowry, an arable field (*serotwana*), also given to a daughter (Schapera, 1938, p. 203), who may plough it together with her husband.[1] This contradicts Radcliffe-Brown's assertion (1950, p. 46; cf. Goody, op. cit., pp. 21-2) that dowry is absent in Africa. More important, though, its presence is not readily attributable to socio-cultural differences which mark the Kgatla off from other Tswana: their structural arrangements, like patterns of differentiation and preferential marriage, are similar; *serotwana* is neither ideologically associated with, nor actually linked to, upward mobility; and the quality of affinal relations here seems comparatively unexceptional. It is true that emphasis is placed upon a bilateral network of kin ties and affinity is highly valued, but this applies to all Tswana (A. Kuper, 1975; Comaroff and Comaroff, forthcoming), including those who transfer bridewealth only, and has more to do with the pattern of close kin marriage than with the nature of prestations.

The Macedonian ethnography also becomes relevant here again. For, in contrast to the expected pattern, the villagers of Skopska appear to deny, rather than stress, affinity. On marriage, a woman crosses the boundary between natal and conjugal households in an abrupt and comprehensive fashion, and retains no rights in the former. When she enters her marital home, she is treated at first as a daughter and only later as a wife and mother, a process of transformation

---

[1] Schapera states that this transfer is voluntary, being within the gift of the father. But it seems that the practice was widespread and not confined to any one social category.

which is symbolically encoded in the composition of her dowry. Significantly, moreover, after her removal, there follow no affinal exchanges, outside ceremonial contexts. Affinity does not merely take second place to agnation, it has markedly limited social currency in absolute terms as well. There is little effective stress upon bilateral kinship linkages either: daughters marry out and leave the unit once and for all, and their children have little claim upon their matrilateral kin. Notwithstanding the problem of characterizing the "strength" of lineality (Lewis, 1965), these Macedonians express their patrilineal ideology with singular commitment. It is beyond coincidence in this respect that they dissociate dowry from inheritance; this makes perfect cultural sense. Devolutionary rights are held exclusively by the corporation and its members. Anyone leaving it, therefore, is to be paid out for their past contribution (i.e. labour) and the renunciation of further rights. This done, the common fund is left intact and corporate boundaries may be sustained in both their ideological and economic aspects. Dowry is seen in precisely these terms; the conceptual distinction between it and inheritance rights represents an opposition between inclusion and exclusion, an opposition which also subsumes the denial of affinity. The Macedonian example, like the Tswana case, then, does not fit the general typification. The same may be said of the Wiru and Melpa, where transfers from a bride's family to the couple (an "analogue of dowry", as Strathern terms it) occur alongside bridewealth. But they have little to do with a woman's standing, or status placement in general; after all, these societies are hardly stratified. Rather, the fund so created, which consists of live animals, produces the wherewithal for subsequent affinal exchanges: it represents the genesis of a new cycle of prestations linking a husband and his wife's kin.

These examples suggest much greater ethnography diversity than is often supposed in "paradigmatic conceptions" of dowry. The point is, however, that the former cannot be represented as variations on a theme or transformations of a model derived primarily, say, from Indian arrangements. Not only are the socio-cultural systems of which they are part quite different, but so too is the way in which the alienation of prestations relates to the constitution and exchange of value in those systems. The problem of arriving at a general typification by the assimilation of correlations and functional associations from specific cases, e.g. between dowry and stratification, pre-mortem inheritance, bilateral kinship and so on, is that it ultimately depends upon the decontextualization of manifest arrangements from the total set of relations which give them meaning. Trading off context for comparison might satisfy a "craving for generality" (Wittgenstein, 1955, p. 17), and sustain the "lingering delusion of a natural science of society" (Needham, 1971b, p. 2), but it leads away from explanation. This is not to say that there have been no insightful accounts of dowry in particular societies, or that our cross-cultural knowledge is worthless. Yet we are a long way from the general "theory" that structural functionalist methodology envisions as possible, precisely because the reductionist procedure by which general description is produced is epistemologically ill-founded.

C. *Bridewealth*

While our knowledge of bridewealth is certainly substantial (Fortes, 1962, p. 9), it too has been typified and explained in markedly uniform terms. There have, admittedly, been efforts to essay its commercial character (see p. 11, f.n. 2), to explore its cultural constitution (Sansom, 1976), and to repudiate established male biases in its analysis (Singer, 1973; Lamphere, 1974). But the dominant interpretative frame of reference remains the functional relationship between these prestations and (i) *structural* arrangements; (ii) the *jural* creation of statuses and alienation of rights; and (iii) the *politico-economic* negotiation of affinity. I consider each of these dimensions in turn.

Generally speaking, bridewealth is viewed as a transfer made between corporate (usually unilineal) groups, or their lower order segments (Goody, op. cit., p. 7; Mair, 1971, pp. 64-5). In the course of exchanging prestations and rights in women, these units create relationships of affinity and debt with each other, affirming their own internal solidarity and mutual interests in the process. The paradigmatic association of bridewealth with corporate (descent) structures has further institutional corollaries. It is seen to "fit" (cf. Goody, op. cit., pp. 2-17) with polygynous marriage; the unity of the sibling group and the formation of houses which, being differentiated by their matrilateral ties, represent foci of segmentary fission and fusion; virilocal residence; the levirate, sororate and other forms of secondary union; and so on. All this, patently, evokes the classical portrayal of the "structure of unilineal descent groups" (Fortes, 1953), and warrants Goody's observation (see above) concerning the descriptive analytical link between bridewealth "systems" and "descent theory". In short, the segmentary lineage model, and its grounding in the pervasive concept of the corporation, looms large in our understanding of these marriage payments.

This does not lack *prima facie* empirical support. Bridewealth, at least in Africa, is common in patrilineal systems, and usually absent or insubstantial in matrilineal and so-called bilateral societies. Where marriage with bridewealth is one option among several, moreover, its non-payment usually entails reduced control over the bride on the part of her husband's kin, the affiliation of her children to her own natal unit, non-agnatic devolution and, perhaps, non-virilocal residence.

Nevertheless, the studies below demonstrate that bridewealth *does* occur in non-unilineal contexts, and sometimes is associated with *intra*-descent group marriage.[1] More important, however, they indicate that its relationship to structural arrangements may be more complex than is suggested by orthodox descent theory. I have already alluded to the Mursi, who share a patrilineal ideology, but among whom descent groups and their internal relationships are given manifest form by the mobilization and distribution of marriage payments. These groups cannot be characterized as bounded unilineal corporations which, being already constituted, then engage with each other in bridewealth transactions; they are the former largely by virtue of the latter. Marriage prestations and unilineal structures, then, are not reducible here to separate institutions which may be conceived or explained in terms of a functional interdependency; they are more accurately described as two transformations of the same socio-cultural rules. The point is taken further by Barnes (Chapter 4), who specifically considers the connection between corporate organization, descent and marriage payments. In Eastern Indonesia,

> Where unilineal descent, affinal alliance and marriage exchanges occur together, they all have an essential part in the constitution of corporations, but each of these features may be present or absent independently of the others. . . . Marriage payments may allocate from one family to another not only

---

[1] Mair (1971, pp. 64-5), who denies this possibility, implies that, where prestations are not transferred between lineages, they are not truly bridewealth. If this is intended, however, it leads to an inescapable circularity; for it defines out of existence any instances which do not sustain the paradigmatic assumptions of descent theory. Gluckman (1950), on the other hand, accepts that bridewealth may be transferred in non-unilineal contexts. But he suggests that such payments ought to be typologically distinguished from those occurring in unilineal systems, and separately explained.

children, but also wives, and in some cases even husbands. Such payments can
be used to establish an exclusive connection, but they may just as well leave an
individual with membership and obligations in two locations.

This does not merely prove wrong the established view that unilineal
principles are the only, or most suitable, means of establishing
corporations or recruiting members to them. It suggests, more
constructively, that descent, alliance and prestations, existing in various
combinations and transformations, are the three elements which
constitute corporate structures.

The Tshidi and Bedouin ethnographies lend support to the general
argument that the relationship between marriage rules, descent
ideologies and exchange arrangements may impart order to the
manifest social universe and the manner in which it is experienced and
negotiated. These systems are characterized by close kin (including
FBD) marriage, a pattern which, for well-established reasons
(Comaroff, Chapter 6), violates the essential principles of "descent
theory". In such systems, social bonds are inherently ambiguous and
overlapping, and everyday life is marked by a stress upon pragmatic
individualism in career management and group formation.
Bridewealth here may have little to do with inter-group affinal ties; in
the absence of exogamic proscriptions, there is no inscribed opposition between kinship and affinity. Thus the Bedouin, for example,
place conspicuous emphasis upon the strategic deployment of marriage
exchanges to configure individuated linkages to advantage, and to
create ties of patronage, clientage and complementarity both within,
and across descent groups. The corporation may be ideologically predicated upon agnation; but, given the logic of the marriage rules, it
takes its manifest form from the negotiated exchange of rights in
persons and wealth.

If the structural aspect of marriage exchanges is oversimplified in
structural functionalist orthodoxy, so too, I suggest, is their jural
dimension. This dimension is central to established anthropological
conceptions: whatever other differences may be expressed concerning
its analysis, the conjugal bond is almost universally regarded as a
jurally constituted and contractually defined relationship, a view
grounded firmly in the concepts of western jurisprudence (Roberts,

1977a, p. 7 ff; 1977b).[1] Despite growing evidence on the shortcomings of the "jural approach",[2] marriage continues to be seen primarily as a "bundle of rights", and bridewealth as the instrument of their production and/or exchange. Broadly speaking, this may be subsumed in four related statements:

(i) Marriage prestations are essential in establishing the legitimacy of a union, it being assumed that a clear distinction is generally made between regular and irregular relationships (Radcliffe-Brown, 1950, p. 46).

(ii) The passage of bridewealth signals the alienation of various kinds of rights in a woman to her husband and his kin; where it is paid in instalments, the movement of such rights occurs in concommitantly reciprocal stages (Evans-Pritchard, 1951, p. 97; A. Kuper, 1970, p. 476-7; Mitchell, 1963).

(iii) Of these, perhaps the most significant concerns the affiliation of children; especially in patrilineal systems, "bride-price is child-price" (Mair, 1971, pp. 51-2).

(iv) The payment marks a transformation of personal and social statuses, not merely for the couple, but also for the wife-givers and takers, who become affines, whatever else they might have been before (Fortes, 1962, p. 1 ff).

This requires one qualification: Fortes (1962, p. 9 ff) suggests that bridewealth has two components, a Prime Prestation and Contingent Prestations, the first being "the *sine qua non* for lawful marriage and therefore, strictly speaking, the sole jural instrument for the transfer of marital rights" (p. 10). Contingent Prestations, in contrast, are negotiable; they are exchanged in the cause of advantageous affinal relations.

---

[1] There is some irony in this since the jurisprudential concept which has perhaps been most difficult to apply in small-scale systems has been none other than a general law of contract. Thus, for example, Gluckman (1955, 2nd edn 1967, pp. 30, 206) found an absence of executory contract among the Barotse. Walker (1968) has argued that the Bamalete do have a law of contract, but Roberts (1970) has offered a cogent refutation. Schapera (1938, p. 239 ff) also speaks of contract among the Tswana; marriage, he suggests, being one kind. However, it appears that Schapera is using the term rather loosely, implying a promisory rather than an executory notion. Indeed, Roberts (1972) has reported a marked absence of contract cases in Tswana customary courts and the wisdom of viewing marriage in this fashion has been seriously called into question (e.g. Roberts, 1977b; Comaroff and Roberts, 1977).

[2] Since some of this evidence is mentioned in my essay, it is not repeated here. However, two manuscripts, made available to me after I wrote that essay, demonstrate convincingly the inadequacy of the jural approach for the analysis of marriage among the Kpelle as well (Bledsoe, in press; Bledsoe and Murphy, unpublished MS).

While these statements may describe the situation in some societies, they certainly do not represent universal similarities. The Melpa and Wiru, for example, invert the priorities of Fortes's generalization (Strathern, Chapter 2). Here the legal dimension of bridewealth is not "primary" in any meaningful sense; it is the so-called contingent aspect — the production of affinal exchange linkages — which represents the dominant value motivating the alienation of prestations. In Fortes's view, people might exchange to marry; but, in the view of the Melpa and Wiru, people marry to exchange.[1]

The Tshidi provide a still more difficult case for the jural approach. Among them, bridewealth has little to do with the validation of unions. Even when it is transferred early in the development cycle, which is rare, it is always possible that a party wishing to eschew the bond will seek to redefine the transaction as having been another type of exchange. Moreover, as in some other systems,[2] it is difficult in everyday contexts to tell whether a couple are "married", or to specify the status of their relationship, an ambiguity which is culturally inscribed in common terminological usage. Consequently, there is no mechanical link between the passage of prestations and rights, including those over the affiliation of children, these rights being seen to develop as an intrinsic property of the growth and perpetuation of any relationship. Furthermore, the notion that marriage and its associated prestations alone generate affinity, or transform other kinds of kinship bond into it, as among the Gisu (La Fontaine, 1962), simply does not apply here. Marriage and affinity are involved in a complex dialectical relationship, each having the capacity to create, privilege or destroy the other.

On the basis of these and other recent ethnographies (see p. 18, f.n. 2) it is impossible to avoid the conclusion that the pervasive influence of the jural approach has had the effect of obscuring important socio-cultural variations in the constitution of marriage, affinity and exchange. Of course, neither the Tshidi nor the Melpa and Wiru conform to the classical African segmentary lineage model. But I am not convinced that the jural approach always applies even in that context. The Tallensi, for example, seem to make no terminological distinction between what Fortes (1949, p. 84 ff) calls "experimental"

[1] This phrasing was suggested by Martin Southwold, although he used it to characterize a contrast between systems rather than to comment upon Fortes's position.
[2] E.g. the Sotho (Murray, 1977) and lakeside Tonga (Van Velsen, 1964, pp. 79-98).

marriages and marriages "proper": the latter, apparently, are merely those which last. Given that "the ideal of marriage as a lifelong and irrevocable bond does not exist" (p. 85), how are regular unions differentiated from irregular ones? They surely must be if marriage is to have any jural force. Fortes suggests that "proper" relationships are distinguishable by the "strict letter of custom", but the customary modes of conjugal formation seem decidedly ambiguous, allowing individuals to establish and dissolve relationships without much (jural) difficulty. Moreover, the question of rights is anything but unequivocal; even where "jural proprieties" have been observed, this merely "gives the husband a weapon with which he can try to assert his rights to and over his wife. It does not give him an absolute guarantee of these rights nor does it ensure the stability of the marriage" (p. 86). What can "right" mean here? In what sense are proprieties *jural* if they neither really convey "rights" nor make them enforceable? The concepts of western jurisprudence may have their appeal, but it is only too easy to construct an analytical artifice with them.

The third dimension of bridewealth arrangements, their pragmatic political and economic character, is subject to less general agreement than the other two. While some ethnographers (see p. 11, f.n. 2) have reduced these arrangements almost entirely to the terms of commerce and bargain, Goody (op. cit.) comes close to denying them any political meaning at all, other than in the maintenance of broadly egalitarian structures.[1] A compromise between these two positions is implied in Fortes's distinction (1962) between the non-negotiable "Prime constituent" and the politically motivated "Contingent element" of bridewealth. But Fortes offers little more than the programmatic suggestion that the latter may be analyzed along the lines suggested by game theory.

The relative lack of an agreed typification of this aspect of bridewealth may be an expression of the stress placed upon its functionality in generating and symbolizing alliance (in the broadest sense of the term). Transactional analyses apart, this tendency has been associated with two theories of value, both of which reduce politics to a residual category. The first is exemplified by Goody's

---

[1] Goody suggests that the use of bridewealth as an instrument of inequality is a "new development" in Africa (p. 13), although elsewhere he echoes Meillassoux's point (see below) that it may be employed by older men to sustain the dependency of younger persons upon them (p. 5).

"quantum of rights" hypothesis, according to which the size of prestations is held to vary in rough proportion to the rights trans-ferred.[1] This suggests that the relationship between the values alienated depends upon the intrinsic worth of those rights, which is normatively given, rather than negotiated in exchange. The second theory invokes the encompassing logic of balanced reciprocity. Thus Leach argues that, while many of the values involved are intangible and not easy to specify (cf. Sahlins, 1965, p. 177), [2] the "exchange account" entailed in the marriage process must ultimately balance. But, as Goody (op. cit., 2) points out, this assumption may end in tautology:

> If we assume immediate reciprocity, whether with regard to women or property, then the two sides of the equation have to balance by definition: assumptions about the 'value' system follow from assumptions about the nature of exchange. The tautology is even more apparent in systems of generalized exchange, where the reciprocity is notional.

Moreover, if balances are always struck, it follows that the flow of exchanges simply sustains the equilibrium of the existing political order, whether it be egalitarian or hierarchical; it can have little in-dependent effect upon that order, a conclusion which is antithetical to all but the most mechanistic and teleological views of politics.

*   *   *   *   *   *

This review of structural functionalist approaches, the constructive implications of which will be considered in due course, reiterates one methodological conclusion above all others: the inadvisability of seeking comparative generalizations by a process of assimilating apparently similar manifest phenomena from different systems to a general typification. At least in programmatic terms, Marxist and structuralist approaches attempt to avoid this problem by appropriating the analysis of marriage prestations to the conceptual-ization of encompassing systems of relations.

[1] Muller (1978) has offered convincing evidence in refutation of this hypothesis.

[2] Sahlins (1965, p. 177 ff) suggests that, in practice, marriage exchanges rarely involve true equi-valence. Apart from all else, the values alienated are not usually given to reckonings of balance — even though, at the level of the total political economy, there may be overall balances struck. In fact, he argues, like others before him, that it is "socially critical" for marriage to entail in-equalities, at least for a time, since indebtedness sustains alliance and affinal complementarity.

Marxist perspectives

Marxist discussion of marriage prestations, which has been limited, appears to have been addressed less to the explanation of the phenomena *per se* than to the problem of typifying pre-capitalist (and, particularly, African) modes of production. Perhaps the best known effort to analyse bridewealth arrangements in this context derives from Meillassoux's account of the Guro economy (1964; cf. also 1960). In it, he suggests that, since "elders" enjoy a monopoly over the type of goods required to enter a union, they may delay the marriages of youths, thereby perpetuating their dependency and retaining their labour services. These "elders" have limited influence in the productive process itself, and cannot sustain their dominance either by physical force or control over the means of production; hence it is in the sphere of marital exchange that their power of command is really grounded. But this also has a more general dimension. As Terray (1972, p. 164) explains in commentary,

> It follows that elders can only perpetuate their supremacy if they control the cir-culation of women and bride-prices, and arrange things so that this reproduces the social structures which sanction this supremacy.

Control over marriage and bridewealth, then, is both a matter of exercising dominance over young people and contriving the exchange of women in such a way as to reproduce *structures* of dependency. If, however, the elders perpetually denied marriage to their sons or appropriated all available wives for themselves, they would threaten the continuity of the community at large. Ultimately, therefore, they expedite the establishment of new unions. This loosens their "indivi-dual authority"; but, as bridewealth passes, the social structure is reproduced (Meillassoux, 1964, p. 223).

Hindess and Hirst (1975, p. 45 ff) dismiss this analysis as naive and egocentric (p. 78): it reduces a system of relations to an epiphen-omenon of the voluntaristic and subjective calculations of elders. Moreover, the systemic nature of these calculations is itself left obscure by the somewhat schematic character of Meillassoux's account. Because the goods used for bridewealth are not fully located within a total set of values, it is never clear what constitutes the range of choices which actually present themselves to elders. For example, may these

objects also be deployed to accumulate clients or establish relations
with other older men both within and outside the local community?
Are they scarce resources which may be put to alternate ends? What,
in other words, is the symbolic connection between the control of this
particular medium of exchange and the politics of status and
elderhood? These questions, which cannot be answered with reference
to the productive process alone, are critical if the Guro system is to be
explained in terms other than those of crude pragmatic individualism.
Still, this ethnography has become the focus for further theoretical
development and debate. Thus Dupré and Rey (1973) use it to
elaborate a notion of structured exploitation in a pre-capitalist context, implying that control over bridewealth may become the basis of
class conflict. For his part, Meillassoux avoids discussion of exploitation and Terray, following him, accuses Dupré and Rey of devaluing
the discriminatory cogency of the concept of class (p. 167).

Nevertheless, Meillassoux does hold that the privilege enjoyed by
elders may be transformed into other modes of dominance (1972,
p. 101): the prerogatives of seniority may be assumed by a "dominant
class, usually an aristocratic lineage". The latter becomes an
aggregation of "lords", who take as tribute the prestations formerly
due to elders; gradually they gain control over marriage and then the
means of production itself. Coquery-Vidrovitch (1976, pp. 95-6)
argues in similar terms:

> . . . this [Guro] system does not rule out a hierarchy of lineages. The numerical
> growth of the collectivity, for example, might involve an extension of the control
> of the elders to larger groups, manifested by the possession of varying symbols of
> prestige . . . An authority transmitted by primogeniture might lead to the pre-
> ponderance of a senior lineage, all of whose members enjoy similar prerogatives,
> transforming the primitive relationship between elders and young men into a
> relationship between patrons and clients (as in Buganda). This is the beginning
> of the hierarchization of social classes . . .

How precisely these transformations might occur remains abstruse, but
the essence of the argument is patent: control over bridewealth
represents the ontogeny of nascent class formations. While Marxist
anthropologists do not all accept Meillassoux's analysis, for some, Guro
arrangements have become a paradigmatic instance from which wider
theoretical inferences may be drawn.

Meillassoux's general observation, that control over bridewealth may allow elders to perpetuate the dependency of young men, is both correct and important (cf. Douglas, 1963, p. 58 ff on the Lele); the systematic relationship between these prestations and the production of differentiation and subordination is certainly worthy of further examination (see above.) However, as the essays below demonstrate, there is considerable cross-cultural diversity in the extent to which marriage payments may be so used. In some societies, it is held to be in the combined interest of father and son (and perhaps others too) for the latter to secure a wife, sometimes as soon as possible. After all, marriage does not bring benefits to the couple alone. Meillassoux's imputation of a simple opposition of interest in this respect between father and son ignores the fact that a union yields value to the former as well. More fundamentally, as Parkin (Chapter 7) indicates, the cultural constitution of exchange processes delimits the manner in which they may be perceived and utilized by all the parties to a marriage. This is no less true among the Guro than anywhere else: the manner in which elders regularly alienate marriage prestations, whether or not they defer doing so in the short-term, is inscribed in the socio-cultural logic of the social division of labour and the process of its reproduction.

In order to demonstrate this, it is necessary first to note an apparent circularity in Meillassoux's analysis. On the one hand, hegemony over the currency of bridewealth is held to constitute the elders' effective power of command; without it, their leadership would merely be "functional" (cf. Terray, op. cit., pp. 132, 166), for they lack the capability to coerce by other means. Yet it is largely by virtue of such authority that they supposedly have the capacity to monopolize the relevant valuables in the first place. In my view, this circularity results, firstly, from reducing marriage exchanges to an expression of inter-generational conflict and the simple logic of dominance and, secondly, from conflating the roles of elder and father. Even if we accept Meillassoux's general frame of reference for the moment, there are more convincing ways of interpreting his data.

Among the Guro, households ("work teams") are the major productive units, and enjoy a measure of economic autonomy. In the agricultural activities from which they obtain most of their livelihood, however, cooperation between these units is necessary. But this occurs within the context of kinship relations: the embracing domain of such cooperation is the lineage segment. Elderhood, in turn, is not simply a function of age. It is a status inscribed in the ideology of descent and refers to segmentary organization. An elder occupies his position by virtue of being the head of an aggregation of semi-interdependent and related "work teams". Now the emergence and definition of these aggregations depends upon a social, not a technological, fact (cf. Friedman, 1975, pp. 167-8), namely the growth and fission of domestic groups. Ontologically at least, it is through this process that fathers, as household heads, become elders, or segment heads. In short, the reproduction of elderhood itself, and its location in the encompassing structure of relations, is entailed in the subdivision of the parent household, and this can only take place with the marriage of its off-spring. Marriage, then, is not merely the means by which sons gain independence. It is also the process whereby the social division of labour at large is reproduced. Just as fathers become elders, so domestic relations are transformed into the wider order of inter-dependency upon which cooperative relations are predicated; these two transformations are entailed in one another. Baldly stated, elders cannot deny marriage or withold bridewealth, for, ultimately, it is through marriage that they become elders.

Nevertheless, there is a potential contradiction in the way that the Guro might themselves *experience* the articulation of household and segment. If Meillassoux is correct, the larger the domestic unit, the better it is able to realize its productive operations, a consideration which might indeed predispose some fathers to seek to delay the marriage of their sons. On the other hand, the elaboration of the larger cooperating segment, which is also a necessary condition of agricultural production, demands that the latter establish their own work teams. Apart from all else, this implies the recruitment of additional women to the segment, thereby increasing its labour force. Thus a man may also feel motivated to alienate his offspring. The final bestowal bridewealth, in other words, may have little to do with abstract appreciation of the need for communal survival; it too may be experienced in entirely pragmatic terms. The general point, then, is that the manifest tendency of some older men to defer marriages, which they do in their social capacity as fathers, not as "elders", would appear to be an expression of a socio-culturally constituted contradiction in the structure of productive relations. It makes little sense to see it in terms of a voluntary desire on the part of elders to sustain control; indeed, elderhood is ultimately predicated upon the independence of sons. Moreover, the compliance of younger men is not assured by witholding prestations, but by the social knowledge that they will inevitably be made available.

Meillassoux's explanation of Guro bridewealth arrangements, therefore, is less than convincing. *A fortiori*, its general applicability, and any attempt to view it as revealing the ontogeny of class formation, must also stand in considerable doubt. However, the major point which emerges from this discussion, i.e., that there is a systematic relationship between the logic of marriage prestations and the reproduction of the social system, has important implications.

Structuralist perspectives

Structuralist discourse, has, in general, also been concerned less with the explanation of bridewealth and dowry *per se* than with the elaboration of higher order models; in this case, of exchange systems. Prestations are seen here as integral elements of such systems, whose motivation lies in the universal principle of reciprocity (Levi-Strauss, 1969, pp. 52-68). Following Mauss (1954), exchange is conceived of as

> . . . a total phenomenon, . . . a total exchange, comprising food, manufactured objects, and that most precious category of goods, women.
> Levi-Strauss *loc. cit.*, 60-1)

The alienations associated with marriage, then, are conceived as related items in a series of reciprocal transfers between groups, the nature of which gives form to the social system. But this assumption may be interpreted in two distinct ways. This first is illustrated in Needham's account of Purum marriage processes (1962, pp. 94-5). These, he argues, involve two opposed cycles; a "feminine cycle", comprising women and certain goods, moves from wife-givers to wife-takers, while a "masculine cycle" transmits valuables, labour and ritual services in the other direction. The complementarity of the two cycles generates an interdependency between the groups concerned, and expresses "a balance between two sets of values, each vital to the total society" (p. 95). As this confirms, prestations are merely one feature of an equation of balance, whose form is enshrined in the symbolic system of the Purum. The central point, though, is that reciprocal equivalence is a condition of, and is contained within, any single series of marriage exchanges.

Needham may be quite correct in stressing that complementarity and balanced reciprocity are culturally inscribed values in Purum alliance exchanges. However, I have already noted the difficulties which arise when it is assumed, as a general principle, that "exchange accounts" must in fact balance at the end of every series of transactions (p. 21, f.n. 2).[1] Levi-Strauss (1969, p. 238) avoids this problem by taking it as axiomatic that women are always exchanged for women, never for goods. Hence, in "marriage by purchase" (i.e. with bridewealth), prestations are not themselves generic objects of exchange. They are "tokens" which guarantee that a wife may be obtained elsewhere for one given, under conditions which preclude direct interchanges. Thus, for any group, balanced reciprocity, the realization of like for like, may be circuitous and delayed; but it is ultimately achieved when the "token" is used. Bridewealth, in short, is a symbolic currency which may mediate the cycle of reciprocities where, in separate transactions, a unit alienates women in one direction and obtains them from another.

As this suggests, the symmetrical exchange of women between groups is inimical to "marriage by purchase". Similarly, in asymmetrical systems where the cycle of alienations is limited and closed (such, for example, that group A gives wives to B, B to C, and C to A), an overall balance of equivalences in wife-giving and taking may visibly be achieved, albeit obliquely. But as the cycle begins to lengthen, prestations are likely to enter the formula of exchange, for they allow flexibility in the realization of reciprocity over increasingly protracted chains of transactions. (In this sense, bridewealth is little more than an "indirect and developed form of marriage by exchange" [p. 470].) Where, under these conditions, cousin unions continue to be sanctioned, the system may retain its elementary structure, if in an extended and more supple form. Once the positive marriage rule is set aside, though, and purchase is substituted for the right to a cousin, generalised exchange will break away from that elementary structure and undergo a transformation towards a complex system.

It is not always clear, however, whether Levi-Strauss sees bridewealth as a cause, an effect, or a corollary of such transformations. This is evident in his celebrated Kachin analysis (loc. cit., p. 234 ff):

---

[1] I hasten to add that Needham appears not to make any such universalist claims, although others have done so (see above).

the lengthening of the asymmetrical cycle here is associated with the tendency of certain groups to alienate or appropriate prestations instead of fulfilling the conditions of alliance. This, in turn, allows "enterprising lineages" to short-circuit the existing cycle and to create advantageous exchange relations in order to accumulate goods and women. As a result, the cycle is ruptured: the essential egalitarianism of Kachin society gives way to anisogamy and hierarchy. This view bears glancing similarity to the assertion of some Marxists (see above) that marriage prestations may have a mediating instrumentality in the movement from egalitarian to hierarchical social orders. But, while an evolutionary position has been imputed to Levi-Strauss in this respect (Barnes, 1971, p. 164, p. 103), he does not deal systematically with the relationship between marriage rules, prestations and political structures. Consequently, the analysis of bridewealth remains securely contained within the formal logic of exchange arrangements.

Levi-Strauss's interpretation of "marriage by purchase" has been censured for its inapplicability in some contexts (e.g. Tardits, 1974)[1] and employed in others to resolve related problems (e.g. de Heusch, 1974). Its evaluation as a generic approach to the subject, however, depends first upon the determination of its theoretical status, a question not explicitly addressed by Levi-Strauss himself. Three possibilities suggest themselves, of which the most ambitious is that it represents a universalist explanation of the genesis of bridewealth. But if this is intended, we are being asked to take on trust — for the proposition is undemonstrable — that every system of "marriage by purchase" originated in an elementary structure and has undergone the same transformation towards the complex form. Of course, this also presupposes that we accept Levi-Strauss's conceptualization of elementary structures, which has been increasingly criticized (e.g. Korn, 1973, pp. 36-8, 140 ff; Leach, 1970, p. 105 ff), and the constitutive logic underlying his taxonomy of systems. Since it is inappropriate here, I have avoided the general debates which surround these paradigmatic issues. But, significantly, the classic case which disconfirms the bridewealth hypothesis, at least in this (supposed) version, does so precisely because it contradicts the ontological assumptions upon which that taxonomy is founded. The point has

---

[1] See also Leach's criticism (1951) of the analysis of the Kachin, to which Levi-Strauss has replied (1969, p. 238 ff).

repeatedly been made: FBD marriage systems, of which the Bedouin and Tshidi systems are variants, do not merely represent an empirical anomaly for the Levi-Straussian scheme. Rather, they deny the assumed universality of the very principle upon which it depends; viz. exogamy as a precondition for the reciprocal exchange of wives. As Bourdieu (1977, p. 30) puts it, they "challenge . . . the theory of marriage as an exchange of one woman against another". Consequently, bridewealth in these societies cannot be reduced to an indirect form of marriage by exchange; nor could its emergence be the corollary of a transformation in a taxonomy between types whose validity it negates.

I find it difficult to believe that Levi-Strauss intended his explanation to be understood in these terms, however. Had he done so, he would surely have confronted some of the obvious problems which it raises. It is one thing, for example, to associate the emergence of bridewealth with a particular mode of systemic transformation, but quite another to demonstrate the manner in which a meaningful reconstitution of the principle of exchange actually occurs. Similarly, the question of variation also stands unresolved: if marriage always involves the alienation of a woman for another, why is it that both prestations and conjugal unions may take diverse forms *within* as well as between systems (cf. Parkin, Chapter 7; Barnes, Chapter 4)?

In the light of these considerations, it is possible that Levi-Strauss was concerned less with the universal genesis of bridewealth than with the proposition that it represents a symbolic currency by means of which the (indirect) exchange of women may be ordered and the principle of reciprocity realized. While this appears more plausible, it does not obviate the intractable issue of patrilateral parallel cousin marriage, or explain those cases in which the mobilization and alienation of gifts appear to *constitute* wife-giving and wife-taking units (see above). Nor, again, does it account for the fact that, in some systems, contrasting kinds of union co-exist, each with its appropriate schedule of payments. In these contexts, as Barnes and Parkin indicate, the various forms of prestation mediate the exchange of a range of different values associated with conjugality and affinity. Their reduction to an undifferentiated symbolic "token", and of marriage to a single class of exchange, does not illuminate their meaning, therefore. Indeed, the explanation of bridewealth in these terms is reminiscent of a simple functionalist logic: the token exists, ultimately, to sustain the equation of balanced alienation, the principle upon which systemic integration is held to depend.

The final possibility is that the analysis of "marriage by purchase" is meant simply as an account of the transformation of elementary structures, and not as a general explanation of bridewealth at all. Even as such, it would not answer all the problems raised thus far, and has been empirically challenged (Tardits op. cit.). But it would be consistent with structuralist methodology in one important respect. Whatever the merits of its particular applications to the question of bridewealth, this methodology typically seeks the meaning of a social phenomenon in terms of its relations to other phenomena within an encompassing system; the discovery of principles from the cross-cultural comparison of decontextualised "institutions" is specifically eschewed. Because marriage payments are conceived as elements within total exchange systems, then, they are not in themselves an independent object of theoretical statement — except in so far as the latter addresses the nature of their encompassment.

This is precisely what both Needham (1962) and Levi-Strauss (1969) imply: marriage alienations derive their meaning by virtue of their location in the embracing logic of cycles of reciprocal giving and taking. While it may not promise a generic "theory" of bridewealth in familiar positivist terms, this does reiterate the constructive importance of the classic assertion that prestations cannot be understood except in so far as they are elements in total socio-cultural systems.

At the same time, much structuralist writing, and Levi-Strauss (1969) is no exception in this respect, violates this very principle. For, on *a priori* grounds, which are assumed rather than established, marriage exchanges are taken to constitute a total and closed system in and of themselves. At both the empirical and theoretical levels — as several of the present contributors indicate (e.g. Strathern, Barnes, Chapters 2 and 4) — this is simply unacceptable: marriage is merely an element in an encompassing exchange system and, therefore, is a moment (or a cycle) within the embracing and interrelated processes generated by that system. Such processes may take a variety of forms, but they often include several other elements; for example, funerary and sacrificial alienations, child payments, matrilateral transfers and so on. In terms of the logic to which structuralist methodology professedly subscribes — and the ontology which it derives from Saussure and Mauss — both the symbolic value and the structural implications of marriage (and its associated prestations) are rendered largely meaningless once they are analytically privileged and/or excised from the context of which the other elements are equally a part.

In total, while affirming a programmatic committment to the analysis of total systems, many structuralists have fallen into the elementary errors of reductionism and decontextualization by treating marriage exchanges as if they constituted a totality, rather than being encompassed in one. Moreover, even if structuralist models did comprehensively address exchange in all its dimensions, there would remain the final question of why "exchange" is equated with "system" in the first place. Is the former not subsumed in a yet higher order, of which the production, distribution and consumption of social and material value are the other components?[1]

II

In summary, then, although each of the three paradigmatic approaches has yielded important insights, none has yet offered a satis-factory general explanation of marriage prestations, albeit for different reasons. Structural functionalist methodology, which envisages such an explanation as possible and has produced most of the available data, has failed in this respect because of a dualism in its heuristic and theory-building procedures. For, while it acknowledges the analytical significance, in any single instance, of the relationship between a given social form and the particularities of its systemic context, this relationship is violated in the cause of higher order ex-planation and generalization: the latter are typically based upon the identification of a synthetic category of largely decontextualized phenomena (e.g. "bridewealth") defined by their surface likenesses and their coexistence with apparently similar organizational features (e.g. "unilineal corporations"). This procedure creates analytical artifice from polythetic class, proceeding from ill-conceived taxonomy to misguided theory.[2] In contrast, neither Marxist nor structuralist

[1] I am particularly indebted to Terence Turner for helping me to clarify a number of the issues addressed in this commentary on structuralism, as well as that on Marxist approaches. Many of his ideas are reflected in these sections (see, e.g. Turner, 1980).

[2] This procedure has also underpinned various efforts to establish correlative generalizations, and led to many of the arguments which have ensued in their wake. The infamous "marriage stability" debate is one well-worn example. I have deliberately avoided re-opening this issue here, both be-cause my commentary on structrual functionalism ought to make it clear, as several other writers have done, why the whole question was theoretically ill-founded in the first place.

approaches allow that marriage prestations are, in themselves, an independent object of theory, although both have ascribed function-ality and analytical privilege to the marriage process at large, and to marriage prestations in particular, in sustaining the integrity of social orders. Moreover, in appropriating such exchanges to systemic models, these approaches have barely begun to comprehend the wide variations in the manifest arrangements that are known to exist.

Given that anthropology is, in theory and practice, concerned alike with ethnographic specificity and comparison, how then is it possible to establish a universe of discourse about any phenomena which embraces both? The most usual answer — since it contradicts the highest precepts of none of the major paradigms — is to reaffirm the value of comparing total systems or processes. Needham (1971b, p. 6), following Leach, applies this dictum directly to the study of marriage:

> The comparison of marriage in different societies needs therefore to be con-textual and ultimately 'total' in a Maussian sense, if we are to be sure that we understand what we are trying to compare.

Laudable though this might appear, it does not address the question of what actually constitutes a "total" system or process; nor does it detail an acceptable methodology of comparison, which, after all, is the problem with which we began. Furthermore, even those writers who have ostensibly sought to contextualize marriage prestations in the manner to which Needham alludes have had limited success. Significantly, this is precisely because they have given theoretical priority to a single motivating process, be it exchange (Levi-Strauss, 1969) or production (Meillassoux, 1960, 1964, 1972), and thereby con-fused these processes for the total systems which encompass them.

Is the inference to be drawn from this that we ought to abandon the attempt to explain marriage prestations in comparative terms, and be satisfied with the conclusion that our key concepts are no more than odd-job words? Or, do we simply ignore the epistemological problems which have been raised, and produce ever more data in the hope that theory will ultimately take care of itself? The present symposium, in spite of its empirical and analytical diversity, suggests the opposite: that a meaningful discourse is both possible and worthwhile. In order, finally, to explore this, let me draw together the various constructive strands which have emerged thus far:

1. The meaning of marriage payments is not to be understood by the cross-cultural comparison of their surface manifestations and their general social correlates, but by first establishing their relations to other organizational elements within encompassing systems.

2. Any such system may be analysed at two levels. On the one hand, it exists as a constitutive order; that is, as a set of related principles which give form to the socio-cultural universe. On the other, it is a lived-in, everyday context which represents itself to individuals and groups in a repertoire of values and contradictions, rules and relationships, interests and ideologies.

3. The marriage process is a fundamental dimension of the reproduction, and potential transformation, of the social system at large.

4. The mobilization, alienation and distribution of prestations, along with other principles and processes, may represent a generative mechanism whereby social units, roles and relationships are actualized, transformed and given their manifest content.

Now these emergent propositions converge in a common theme which runs through all the essays, albeit in a variety of ways. It may be summarized thus: the transfer of material objects, an interrelated class of alienations, of which marriage prestations are one element[1], represents a point of articulation between the organizational principles which underlie and constitute a socio-cultural system and the surface forms and processes which together comprise the lived-in universe. Let me elaborate on this.

Few anthropologists would disagree that an analytical distinction is to be drawn between the surface forms and processes of everyday life and those structural principles which lie behind them. There may be disagreement over the ontology of the latter, and the exact nature of their interrelationship, but there is no doubting the constitutive status attributed to such organizing principles as descent and affinity, marriage rules and alliance, sex and age, devolution and rank, ceremonial exchange, and so on.[2] However, if the implied distinction between systemic levels is to be given adequate theoretical recognition,

---

[1] "Alienation" is defined here as any voluntary or involuntary transfer (of a material object). Following Mauss, such transfers might also betoken the symbolic alienation of part of the self.

[2] Marxist anthropology might appear to represent an exception to this statement. But the so-called "technicists" and "vulgar materialists" apart, many writers in this tradition have shown a reluctance to deny the ontological status of the social in pre-capitalist systems. This issue runs to the very heart of Marxist discourse, however; it is too complex to be dealt with adequately here.

it is necessary to pose a number of contingent questions. How, for example, are these constitutive principles in fact actualized? How do they give form to the surface realities of everyday life? And, conversely, how may such manifest activities transform and reconstitute organizational principles, as they must if social systems are to be accorded any historical existence? In other words, wherein lies the dialectical relationship between the two primary levels which comprise a socio-cultural system? It goes without saying that the formulation of the questions in these terms connotes a theoretical orientation which differs markedly from structural functionalist, structuralist or Marxist orthodoxy. Nevertheless, I would suggest that it offers new insights into familiar problems concerning the comparative analysis of socio-cultural systems in general and marriage exchanges in particular.

Significantly, some of those who have sought answers to these questions have tended to do so, either implicitly or explicitly, with reference to the order of material exchanges (cf. Evans-Pritchard, 1940, p. 89). Thus Sahlins suggests that ". . . the system of object-values is a realization, on the level of concrete distinctions, of the main relationships of the cultural order."[1] This statement foreshadows my central point that the logic of alienation and the transfer of property[2] underlies the articulation of constitutive social principles and surface forms and processes. This view has sometimes been implicit in analyses of devolution and its relationship to the internal elaboration of descent groupings. It posits that the ideology of descent might represent a culturally inscribed order in terms of which status and segmentary relations are categorically mapped; but it is with reference to the devolutionary process[3], whether or not it is explicitly regarded from within as a context for strategic activity, that members acquire their rank and location within fields of relationships, that the social definition of linkages between them are negotiated and expressed, and

---

[1] I am indebted to Marshall Sahlins for allowing me to quote this passage from his unpublished paper, "A Synthesis of Riches: Raw Women and Cooked Men and other 'Great Things' of Fiji" (November 1978).

[2] I stress alienation rather than exchange, since the first is prior to the second; that is alienation can occur without exchange, but not vice versa. In this sense, exchange is contingent upon, and a compound form of, alienation.

[3] Note that it is to the devolutionary process, and not (death-centred) inheritance, that I refer. This process, in many societies, begins at the moment a domestic unit is established (and before some of those who will be involved are yet born). For the very creation of such a unit typically involves the allocation of property which will become part of the inter-generational flow of material holdings (Roberts and Comaroff, 1979; Comaroff and Roberts, forthcoming).

that segmentary alignments gain their manifest shape.

The devolutionary process is not the only one in which intra-group relations are configured, however. Marriage payments may equally be involved in this, as the Mursi ethnography vividly demonstrates (see above). Indeed, in any system where explicit rules delimit the contributors to, and recipients of, prestations by kinship category, their alienation represents a symbolic context in which relevant linkages are construed and, perhaps, negotiated. Existing definitions of these linkages may simply be reaffirmed, or they may be contested; but, in either case, a manifest universe of effective relations is ordered in the process. Even where explicit rules are absent, moreover, the alienation of goods or animals, be it as a donation to a marriage payment or as a distributive gesture by its recipient, is a symbolic act of social definition; one which, as Evans-Pritchard (ibid) would have it, "builds up" relations, just as non-giving may cause them to lapse. Returning to Sahlins' insight, it is one of the processes in which the categories of a socio-cultural order are realised and given surface form as (living and dead) persons are located within them; indeed, according to Peters it is *the* process in which effective patterns of relationship are configured among the Bedouin.[1] The same, of course, is true of extra-group affinal relations, whether or not these are predicated upon positive marriage rules (cf. Barnes, Peters, Strathern, Chapters 4, 5, and 2).

This is perhaps the most elementary, and, indeed, well-recognised, sense in which marriage alienations, as integral to a system of alienations, articulate the different levels of a socio-cultural order. I have chosen it to exemplify my argument, however, because it suggests a line of enquiry which, when placed in the context of the present symposium, has a number of illuminating implications.

The first addresses the relationship between marriage and prestations. With few exceptions, there has been a general tendency, within all the major paradigms, to make a functional distinction, effectively if not programmatically, between them. Marriage is seen as

---

[1] Significantly, Peters points out that a new affinal tie commands higher bridewealth than do older ones, a pattern also found in some other societies. As affinal links are gradually reinforced by further unions, the amount alienated "goes down progressively until a kinship structure has been erected." This provides a vivid illustration of my point, since it suggests that marriage alienations continue as long as an order of relations is in the process of being realized; once it has actually been realized, further alienations become unnecessary.

structurally prior, and prestations largely as its institutionalized mode of facilitation. It is as if the primary reason that marriage payments exist is to expedite or regulate proper marriage exchanges, whether it be to mediate symbolically the indirect flow of women where their reciprocal alienation is impossible (Levi-Strauss), to realize the rights and duties which are inherent in the conjugal bond (Fortes, 1953, 1962), or to control the timing of espousal (Meillassoux). Now this emphasis upon teleology typically depends upon treating "marriage" as a single and undifferentiated category of relationship; it assumes *a priori* that all conjugal unions are of a kind and have broadly the same structural significance. If other types of union are dealt with at all, they are usually regarded as "informal" and, therefore, structurally residual.

Such a view might fit well with established jural orthodoxy (see above), and with alliance models; but it leads to a gross oversimplification, and necessarily obscures the semantic logic of marriage payments. For, in most social systems, there exists some form of taxonomy, however rudimentary, according to which unions may be classified; indeed, unless mating and marriage were held indigenously to be coterminous, it is difficult to see how it could be otherwise. Moreover, while in some instances such taxonomies may have only two component classes (which a crude jural logic might gloss as "legitimate:illegitimate"), others are more complex (Parkin, Barnes, Comaroff). Whatever their degree of elaboration, however, such taxonomies imply the same thing: that each category of union within them entails a different normative configuration of domestic, affinal and kin relations; each has different structural implications; and each yields different values to those involved. I stress that this is *not* the same as saying merely that some unions are "valid" or "recognized" and others are not; for indigenous distinctions may not be drawn in legalistic terms akin to our own, even in those contexts where established taxonomies have only two classes. Rather, the various categories represent contrasting ways of defining and locating unions and their offspring in a social universe (Barnes, Parkin).

The meaning of marriage prestations, then, begins with the fact that, where they exist, they represent a critical element in the symbolic order with reference to which unions are classified and invested with social currency. In simple (two-category) systems, the act of giving or witholding may itself index the definition of a union; in more complex ones, there are a plurality of available modes of alienation. In short, prestations transform mating, which in itself may have no intrinsic social value, into a socially meaningful process, and thereby locate it in a universe of relations. As Parkin demonstrates for the Mijikenda peoples, the semantic logic of prestations may be expressed as a "grammar" which underlies systematic variations in the relationship between marriage and the ordering of affinal, familial and devolutionary patterns. This is also exemplified by the case of the Buna (Barnes) who, as I have already noted, recognize two primary forms of union, each being marked by its own schedule of prestations. The one form is associated with MBD marriage and an order of prescriptive assymmetrical alliances linking descent groups; the second, with marriages ouside of this order. In the first type, in which relations between affines are marked by the complementary flow of gifts, bride-wealth is not merely given to wife-givers, but also to wife-givers of wife-takers, thereby locating the union securely within a total marriage cycle and an encompassing pattern of alliances. The second form, in contrast, involves none of this: it brings about uxorilocal residence and matrifiliation (see above) and a quite different configuration of relations.

Parkin's conclusion is of general importance, therefore, in that it addresses the crucial connection between the semantic dimension of these prestations and the systemic implications of their alienation. The former dimension orders the range of alternatives in terms of which manifest relations and aggregations may potentially be actualized in the marriage process;[1] as such, it constitutes a repertoire of values and goals which actors may perceive to motivate their choices, and in respect of which they may seek to contrive their careers and social situations. But, by definition, any range of alternatives may be realized in more than one way; as I have stressed, the implications of marriage alienations are to be distinguished from their motivation. This, of course, is one reason why two systems with identical rules and categories may exhibit markedly different statistical patterns "on the ground", as may a single system at different historical moments. *Pace* transactional theory, however, the structure of these systems is not the

---

[1] It is important to emphasize that this refers specifically to the marriage process. Ultimately, the full range of potential surface forms can never be determined by marriage arrangements alone; it depends, as I have already stated, upon the total set of constitutive principles in any system. The point is developed further below.

product of choice. Quite the opposite: the logic of choice is inscribed in
their constitutive principles. And its aggregative implications — the so-
called "emergent" forms yielded by transactional processes — are in
fact particular historical realizations, at the level of gross surface
arrangements, of the generative and transformational properties of
any such system. But this anticipates a later stage of the discussion, for
it raises, at least by implication, the problem of the relationship
between marriage and the other constitutive principles which underlie
a socio-cultural order.

As all this suggests, then, marriage prestations are not ontologically
separable from marriage. Rather, they are complementary elements of
the same thing: a meaningful order with reference to which the
physical fact of cohabitation is transformed into a social fact. This is
well illustrated by the fact that, in those systems in which prestations
are regularly presented late in the development cycle — the Tshidi
provide one example here — the terms relevant to the definition of
unions (such as "marriage", "husband" or "wife") are unmarked; they
cannot be lexically separated from what we might equally translate as,
say, "temporary liaison", "man" or "woman". In these systems it is
typically very difficult to establish, in the abstract, the status of an
everyday union (Comaroff, Chapter 6). But the alienation of
prestations, when it is agreed to have occurred, removes the ambiguity, finally defines the status of the union, and locates its offspring in a genealogically ordered social field. Similarly, in those
contexts where a union is defined by an initial payment, but where the
remainder is given in instalments, as in the Bedouin case, the ideology
of affinity is closely associated with the concept of debt; the debt, as
the saying goes, is the relationship. Here, as in other systems where the
link between affinity and debt is culturally emphasized, marriage tends
to be viewed as a process of becoming rather than as a state of being. In
short, the alienation of prestations marks the progressive realization of
a categorically inscribed relationship.

In dealing with this initial dimension of the meaning of marriage
prestations, I reiterate that it is not my intention to suggest that, from
within any system, they are perceived solely as a classificatory device.
The manner in which the logic of these prestations is experienced in a
particular society — for example, whether they are integral to an
ideology of exchange (as among, say, Melpa and Wiru) or not (as in
Macedonia), or whether they are the object of strategic manipulation

(Bedouin, Tshidi) or not (Mursi) — depends equally upon another level of their meaning. This, as I have already implied, is to be found in the relationship between marriage (in the broadest sense) and the other constitutive principles with which it coexists.

It would seem self-evident that the meaning of marriage prestations, given their semantic relationship to marriage, depends in large measure upon the location of the latter in any constitutive order. Yet it has been the tendency to ignore this which has led to many of the theoretical problems discussed earlier. Now it is hardly necessary to emphasize that marriage rules are themselves always an element in the set of organizing principles upon which a socio-cultural system is founded: in their absence, the constructs of family, kinship or descent would have little meaning, just as, without them, there could be no systematic reproduction of a social universe. Accounting for the particularity of any system, therefore, depends first upon establishing the relations between these principles. As Strathern's analysis of the Melpa and Wiru ethnography indicates, where such relations vary across societies, prestations will have a different structural value (in the Sausserian sense), whether or not they share the diacritica which we gloss in such labels as "bridewealth" or "dowry". This, again, is also demonstrated by Barnes in his comparison of a range of systems in which the relationship between the principles subsumed in descent, alliance and marriage occur in a number of combinative transformations. Not only are there concommitant variations in the meaning of bridewealth, but also in the surface structures, corporate arrangements and social forms which may be realized by its alienation.

The general point is taken an important step further by contrasting so-called "endogamous" systems, of which the Bedouin and Tshidi are two variants, with more familiar exogamous patrilineal ones. The differences are marked, being manifest particularly in the nature of social aggregation, the ideology and ethos of social action and the organization of political processes and economic relations. For reasons which are explained in my own essay below, "endogamous" systems such as these tend to be experienced from within as highly individualistic and competitive. Group boundaries are constantly mitigated by intra-descent group unions and the onus thrown upon the individual to contrive his relations and alliances. Consequently, the effective universe of kin tends to be drawn from a bilateral kindred which is pragmatically constructed in the course of the social process (see above). Here, then, the logic of patrilateral parallel cousin marriage, in its relation to the other organizing principles, necessarily generates a fluid and enigmatic social environment, in which categorical linkages overlap and entail normative contradictions which demand social management; even inactivity affects the social field and may be construed as strategically motivated. Under these conditions, as Peters shows, prestations do not merely index different marriage choices. They also become an instrument used by individuals in politically and economically inspired efforts to shape social networks to advantage, and to control other persons within them. As such, these prestations may have little to do with the establishment of affinal ties between units, or with groups at all, this being quite unlike the pattern typically described for exogamous unilineal systems, where their symbolism has centrally to do with the incorporation of brides, the affirmation of inter-group relations, and so on.

Although I have only drawn the contrast in the broadest of terms, this is enough to make its implications clear. Not only does the total order of constitutive principles impart meaning to marriage payments in any society. It also gives form to the manner in which its members experience their social universe, and conceive the dominant ideology and order of values in terms of which action is motivated within it. It is only by confronting the full theoretical moment of all this that it becomes possible to explain why, for example, despite sharing largely the same definitional and substantive features, dowry in Macedonia is so different in its structural, ideological and politico-economic aspects from its Indian counterparts (see above). The same, of course, may be said for the variations described in respect of the Mijikenda peoples, the Melpa and Wiru, or the societies of Eastern Indonesia. Once again, there is no need to labour the point, since these analyses speak cogently for it. But it does have two general analytical implications worthy of note.

The first refers to the question of whether or not prestations have a commercial character, a long-standing issue which refuses to die (see p. 11 f.n. 2). It follows from the discussion thus far that the values which are indigenously held to motivate marriage transactions within a system, be they conceived in terms of utility or reciprocity, bargain or balanced exchange, depend upon its socio-cultural constitution. And there appears to be considerable cross-cultural variability in this respect. Thus, for example, Melpa marriage alienations are one element in a total exchange system in which successful accumulation is an ideologically stressed objective, while marriage and dowry in Macedonia are barely regarded as involving exchange at all; Mursi seem compelled to give as much as they have, while Swazi (royals) attempt to obtain as much as possible; Tshidi typically give the same (relatively small) amount for all unions, while Bedouin bridewealth varies markedly in size; and some Eastern Indonesians appear to believe that marriage really is uncommonly like a commercial transaction in women, a perception they sometimes seek to mystify. As this suggests, marriage prestations cannot be *explained* in utilitarian or commercial terms, since their utilitarian quality is a culturally constituted variable; but nor can it be claimed, as a universal, that they never have a commercial character. What does need to be explained, however, are the systemic conditions which generate ideologies and value orders of contrasting kinds.[1]

The second implication concerns the relationship between marriage exchanges and group boundaries. This is a significant issue for both structuralist and structural functionalist theory, of course, since both assume *a priori* that marriage typically involves bounded units; indeed, this assumption underlies their respective approaches to the analysis of marriage rules and the structural implications of affinity at large. It seems to me, however, that the converse may be true: that group boundaries do not necessarily regulate the marriage process but are its symbolic product, at least in those systems whose organizing principles entail a potentiality for the generation of discrete units. However, this potentiality is certainly not found in all systems, nor, as Barnes points out, ought we expect that it should be. As will be clear by now, for example, where FBD unions are permitted, discreteness is not a necessary characteristic of groups, for the marriage process itself actualizes complex configurations of overlapping relations, which is why the established theoretical paradigms have had so much difficulty comprehending such arrangements. As the Eastern Indonesian ethnography shows, moreover, there are many other structural conditions which may mitigate the formation of boundaries in a social universe.

Even where the quality of boundedness is a potentiality inscribed in

---

[1] Exactly the same may be said of the legal aspect of marriage, and the ideology of right and liability. This ideology, which requires explanation rather than offers it, is again of variable cross-cultural significance (see above; Comaroff, Chapter 6).

a system, as it may be when the principle of exogamy coexists with exclusive (though not necessarily unilineal; cf. Barnes, Chapter 4) rules
of affiliation, everyday social ties are often intrinsically ambiguous,
particularly at the margins of social units. As Peters reminds us in
respect of the Nuer, the exigencies of territorial arrangements, the
compounding of local ties and a degree of mobility may result in highly
complex patterns of relationship. In this context, the lines of cleavage
between higher order segments tend to be anything but sharply
demarcated, which we might expect them to be if the rule of exogamy
really did mediate marriage choice in pragmatic terms. In other
words, it is doubtful whether, under such conditions (and they are not
uncommon), those involved in the creation of any union are expressly
motivated by the calculus of exogamy. It is as likely, on the available
evidence (cf. Peters, Chapter 5), that the relevant kin of nubile young
people seek prospective affines first and contrive the definition of their
relationship to them thereafter. As is well-known, this is culturally
recognised in some societies where, if a kinship tie is held to exist
between the spouses-to-be, it may be ritually severed. The conclusion
which flows from all this is that the rules of exogamy and affiliation
give form to a categorical order whose logical construction entails a
prescriptive opposition between consanguinity and affinity, which, in
its social aspect, must necessarily be expressed in the discreteness of
those units involved in the conjugal process. Group boundedness,
therefore, is a corollary of a categorical order based upon these constitutive principles, and not itself an ontological feature of a social
system. Thus, whatever the state of relations which obtain between
units in advance of marriage, the latter realizes a boundary between
them. The passage of bridewealth, then, in so far as it indexes a union
of a certain kind and actualizes a concomitant field of social relations,
is a symbolic medium in terms of which this process of realization
takes place.

The theoretical implications of this, significant though they
obviously are, cannot be pursued here, except to note one point of
general importance which emerges in two of the essays below. It
concerns the relationship between the constitutive and "lived-in"
orders, with particular reference to the elaboration of social units.
Barnes notes that the introduction of marriage prestations where they
did not exist before in Eastern Indonesia may lead to a development
from individual to corporate responsibility. He goes on to state that:

> Since such payments have much to do with the nature of corporations, it is conceivable, though impossible to prove at the moment, that they might be closely involved in a causal sequence leading to changes in rules of descent.

Similarly, Parkin shows that the introduction of cash into bridewealth among the Mijikenda peoples, the particular effect of which is mediated by the pre-existing nature of marriage prestations, may reconstitute the fundamental principles upon which these systems are based, with or without the volition of individual actors.

Now this informs a question raised earlier. For it confirms that the relationship between the constitutive principles and the "lived-in" universe is ultimately a dialectical one, in that each order may reproduce, transform or reconstitute the other, Indeed, it is this relationship which underpins the historicity of any socio-cultural system, whether it continues to be reproduced, changes from within, or is changed by virtue of exogenous forces (which themselves require symbolic mediation if they are to be internalized and given social currency). In this respect, the alienation of material objects, because it represents the point of articulation between systemic levels, is clearly a critical element in the dialectic. As Barnes implies, the full force of this is yet to be explored, but it leads towards an approach which encompasses not merely the comparison of synchronic systems in space, but also of their dialectical movement through time.

*   *   *

It is unnecessary to summarize my discussion, since this discussion is itself a summary statement of a position. In formulating it as I have done, I have drawn freely upon the essays below. I do not pretend, however, that their authors would necessarily endorse my approach, or those of each other, just as I do not feel compelled to agree myself with each analysis in all of its dimensions. My intention, then, has specifically not been to seek points of consensus between the contributors. Rather, it has been to show, by drawing out the implications of their studies, that it is indeed possible to establish a constructive universe of discourse about the meaning of marriage payments without retreading the pathways towards old epistemological traps, or abandoning comparison entirely. In this respect, it has been central to my argument that, by conceptualizing socio-cultural systems as involving a dialectical relationship between their constitutive and lived-in orders, we may begin to engage in meaningful systemic comparison. By that token, although it is largely programmatic and certainly not exhaustive of its subject matter, this discussion has as much relevance for anthropological method in general as it does for the analysis of marriage payments in particular.

Bibliography

Ardener, E. W. (1971). The new anthropology and its critics. *Man*, (N.S.), **6**, 449-467.

Barnes, J. (1971). "Three Styles in the Study of Kinship". Tavistock, London.

Barth, F. (1966). "Models of Social Organization". Royal Anthropological Institute (Occasional Paper No. 23), London.

Barth, F. (1973). Descent and marriage reconsidered. *In* "The Character of Kinship" (Ed. J. Goody). Cambridge University Press, London.

Berreman, G. D. (1962). Pahan polyandry: a comparison. *American Anthropologist*, **64**, 1, 60-75.

Blau, P. (1964). "Exchange and Power". Wiley, New York.

Bledsoe, C. "Women and Marriage in Kpelle Society". Stanford University Press, Stanford, (in press).

Bledsoe, C. and Murphy, W. P. The Kpelle Negotiation of Marriage and Matrilateral Ties (unpublished MS).

Bourdieu, P. (1977). "Outline of a Theory of Practice" translated by R. Nice). Cambridge University Press, London.

Chaney, R. P. (1978). Polythematic expansion: remarks on Needham's polythetic classification. *Current Anthropology*, **19**, 1, 139-143.

Comaroff, Jean (1978). Medicine and culture: some anthropological perspectives. *Social Science and Medicine*, **12B**, 247-254.

Comaroff, J. L. and Comaroff, J. The management of marriage in a Tswana chiefdom. *In* "Essays on African Marriage in Southern Africa" (Eds. E. J. Krige and J. L. Comaroff). Forthcoming.

Comaroff, J. L. and Roberts, S. A. (1977). Marriage and extra-marital sexuality: the dialectics of legal change among the Kgatla. *Journal of African Law*, **21**, 1, 97-123.

Comaroff, J. L. and Roberts, S. A. "Rules and processes: the cultural logic of dispute in an African context". Forthcoming.

Coquery-Vidrovitch, C. (1976). The political economy of the African peasantry and modes of production. *In* "The Political Economy of Contemporary Africa" (Eds. P. W. Gutkind and E. Wallerstein). Sage Series on African Modernization and Development, vol. 1. Sage Publications, Beverley Hills and London.

Crick, M. (1976). "Explorations in Language and Meaning: towards a Semantic Anthropology". Malaby Press, London.

De Heusch, L. (1974). The debt of the maternal uncle. *Man*, (N.S.), **9**, 4, 609-616.

Douglas, M. (1963). "The Lele of the Kasai". Oxford University Press for the International African Institute, London.

Dumont, L. (1971). "Introduction à Deux Théories d'Anthropologie Sociale". Mouton, Paris and the Hague.

Dupré, G. and Rey, R. P. (1973). Reflections on the pertinence of a theory of the history of exchange. *Economy & Science*, **2**, 2, 131-163.

Evans-Pritchard, E. E. (1934). Social character of bridewealth with special reference to the Azande. *Man*, 34, 194, 172-175.

Evans-Pritchard, E. E. (1940). "The Nuer". Clarendon Press, Oxford.

Evans-Pritchard, E. E. (1951). "Kinship and Marriage Among the Nuer". Clarendon Press, Oxford.

Fallers, L. A. (1973). "Inequality: Social Stratifications Reconsidered". University of Chicago Press, Chicago.

Fortes, M. (1949). "The Web of Kinship Among the Tallensi". Oxford University Press for the International African Institute, London.

Fortes, M. (1953). The structure of unilineal descent groups. *American Anthropologist*, 55, 1, 17-41. (Reprinted in M. Fortes (1970). "Time and Social Structure and Other Essays". Athlone Press, London.)

Fortes, M. (1961). Comment on S. N. Eisenstadt, "Studies of Complex Societies". *Current Anthropology*, 2, 211-212.

Fortes, M. (1962). Introduction. *In* "Marriage in Tribal Societies" (Ed. M. Fortes). Cambridge Papers in Social Anthropology No. 3. Cambridge University Press, London.

Friedman, J. (1975). Tribes, states, and transformations. *In* "Marxist Analyses and Social Anthropology" (Ed. M. Bloch). A.S.A. Studies No. 2. Malaby Press, London.

Geertz, C. (1973). "The Interpretation of Cultures". Basic Books, New York.

Gluckman, M. (1950). Kinship and marriage among the Lozi of Northern Rhodesia and the Zulu of Natal. *In* "African Systems of Kinship and Marriage" (Eds. A. R. Radcliffe-Brown and D. Forde). Oxford University Press for the International African Institute, London.

Gluckman, M. (1955). "The Judicial Process Among the Barotse" (2nd edn 1967). Manchester University Press, Manchester.

Goldschmidt, W. (1969). Game theory, cultural values and brideprice in Africa. *In* "Game Theory in the Social Sciences" (Eds. I. R. Buchler and H. G. Nutini). University of Pittsburgh Press, Pittsburgh.

Goldschmidt, W. (1974). The economics of brideprice among the Sebei and in East Africa. *Ethnology*, 13, 4, 311-331.

Goody, J. (1973). Bridewealth and dowry in Africa and Eurasia. *In* "Bridewealth and Dowry" (Eds J. Goody and S. J. Tambiah). Cambridge Papers in Social Anthropology No. 7. Cambridge University Press, London.

Gray, R. F. (1960). Sonjo bride-price and the question of African 'wife purchase'. *American Anthropologist*, 62, 1, 34-57.

Hindess, B. and Hirst, P. Q. (1975). "Pre-Capitalist Modes of Production". Routledge & Kegan Paul, London.

Jarvie, I. C. (1964). "The Revolution in Anthropology". Routledge & Kegan Paul, London.

Jarvie, I. C. (1965). Limits to functionalism and alternatives to it in anthropology. *In* "Functionalism in the Social Sciences" (Ed. D. Martindale). Monograph No. 5, American Academy of Political and Social Science.

Kapferer, B. (Ed.). (1976). "Transaction and Meaning". A. S. A. Essays in Social Anthropology No. 1. Institute for the Study of Human Issues, Philadelphia.

Korn, F. (1973). "Elementary Structures Reconsidered". Tavistock, London.

Kuper, A. (1970). The Kgalagari and the jural consequences of marriage. *Man* (N.S.), 5, 3, 466-482.

Kuper, A. (1975). The social structure of the Sotho-speaking peoples of Southern Africa. *Africa*, 45, 1 and 2, 67-81; 139-149.

Kuper, A. (1978). Rank and preferential marriage in Southern Africa: the Swazi. *Man*, (N.S.), 13, 4, 567-579.

Kuper, H. (1949). "An African Aristocracy". Oxford University Press, London.

La Fontaine, J. S. (1962). Gisu marriage and affinal relations. *In* "Marriage in Tribal Societies" (Ed. M. Fortes). Cambridge Papers in Social Anthropology No. 3. Cambridge University Press, London.

Lamphere, L. (1974). Strategies, cooperation, and conflict among women in domestic groups. *In*

"Woman, Culture and Society". (Eds. M. Z. Rosaldo and L. Lamphere). Stanford University Press, Stanford.

Laughlin, C. D. (1973). Maximation, marriage and residence among the So. *The Canadian Review of Sociology and Anthropology*, 10, 3, 199-213.

Leach, E. R. (1951). The structural implications of matrilateral cross-cousin marriage. *Journal of the Royal Anthropological Institute*, 81, 23-55. (Reprinted in E. R. Leach (1961). "Rethinking Anthropology". Athlone Press, London.)

Leach, E. R. (1955). Polyandry, inheritance and the definition of marriage. *Man*, 54, 182-186. (Reprinted in "Rethinking Anthropology". Athlone Press, London.)

Leach, E. R. (1961). "Rethinking Anthropology". Athlone Press, London.

Leach, E. R. (1970). "Levi-Strauss". Collins, London.

Levi-Strauss, C. (1969). "The Elementary Structures of Kinship" (translated by J. H. Bell, J. R. von Sturmer and R. Needham). Eyre & Spottiswoode, London.

Lewis, I. M. (1965). Problems in the comparative study of unilineal descent. *In* "The Relevance of Models for Social Anthropology" (Ed. M. Banton). A.S.A. monographs No. 1, Tavistock, London.

Lewis, I. M. (1973). "The Anthropologist's Muse". Inaugural lecture London School of Economics, London.

Loudon, J. B. (1976). Introduction. *In* "Social Anthropology and Medicine" (Ed. J. B. Loudon). A.S.A. Monograph No. 13. Academic Press, London.

Madan, T. N. (1965). "Family and Kinship: a Study of the Pandits of Rural Kashmir". Asia Publishing House, New York.

Mair, L. P. (1971). "Marriage". Penguin, Harmondsworth.

Mauss, M. (1954). "The Gift: Forms and Functions of Exchange in Archaic Societies" (translated by I. Cunnison). Cohen & West, London.

Meillassoux, C. (1960). Essai d'interprétation du phénomène économique dans les sociétés traditionelles d'autosubsistence. *Cahiers d'Etudes Africaines*, 4, 38-67.

Meillassoux, C. (1964). "Anthropologie Economique des Gouro de Côte d'Ivoire". Mouton, Paris and The Hague.

Meillassoux, C. (1972). From reproduction to production. *Economy and Society*, 1, 1, 93-105.

Mitchell, J. C. (1963). Marriage, matriliny and social structure among the Yao. *In* "Family and Marriage" (Ed. J. Mogey). Brill, Leiden.

Muller, J. C. (1978). On bridewealth and meaning among the Rukuba, Plateau State, Nigeria. *Africa*, 48, 2, 161-175.

Murray, C. (1977). High bridewealth, migrant labour and the position of women in Lesotho. *Journal of African Law*, 21, 1, 79-96.

Nash, J. (1978). A note on groomprice. *American Anthropologist*, 80, 1, 106-108.

Needham, R. (1962). "Structure and Sentiment: a Test Case in Social Anthropology". University of Chicago Press, Chicago.

Needham, R. (1971a). Introduction. *In* "Rethinking Kinship and Marriage" (Ed. R. Needham). A.S.A. Monograph No. 11. Tavistock, London.

Needham, R. (1971b). Remarks on the analysis of kinship and marriage. *In* "Rethinking Kinship and Marriage" (Ed. R. Needham). A.S.A. Monograph No. 11. Tavistock, London.

Needham, R. (1975). Polythetic classification: convergence and consequences. *Man* (N.S.), 10, 3, 349-369.

Radcliffe-Brown, A. R. (1950). Introduction. *In* "African Systems of Kinship and Marriage" (Eds. A. R. Radcliffe-Brown and D. Forde). Oxford University Press for the International African Institutes, London.

Rivière, P. G. (1971). Marriage: a reassessment. *In* "Rethinking Kinship and Marriage (Ed. R. Needham). A.S.A. Monograph No. 11. Tavistock, London.

Roberts, S. A. (1970). The Malete law of contract: a reply. *Botswana Notes & Records*, 2, 62-63.

Roberts, S. A. (1972). The survival of the traditional Tswana courts in the national legal system of Botswana. *Journal of African Law*, 16, 111-113.

Roberts, S. A. (1977a). Introduction. *In* "Law and the Family in Africa" (Ed. S. A. Roberts). Mouton, The Hague.

Roberts, S. A. (1977b). The Kgatla marriage: concepts of validity. *In* "Law and the Family in

Africa" (Ed. S. A. Roberts). Mouton, The Hague.

Roberts, S. A. and Comaroff, J. L. (1979). Chiefly decision and the devolution of property in a Tswana chiefdom. *In* "Power in Leadership" (Eds. W. Shack and P. Cohen). Clarendon Press, Oxford.

Sahlins, M. (1965). On the sociology of primitive exchange. *In* "The Relevance of Models for Social Anthropology" (Ed. M. Banton). A.S.A. Monographs No. 1. Tavistock, London.

Sahlins, M. (1976). "Culture and Practical Reason". University of Chicago Press, Chicago.

Sansom, B. (1976). A signal transaction and its currency. *In* "Transaction and Meaning" (Ed. B. Kapferer). A.S.A. Essays in Social Anthropology No. 1. Institute for the Study of Human Issues, Philadelphia.

Schapera, I. (1938). "A Handbook of Tswana Law and Custom". Oxford University Press for the International African Institute, London.

Singer, A. (1973). Marriage payments and the exchange of people. *Man* (N.S.), 8, 1, 80-92.

Spiro, M. (1975). Marriage payments: a paradigm from the Burmese perspective. *Journal of Anthropological Research*, 31, 89-115.

Tambiah, S. J. (1973). Dowry and bridewealth and the property rights of women in South Asia. *In* "Bridewealth and Dowry" (Eds. J. Goody and S. J. Tambiah). Cambridge Papers in Social Anthropology No. 7. Cambridge University Press, London.

Tardits, C. (1974). Prix de la femme et mariage entre cousins croisés. Le cas des Bemba d'Afrique Centrale. *L'homme*, 14, 2, 5-30.

Terray, E. (1972). "Marxism and 'Primitive' Societies", Monthly Review Press, New York.

Turner, T. Kinship, household and community structure among the Kayapo. *In* "Dialectical Societies" (Ed. D. Maybury-Lewis). Harvard University Press, Cambridge, Mass. (1980).

Van Velsen, J. (1964). "The Politics of Kinship". Manchester University Press, Manchester.

Walker, J. M. (1968). Bamalete contract law. *Botswana Notes and Records*, 1, 65-76.

Wittgenstein, L. (1955). "The Blue and Brown Books". Blackwell, Oxford.

Yalman, N. (1967). "Under the Bo Tree". University of California Press, Berkeley and Los Angeles.

Acknowledgements

David Rheubottom, Keith Maxwell, Terence Turner, Jane Fajans and Jean Comaroff read earlier drafts of the manuscript and made valuable comment upon it. Marjorie Kirkpatrick assisted me in background research, and Nancy Munn helped me clarify many of the issues discussed here. I should like to express my gratitude to all of them.

2 The Central and the Contingent: Bridewealth among the Melpa and the Wiru

ANDREW STRATHERN

Introduction

In this chapter I intend to examine some aspects of bridewealth transactions in two areas of the Highlands of Papua New Guinea, those of
the Melpa and Wiru. Basic ethnographic material on the Melpa has
been published elsewhere (e.g. A. and M. Strathern, 1969; M. Strathern,
1972). Here I am more concerned with comparative problems. By
referring to perspectives on bridewealth in Africa and Asia discussed
by Fortes (1962) and Goody and Tambiah (1973) I will introduce the
themes I propose to discuss.

In his Introduction to "Marriage in Tribal Societies" (1962), Fortes
adds to his long-standing concern with the social legitimisation of
changing statuses and roles in the life-cycle a further interest in the
bargaining or manipulative aspects of bridewealth negotiations. He
suggests that "game" theory may profitably be applied to the analysis
of the bargaining which sometimes takes place on occasions of
bridewealth transfer, when the groom's and the bride's sides meet and
discuss the scale of payments to be made: "The 'game' requires that
they be defined as opponents, each aiming at profiting rather than
losing by the outcome" (p. 3).

He goes on to make a further distinction between what he calls the
"Capital Value" and "Ancillary Values" at stake in such negotiations,

and expresses these also in the terms of Prime Prestation and Contingent Prestation. Prime prestation corresponds to capital value, i.e. "the set of rights in the bride's sexual and procreative capacities and the domestic services that go with them" (p. 3). Hence, according to Fortes:

> The prime prestation is stipulated by the marriage laws. It is normally fixed in kind and amount, and is often restricted to the context of marriage as regards its disposal by the recipient . . . It is the part of the marriage payments which constitutes the *sine qua non* for lawful marriage and which is therefore strictly speaking the sole jural instrument for the transfer of marital rights . . . Bargaining cannot enter into this. For no matter what its economic worth may be its significance lies in its binding power as a jural instrument (p. 10).

The formulation here resembles Sansom's notions of "signal value" and "jural tender" (Sansom, 1976). The contingent prestations, by contrast, are "often open to bargaining" since

> they are not a jural instrument for the transfer of rights but a means of winning and preserving the goodwill of those with the power to transfer marital rights . . . They are the medium through which affinal relations are established and maintained (p. 10).

These generalizations are derived from African societies. As has often been found in comparisons between Africa and New Guinea (cf. e.g. Barnes, 1962), they are awkward to apply when we come to consider the Melpa and Wiru, for among these two peoples the concern with setting up relations with affines through bridewealth cannot be said to be contingent or peripheral by contrast with a central "jural purpose" of the payments. Instead, relations with affines are central, and it will be the main point of this chapter to explain in more detail how this is so.

Again, before doing so, let me draw some further points for investigation from Goody and Tambiah (1973). In his essay, Goody pursues an interest in transfers of material property as central to the analysis of "corporacy" and unilineal descent groups, and rightly points out that there is a whole area for close analysis "in terms of the size of the payment, its material content, the personnel involved in the giving and receiving and the use made of the objects received" (p. 3). All of these matters were fairly closely canvassed in Fortes's volume, but Goody adds to this a further problem: the relationship between bridewealth, dowry and inheritance practices, in particular the inheritance rights of women — a problem also taken up by Tambiah. The issues which I shall particularly draw upon for comparison are:

1. The use of bridewealth, and dowry in particular, in forming a conjugal fund, held separately or together by the spouses, and the creation of new productive units at marriage.
2. The linking of bridewealth received for a sister with that given for her brother's wife (Goody, 1973, p. 7).
3. The importance of what Goody calls "diverging devolution" — most significantly, the inheritance of important kinds of productive property by daughters from their parents — in influencing marriage arrangements. For comparative purposes, we may be especially interested here in the question of women's land rights after marriage, and in the related question of the meaning of uxorilocal residence patterns. In our New Guinea cases, does uxorilocal residence mean what it does in the case of *diga/binna* marriage in Sri Lanka as described by Leach, Tambiah, Yalman and others? Is it practised in order to obtain an heir for an estate or to add to a senior householder's work-force (cf. e.g. Goody and Tambiah, 1973, p. 135)?

Tambiah, in his contribution to the same volume, examines women's property rights in South Asia in some detail. He stresses the position of the "appointed daughter", who, in the absence of male issue to her father, may marry uxorilocally and produce a son who in turn becomes an heir to the joint family property (p. 79). He states that this "is an established and customary occurrence in India". In general, given the dominant ideas of status hierarchy linked with marriage in this part of the world, he notes that dowry is partly a matter of maintaining the status of daughters by giving them movable wealth, entailing, except in the case of uxorilocal marriage, "a concomitant exclusion from a formal share in the patrimony, especially land" (p. 93). Finally, he observes an emphasis on affinal alliance, expressed either in the repetition of marriage or by elaborating a cycle of prestations between families once a marriage has been contracted.

This last point brings us back to New Guinea societies, for in these also there is a strong emphasis on the continuity of prestations. Indeed, while it is valid enough to separate "bridewealth proper" from the rest of the series of payments for some analytical purposes, the people's own view of the "meaning" of these transfers can only be fully comprehended in the context of the total exchange cycle, both in terms of the wider political economy of New Guinea societies and in terms of the longer life-cycle of the individuals making the payments or having them made for them. These exchange relations depend both on a successful minimal payment of goods and, equally, on the creation of a further network of exchanges for the future, based upon partnerships either created anew at the time of a marriage or established earlier and given new impetus by the fresh ties and potential ties which a marriage brings.

Specific problems and their wider context

The political economy involved here is one in which the exchange of valuables of the same kind as those used in bridewealth is an enduring concern of the people. The goods employed have been subject to varying conditions of production over time. The chief items are: pigs, pork, shell valuables and money (Australian and subsequently Papua New Guinean). In pre-colonial times access to shell valuables was highly restricted — they came in by trading networks long distances from the coast to the Highlands. Europeans brought in large numbers of shells from the 1930s through to the 1950s, when cash-cropping, trade-stores and road-construction were introduced along with Local Government Councils and head-tax. The breed of pigs was modified by crossing, again from the 1930s, with Black Berkshires and Red Tamworths. The growth of monetary income has varied with the success or otherwise of cash crops, government loans for business enterprise, and the world market price of the major crops, coffee and, to a lesser extent, tea. Throughout such fluctuations — reflected in periods of increase in the size and content of bridewealth and other payments in the ceremonial nexus, followed in the 1960s by official attempts by Councils to limit the number of goods to be used in these payments — there has been a consistency between the items used in bridewealth and in other prestations, and thus the bridewealth nexus has never been cut off from the wider context of the economy. This point has two consequences relevant to the first two points for comparison raised from Goody's analysis of bridewealth in Africa.

A. *Is there a conjugal fund?*

First, is a conjugal fund created at marriage on behalf of the married pair as a productive unit? Men need more land on which to garden when they marry, but the apportionment of land claims is likely to be informal and continuous, occurring both before and increasingly after their first marriage. No definite carving out of a finite estate is envisaged. Instead, a man takes and uses what he needs, along with his brothers. Similarly, women informally retain claims, mediated through their male kin, on garden land at their natal places, and may continue to exercise these to a greater or lesser degree for many years. Their own *residence* and that of their children will determine where the major claims are ultimately inherited. If they stay at their husband's place, their sons will inherit there; but if they go back to their brothers' place, the sons can stay and inherit from their mother's brothers. Choice thus depends on residence. The conjugal fund in respect of land, then, should be viewed as a continuing bundle of claims varyingly passed down to children rather than the continuous division of fixed garden sites, except perhaps in a few places where land shortage is currently at its greatest.

Another contribution to the conjugal productive unit is the endowment of the couple at marriage with pigs for breeding. This is specifically seen as coming from the girl's side and therefore is an analogue of dowry.

In the Melpa case there are three main stages in bridewealth negotiations: (1) *kuim ngoromen*, an initial showing of items by the groom's people; (2) the *penal kng*, when these items are formally exchanged by the two sides, men make speeches and redistribute goods, including cooked pork (supplied by the groom's kin); and (3) *mangal kng*, a much more private occasion held some days later when the groom and bride visit her parents, bearing more gifts of cooked pork, and return with "female property" in netbags and oil-flasks in addition to small pigs as a nucleus for a herd. At the *penal kng*, also, some pigs for which the bride's kin make reciprocal return are designated as an exchange for *kng mbo*, "breeding pigs" for the couple's use. Now the purpose of this "endowment" with movables is quite different from the endowment with jewellery and clothes which Tambiah remarks on as a component of dowry in South East Asia, and which has as a function "the maintenance of the daughter's status".

It is rather to provide the basic means of production for exchangeable wealth and to foster the prospect of a further transfer of wealth by the husband and his wife to her kin. That is why it appears as an endowment of *live* pigs from her side in return for *pork*, which is eaten, coming from the groom's side; and also because it is recognised that women do much of the basic work in feeding and caring for pigs. If the bride's family start her off with a herd, she will press her husband to give back more later and her claims on him to do so will be the stronger in that not only the work but the breeding materials come from herself and her kin. So the 'conjugal fund' aspect of bridewealth is best seen as a means of priming the future exchange relations between affines rather than as creating an estate for eventual inheritance by children.

B. *Brother-sister interdependence*

The goods used in bridewealth thus circulate widely in other transactions also, and, indeed, some of the exchanges involved are seen as directly leading into, or being part of, the society-wide ceremonial nexus of *moka* transaction (cf. A. J. Strathern, 1971a). These are such that people can by various methods obtain wealth, including pigs for breeding, on credit, and later make repayments, albeit with interest. The sources of obtaining goods for bridewealth are diversified, the more so since opportunities for earning cash have increased and cash has become an ordinary part of such payments. Hence it is unlikely to be literally the case that a man is directly dependent on the particular bridewealth given for his sister(s) as a means of obtaining a wife for himself. As an idiom of speech, or a way of referring to the general interdependence of a man and his sisters, Hageners may say that men are beholden in this manner. They also say that when they have received a *moka* of pigs and shells they use these to get new wives who will rear more pigs for them. What actually happens is much more complex and variable. In some circumstances a man may actually use pigs given for his sister in this way. More often, he depends on his sister throughout his life for help with his exchange obligations and reciprocally assists her and her husband. The idea of brother-sister interdependence is recognised by both Melpa (Hageners) and Wiru. Indeed, in the latter case it appears even more strongly, as I shall describe later. The notion of the brother marrying with his sister's bridewealth is thus to be seen in symbolic terms; whereas, in some African cases where goods were scarce and circulated at fixed rates solely in a bridewealth nexus, it may have been true in practice as well. Among the Maring, also, the dependence of a brother on his sister in the context of marriage exchanges is quite explicit (Rappaport, 1969, p. 124).

C. *Uxorilocality*

The argument so far has been that the concepts of "conjugal fund" and "brother-sister interdependence" must be analysed in the context of exchange between intermarrying groups or sets of families. Explication of that point has entailed a preliminary reference to inheritance patterns and to residence at marriage. Here I shall discuss again uxorilocality. Among the Melpa the bulk of marriages result in (patri)virilocal residence and patrifilial inheritance. In the Wiru case the pattern is not so clear-cut, since, instead of dispersed settlements scattered through defined clan-territories, we find the members of a number of exogamous segments all living together in villages. The contemporary nucleated villages of several hundred persons are a product of recent responses to administrative policy since 1962. But in earlier times also peoples of diverse clans lived nearby to each other within hamlets, and intermarriage regularly took place between them. In such a residential situation the distinction between patrivirilocal and patriuxorilocal residence patterns is less significant and, in practice, women more regularly maintain gardens in their own father's place (and their mother's brother's place often), regardless of their residence, simply because the gardens of many of their kin are all nearby. In neither the Melpa nor the Wiru case, however, is it true that uxorilocal residence occurs for the reasons reported in Africa and South-East Asia. That is, it is not practised as an alternative to the payment of bridewealth, nor is it arranged to obviate a lack of sons on the part of the wife's father. Indeed, in one case from Hagen, a man of rather low status but not deprived in family circumstances, paid a high bridewealth for his wife with whom he moved into residence at her father's place, saying he was ashamed and hence felt he should pay more. He also subsequently made child-payments for each of his children, yet the formal affiliation in group terms of these was still uncertain as they were growing up in 1970. The "shame" involved here partly reflects the norm that in-laws should avoid each other. This is harder when they live together. The reason why uxorilocal residence was adopted was not that the husband had no land and hence his father-in-law would be his overlord. It was simply that the wife was a strong personality and persisted in "pulling" her husband to live at her place where she herself preferred to be. Nor was her father short of sons. The husband was not totally beholden to his father-in-law. He could find pigs and make *moka* by himself. In other cases a further reason does appear. A big-man, or leader in *moka*, may deliberately attract sons-in-law to stay with him and help him in his exchanges and garden work. Where land is not short, such a strategy can be employed without disadvantages. The big-man's settlement is swelled. The son-in-law does not exactly work for him, but "helps" him. In the circumstances he is likely to help in this way rather more than if he lived at his own place with his natal kin, although the arrangement does not cut him off from his own people entirely. In this formulation, one point should be further noted: a slight stigma does attach to the practice from the husband's point of view, not because he does not pay bridewealth but because of the implication that his wife has "pulled" him; that is, has shown herself stronger than he is in terms of personality, whereas men declare that the reverse should be so. The focus of concern in this arrangement has to do, then, not with bridewealth as such, or the inheritance of property, or even conclusively with group affiliation. Where a sociological pattern can be found, it is rather in the recruiting activities of "big-men", with an eye to status in the *moka* exchange system. In the New Guinea Highlands societies, this ascendancy of big-men does not appear to amount significantly to an "overlord" relationship with uxorilocal sons-in-law, nor is there such a concern with maintaining a line of inheritance of fixed assets in land. In other words, we are not dealing with the kind of stratification system found in India. The fact that bridewealth *is* paid underlines the point that the son-in-law in uxorilocal marriage is not simply a peasant client of his richer father-in-law.

The central and the contingent reconsidered

A. *Capital value among the Melpa*

This completes my set of contrasts derived from Goody and Tambiah's (1973) work. In a sense the points so far are negative ones. I want to return now to Fortes's ideas and thence to work forward to a further contrast, this time at a micro-level, between the Melpa and Wiru, in terms of the meaning of marriage payments.

Earlier on, I noted that the distinction between Prime and Contingent Prestations can be made in analytical terms for the New Guinea materials, but is potentially misleading. For it tends to concentrate attention, in the Fortesian manner, on the "prime" components, and these are not necessarily "central" from the people's own point of view. It is quite true that, in the categorization of items, some are conceptually related to the "capital value" represented in the bride. Thus, in Melpa, some of the shells (not those exchanged, but those which go unreciprocated to the girl's people) are called *peng pokla*, i.e. they "cut off the head" of the girl. In other words, they "sever" her in terms of "identity" from her kin (the severance is not complete, of course). Homologously, certain of the pigs are described as *kem kng*, which, broadly translated, is equivalent to "pigs for the girl's vagina", i.e. for the husband's new sexual access to her. Others are *kokla kng*, "pigs for exchange". A special pig must be provided for the girl's mother, and it must be a big one, the *mam peng kng*, "the mother's head pig". There is trouble if it is not there, and men on either side argue about the required size of pig for this category. Contrary to Fortes's schema, bargaining is found even in relation to "prime" components, although, in accordance with his views, this bargaining is not about whether these obligatory items should be given or not, but about their size and quality. Each of the items given is categorized in a specific manner, and argument takes place about the numbers of pigs or shells to be categorized in this or that way. For example, the bride's kin may argue that a particular large pig should be designated as *tembokl kng* ("stick pig"), that is, a pig, to be handed over live to the bride's father by the groom's side, for which the groom's people will then find a further equivalent pig and cook it for later presentation to the bride's people. As the bride's people have to divide out pork to their numerous visitors at the *penal kng* occasion, it is in their advantage to claim a large pig for cooking in this way. The groom's people, however, may have wished the large pig they initially displayed to be the one for the mother, i.e. the "mother's head pig". If the bride's people get their way they may subsequently turn round and complain that no pig was provided for the mother, and is this not a disgrace? Recriminations are then likely to follow. The overall context in which bargaining occurs is described by Marilyn Strathern (1972, p. 103) as follows:

> The bride's father is faced with a specific number of items which he must allocate among his watching relatives, whose hopes are always too high. It is under this pressure that the bride's kin negotiate for more. Their tactics of attrition are recognized in the phrase *amb pek rui*, 'to scrape for the woman' — in pressing for extra valuables they gradually wear away the opposition till the groom's side yields.

The situation here is exactly analogous to that which arises when a man displays pigs to give away in *moka*. His creditors cluster round, and usually there are too many of them, so that tension automatically arises. At a bridewealth exchange, the bride's father's kin and affines from other places are likely to be his *moka* partners too, and the wealth given may also flow immediately into the nexus of *moka* payments. Thus the pressure for bargaining derives not so much from a notion of a varying or constantly high capital value of the bride — this is certainly implicitly understood between the two sides but does not necessarily receive explicit mention — as from the general competitive context of *moka* exchange arrangements. It is true that the mother's pig must be big and must not be omitted and that it is given explicitly to compensate her for the loss of her daughter's help. Similarly, in symbolic terms the *kem kng*, or "pigs for the vagina", do represent a part of the capital value in Fortes's terms. Hageners say that a wife is a "strong thing", for she will work and bear children for the husband, so in that sense, again, they do recognize the idea of capital value. Furthermore, they are quite aware that girls differ in their character, skills, and comeliness, and that families differ in their overall status and wealth. All these considerations undoubtedly enter in when marriage negotiations are set in motion. Big-men definitely do expect to receive more wealth for their daughters and probably to give more on behalf of their sons, but there is no pattern of exclusive alliance between big-men via marriages; and a further point must be made in modification of the view that big-men are "out to get" more than others. That is, they must, to maintain their status, also make generous returns to the wife-takers in terms of "Exchange pigs" and "breeding pigs". Otherwise, their own status as big-men will be impugned. Indeed both sides are anxious to put on a good showing, the groom's side to supply plenty of wealth items initially (without perhaps totally impoverishing themselves or incapacitating themselves for meeting other obligations they have), the bride's side to make adequate reciprocation for these on the spot or later and to meet the further claims of their watching kin who gather at the time of the *penal* presentation. The anxiety and bargaining are thus not to be seen primarily as having to do with the economic "value" of the bride but as being about the social value of maintaining, extending and recreating affinal ties between networks of people. Thus, while Fortes's concepts of the Capital Value and Prime Prestation do have some obvious application it would be wrong to accept fully the emphasis of his terms Ancillary Values and Contingent Prestations, because of the highly central — indeed, if you like, "prime" — stress which Hageners place on the overall significance of bridewealth payments in setting up good exchange relations between the parties; their role in creating a "road" that the affines can "see" between themselves from then onwards, as Hageners put it (cf. M. Strathern, 1972, p. 119).

B. *Bridewealth and childwealth among the Wiru:*
   exchanging wealth for the body

I have now indicated the way in which Fortes's generalizations must be modified if we wish to understand the meaning of marriage payments among the Melpa or Hageners. Most of my general points apply equally well to the Wiru people of the Southern Highlands. However, there are some differences of emphasis in bridewealth payments between the Melpa and the Wiru. I now turn to these as a counterpoint, in micro-level comparison, to the major contrasts I have tried to draw out between the African and South-East Asian materials and data from the New Guinea Highlands.

The Wiru are a single language group of some 16,000 people living south of Mount Ialibu in the Southern Highlands Province. Although first subjected to administrative influence only in the early 1960s, they rapidly abandoned all their traditional cults (involving pig-killings), changed much of their clothing and consolidated their hamlets into villages of anything from 50 to 500 or so persons, all in response to administrative and mission pressures. They retain periodic pig-kills, unaccompanied by salient forms of religious ritual. The pig-kills occur at intervals of roughly four or five years, and Wiru men say that they depend on rearing their own pigs for these occasions. Although the pace of social change in the Wiru area in the last decade makes it difficult to characterise the pre-contact Wiru political economy in overall terms, it is clear that, in terms of a distinction I have earlier suggested (A. J. Strathern, 1969) for the part-classification of Highlands exchange economies, "production" is more important than "finance" among the Wiru; that consequently, perhaps, the big-man complex, while structurally present, is not so highly developed; and that in general the economy has not experienced such marked inflation and overall growth among the Wiru as in Hagen.

A nexus of exchanges which has continued, however, to be centrally important and comes into play constantly both at and in between the larger pig-kills is that which centres on the life-cycle and involves bridewealth, child-payments, and death-payments. This same nexus appears in Hagen also, but among the Wiru it is, at any rate nowadays, thrown more sharply into relief. Just as I argued that bridewealth has to be seen as a part of wider *moka* exchanges in Hagen, so for the Wiru I suggest that it must be placed in the diachronic nexus of ideologically stressed life-cycle payments.

The chief emphasis in these life-cycle payments is on child-payments to matrilateral kin, known simply as *marikiri-ke mereko*, "he gives for the children" (cf. A. J. Strathern, 1971b). These are payments for the "skin" (*tingini* or *tingine*) or "body" of the person, and most people regard them as obligatory. They are said to safeguard the condition of the person's "skin", that is, his or her health; for, if they are not made, the mother's brothers will be angry and cause sickness to fall on one. The uncle's *ipono* or spirit attacks the defaulting man's children and they become ill. A father should therefore make these payments for his children. The function of the payments goes beyond that of recruitment of the children to the father's group, as stressed by Roy Wagner for the neighbouring Daribi people of Karimui (Wagner, 1967), since a person continues to make such payments throughout his or her life; and after a death the final payments to maternal kin have to be completed by the deceased's surviving co-residential kin. In Hagen such payments are either completed earlier or are extended into *moka*-style exchanges linking sets of men together under the influence of big-men. In the Wiru case the payments are partly reciprocated, but do not form part of a wider *moka*-like nexus, for there is no full equivalent of the *moka* in Wiru. An adult man or woman at a pig-kill may use some of the pork or a valuable to make a child-payment or a "self-payment" of this kind. Each person does so individually and separately from any concerted presentations taking place between local groups on the same occasion.

How this point applies to the meaning we should attribute to bride-wealth can be seen by brief reference to the way items are categorized in Wiru bridewealth payments. As with the Melpa, some items are for return (*topo tiki*, "they exchange"), some are specifically seen as going from the bride's folk to the groom's, and shells and large packs of ash-salt may be filled into her netbag for her to carry over to the groom's people in public when all items are displayed (*aroa urukaki* or *aroa urukoa mereki*). Men of status are particularly concerned to "fill up their daughter's netbag" in this way, and the motivation is the same as in Hagen: to establish goodwill, to pave the way for future exchanges with the new affines. The fathers on either side are usually very central to the negotiations, slightly more so than in Hagen, where support and participation by wider sub-clan kinsmen tends to be greater. Certain pigs are also given by the bride's kin for cooking and distribution by the groom's kin (*taluai yoroko kai*, "the pig which heats the stones" [for cooking in an earth-oven]). Two further categories are especially important to notice here.

The first is called *tuu piko*, "he places (or gives) marsupials". When the main bridewealth has been given and the girl goes to the boy's home, the two may have licit sexual intercourse. Immediately after or just before this happens they should travel back together to the girl's parents' place and take a gift described as "marsupials" but perhaps containing other wealth items as well. This is explicitly to encourage the fertility of the marriage, seen as controlled by the girl's father. For him to bless them he must receive "marsupials". The symbolism here can be derived from dream interpretations which the Wiru make. If one dreams of having intercourse with a dark-skinned girl, this is taken to mean that a marsupial with dark fur has fallen into a trap one has set for it in the forest the evening before. Conversely if one dreams of finding such a marsupial, it means one will have intercourse with a dark girl. Marsupials and sexuality are thus, it seems, metaphorically synonymous. No specific equivalent category of gift is made in Hagen, although of course men do expect children from their marriages. This special signalling of sexuality and fertility as desired aims, coupled with the paying of respect in this regard to the girl's father at an early stage of the marriage, may seem a minor point of emphasis, but it gains greater significance when one realizes that the advent of children in a marriage will mean a stimulus to the continuity of exchanges between in-laws, and in particular will lead to the offer of more payments from the husband to his wife's father and brothers.

It is interesting, secondly, to note that the category term for those pigs which the groom's kin give "for no return", i.e. directly for the bride, is in Wiru *tingini* or *tingine kai*, "pigs for the skin". Here again there is a divergence from the exact form of the Melpa term, although the general import is the same. In Melpa these pigs are bluntly described as *kem kng*, "pigs for the (girl's) vagina"; in Wiru they are "for her skin" or "for her body". Her father is likely in turn to give one or some of them to his own wife's brother, the girl's mother's brother; and the wife will continue to make payments "for her skin" to her own maternal kin in subsequent years. In Melpa child-payments and payments to mother's folk are all differentiated by separate terms and not assimilated into those used for the symbolic prime prestation in bridewealth as they are here in Wiru. A man gives "for his wife's body" to her father, who is seen as the possessor or owner of her body until her marriage; he continues to pay "for his children's bodies" to her brothers; and the children eventually pay "for their own bodies", as maternally-derived, throughout their lifetimes. The linguistic part-equation of bridewealth with successive life-cycle payments emphasizes, then, the social fact that in practice these payments are all concatenated together in a very explicit way.[1] The "prime prestation" in return for the "sexual gift", then, in Wiru is not to be seen as simply transferring a set of jural rights including sexual access over to the husband. It does do this; but in addition it looks forward to a continuing, indeed never-ending set of exchanges set up through this transaction in the bride's body. Once again, as with the Melpa, but with an altered emphasis, we find that the meaning of marriage payments has centrally, and not contingently or peripherally, to do

---

[1] An alternative term for the payments made for one's "skin" is *yangi*. This again is a term also used in the context of bridewealth, for an exchange of pork between the two sides, with prime emphasis on *aroa yangi kai*, pork given to the girl's kin by the man's side. Such gifts of pork and also pearl shells are expected to continue over time throughout the marriage, and the term *yangi* thus easily carries over into the realm of child-payments. Returns for shell payments are expected from a wife's kin when they hold a major pig-kill, in the form of "ribcages of cooked pork" (*kai luneri*). These are the centre-pieces of the pig's body (*tingine*) and might, if a trifle fancifully, be seen as suitably making recompense for wealth which is payment for a woman's body.

When maternal kin cause sickness, they are said to do it by sending their spirit, *ipono*, to eat the inner parts of their relative's body, the liver, lungs, etc. located in the trunk, for these are the parts they especially "own".

with the aim of creating long-term exchange relations between affines.[1]

Conclusion

Methods of making comparisons in anthropology differ widely. Here I may claim to have done no more than to have proffered a preliminary comparative sketch on two quite separate levels, one inter-continental and the other inter-tribal. Why choose such an approach?

First, much of the theorising and generalizations on bridewealth and marriage emerged in anthropological writings on Africa, and a little later from work by alliance theorists on Indian society. One possibility is that the concerns which underlie exchanges at marriage in African and Indian societies may themselves vary. Both Goody and Tambiah have worked extensively on this theme (Goody and Tambiah, 1973; Goody, 1977). Yet in both cases one can detect a focus on the continuation of status-relations in society as expressed between the generations through inheritance and succession. Hence the themes of "the appointed daughter" and "maintaining a daughter's status", and the particular significance of uxorilocal residence at marriage. While clear contrasts between African and Asian practices do emerge, as Goody has demonstrated, the overall themes and conclusions show an

---

[1] Further aspects of the Wiru situation are of interest for comparison with Hagen. The prominence of the father of the bride among the Wiru is accompanied by apparent anxiety on the father's part about his daughter's sexual activities. Big-men in particular wish to control their daughter's sexual affairs, the more so since Wiru girls tend more often to be rebellious and seek out pre-marital and extra-marital affairs than girls generally do in Hagen. A Wiru father in fact depends on his daughter marrying properly and producing children for the ordered continuity of his exchange relations through her. In Hagen exchange relations do depend considerably on links established through marriages, but not exclusively and not so specifically on the production of children. In pre-colonial times in both areas men could threaten women with physical force if they refused to obey more easily than they can do nowadays in the context of administration and magistrates' courts. The land claims maintained by women among the Wiru are also of note. They freely continue, if they wish, to garden at their father's or their mother's brother's places (the father denies this only if he disapproves of his daughter's marriage or sexual transgressions). This practice is further reinforced by the active role which women play in their own right as distributors of vegetable foods, which they have grown, among their kin. In the role of cousin, in particular, a woman expects to make *langi* gifts to her mother's brother's sons. So she gives back the produce she has perhaps grown on their land. In return the cousins may eventually give a shell valuable to the woman and her husband. She may take this and "pay for her skin" with it by giving it to further matrilateral kin. The active part which women take in "paying for themselves" — just as in Hagen they raise pigs to go back in *moka* to their own kin — clearly helps to keep the whole nexus of transactions going. In both Hagen and Wiru the "endowment" of a daughter with resources fuels not so much the intergenerational *transmission* of material property as the intergenerational flow of *reciprocal* material exchanges.

awkward lack of fit with what we know of many Melanesian societies. Hence my first aim was to establish what is distinctive about Melanesian cases by indicating how generalizations derived from other contexts may fail when we apply them to these. Continuity through exchange of wealth, and not via exclusive adherence to rules of descent or the creation of estates of scarce property, is the keynote, at least for the Highlands societies of Papua New Guinea.

But, given this, we must not try to press the contrasts too hard. At least one ethnographer of Highlands societies, Meggitt, in his most recent book (1977), continues to stress the importance of access to land — and hence the overall dimension of inheritance — in Mae Enga society:

> The Mae do not compete for prestige for its own sake . . . The basic pre-occupation of the Mae is with the possession and defence of clan land. Participation in the Te (exchange cycle), as in other prestations, is but a means to this end (p. 9).

Clearly, more rigorously based statements of comparison between different Highlands societies would be needed to place this view further into context, and such has not been my purpose here. Rather, I have been concerned to draw out a more limited comparison between two Highlands areas in which I have worked, in order to show how the same total concern with exchange relations may be expressed differently in the two cases. An approach to the question can effectively be made through the categories of payment recognized by the people themselves as forming "bridewealth". In these terms it is possible indeed, in both cases, to recognize traces of the conceptual distinctions proposed by Fortes between capital and ancillary values and between prime and contingent prestations. Thus both Melpa and Wiru distinguish between items "for the girl's vagina" (or body) and items "for exchange". Yet a payment of the former items only would not make a marriage. Moreover, bargaining takes place over the former category as well as over the latter. Since a marriage itself is seen as but one "item" or "event" in a much larger process of exchanges between people, the aspect of marriage as a focus for regenerating exchange relations is centrally important. Hence the prestations which would be regarded as contingent, optional or peripheral in the Fortesian scheme, centred as it is on a jural view of rights established through individual acts of marriage, may in terms of an exchange model be rather regarded as central. For certain purposes of analysis it may still be useful at least to pose the questions which are proper to jural analysis: what rights are conveyed by means of marriage payments, how do these payments alter the status of the couples married, and so forth. One would have to remember two points, however: that the payments themselves may not be the sole means of such transfers of rights, since they can be understood only by linking them to other payments in a wider complex; and that, for the same reason, the rights involved have to be seen as contingent, rather than absolute.

Looking at the Melpa and Wiru materials in such a wider context of payments, then, we find that in the Melpa case bridewealth is much influenced through its close articulation with the *moka* exchange nexus. First, the pressure to increase the size of bridewealth is linked to the demands of *moka* exchange partners on recipient kin. And secondly, the endowment of pigs which a newly-married pair receive from the bride's side is to enable them to breed pigs for use in further, continuous exchanges with her people. In Wiru, the same interest in continuity shows, and pigs are similarly sent with the bride for breeding. But in addition there is a specially marked emphasis on child-bearing and on the place of bridewealth in a cycle of "payments for the body" which go to matrilateral kin. Child-payments are also certainly made in Hagen, but are not so prominent as among the Wiru. From the people's point of view, then, one might say that among the Melpa a marriage is fully established when the affines make *moka* with the breeding pigs a young couple have been endowed with; whereas among the Wiru it is properly established when the couple have a child and enter into the nexus of payments for pearl shells in return for ribcages of pork which is signalled at pig-killings by formal chants reaffirming the ties between exchange partners (cf. A. J. Strathern, 1978).

Bibliography

Barnes, J. A. (1962). African models in the New Guinea Highlands. *Man*, 62, 5-9.
Fortes, M. (Ed.). (1962). "Marriage in Tribal Societies". Cambridge University Press, London.
Glasse, R. and Meggitt, M. J. (eds.). (1969). "Pigs, Pearlshells and Women". Prentice-Hall, Englewood Cliffs, New Jersey.
Goody, J. and Tambiah, S. J. (1973). "Bridewealth and Dowry". Cambridge University Press, London.
Goody, J. (1977). "Production and Reproduction". Cambridge University Press, London.

Meggitt, M. J. (1977). "Blood is their Argument". Mayfield Publishing Company, Palo Alto.

Rappaport, R. (1969). Marriage among the Maring. *In* "Pigs, Pearlshells and Women" (Eds. R. Glasse and M. J. Meggitt). Prentice-Hall, Englewood Cliffs, New Jersey.

Sansom, B. (1976). A signal transaction and its currency. *In* "Transaction and Meaning" (Ed. B. Kapferer). A.S.A. Essays in Social Anthropology No. 1. Institute for the Study of Human Issues, Philadelphia.

Strathern, A. J. (1969). Finance and production: two strategies in New Guinea Highlands exchange systems. *Oceania*, **40**, 42-67.

Strathern, A. J. (1971a). "The Rope of Moka". Cambridge University Press, London.

Strathern, A. J. (1971b). Wiru and Daribi matrilateral payments. *Journal of the Polynesian Society*, **80**, 449-462.

Strathern, A. J. and Strathern, A. M. (1969). Marriage among the Melpa. *In* "Pigs, Pearlshells and Women" (Eds. R. Glasse and M. J. Meggitt). Prentice-Hall, Englewood Cliffs, New Jersey.

Strathern, A. J. (1978). Finance and production revisited: in pursuit of a comparison. *In* "Research in Economic Anthropology" (Ed. G. Dalton), vol. I, pp. 73-104. JAI Press.

Strathern, A. M. (1972). "Women in Between: Female Roles in a Male World". Seminar Press, London.

Wagner, R. (1967). "The Curse of Souw: Principles of Daribi Clan Definition and Alliance in New Guinea". University of Chicago Press, Chicago.

Acknowledgements

I am most grateful to Marilyn Strathern for discussion on the topic of this paper. I have also benefited greatly from her systematic account of Hagen bridewealth practices in Chapter 5 of "Women in Between" (1972). Fieldwork among the Melpa and the Wiru has been carried out at various times between 1964 and 1978, with generous help from Cambridge University, the Australian National University, the University of Papua New Guinea, the Social Science Research Council and University College London.

3 The Economics of Mursi Bridewealth: A Comparative Perspective

DAVID TURTON

I

The Mursi are transhumant cattle herders and cultivators who live in the lower valley of the River Omo, in southwestern Ethiopia, about sixty miles north of Lake Turkana. Bridewealth consists, ideally, of thirty-eight head of cattle, and represents, in practice, by far the most significant transaction in the Mursi economy. And yet, by comparison with some other East African herding peoples among whom bridewealth is economically much less significant, the Mursi are poorly off for stock, having no more than one head of cattle per head of human population, and considerably fewer goats and sheep. I shall argue here that this state of affairs is susceptible to a straightforward economic interpretation and that it does not, therefore, require any assumptions to be made about a "cultural obsession" of the Mursi with cattle. Since this argument will involve comparing the bridewealth practices of the Mursi with those of some other East African herders, it is as well to begin by making clear what I see as the limits and validity of this comparison.

The essays contained in this book lead to at least one predictable conclusion, namely that it would be pointless to attempt to say precisely "what is" bridewealth or dowry, so heterogenous are the phenomena to which these terms are commonly applied. Nor is it any solution to use the global expression "marriage payments", since the term "marriage" is also applied to phenomena which are far from homogeneous. Each of these terms designates what Needham (1975) has called a "polythetic class": that is, they class together phenomena having the highest *overall* similarity, which means that no single feature, or set of features, is either a necessary or a sufficient criterion for membership of the class. (This is in contrast to a "monothetic class", for which there does exist such a unique set of features). It follows that it would be futile to search for important common char-acteristics of *all* the phenomena to which any of these terms have been applied, and none of them, therefore, can be taken as designating an analytic category. It does not, of course, follow that they are useless; only that their true usefulness needs to be understood and respected. Needham has again clarified matters here by calling such terms (following Wittgenstein) "odd-job words" (Needham, 1971, p. 5). That is, they designate more or less vaguely defined ranges of behaviour, it being their very indeterminacy which makes them not only useful but indispensable for effective communication. Thus, as an odd-job word, the "bridewealth" of my title refers to a range of behav-iour which may well need to be sorted differently in the light of closer study and analysis. I use it in order to draw attention to what seems, initially at least, to be an institutionalised transaction whereby a man hands over goods to the kin of a woman, a transaction which is a *sine qua non* of the establishment of a particular kind of relationship between the man and the woman in question, this relationship being usually referred to by the odd-job word, "marriage".

The difficulties which are likely to arise from treating a polythetic class as though it were a monothetic one, are illustrated by a recent essay of Goody's (1973) in which he attempts to set out the "different implications" of what he calls "the two major types of marriage trans-actions", bridewealth and dowry. After stressing the need to focus on "differences within those payments described as bridewealth" and on "the relationship of these differences to the rest of the social system, in particular the economy", he nevertheless goes on to remark that "In Africa, the relative size of payment is in a general sense linked with the quantum of rights transferred" (op. cit., pp. 2-3). It is not clear, of course, what exactly is intended by the phrase "in a general sense" but, as will appear later, there can be very great differences in the economic burden represented by bridewealth among East African herders, who share an ideology of patrilineal descent, which it would be very difficult to link with "the quantum of rights transferred". The particular comparison Goody has in mind emerges from his next sentence: "In systems of matrilineal descent groups, where rights in a woman's procreative powers remain with her natal lineage, the amounts are comparatively less than in other societies". The trouble here is that it is at least doubtful whether, for example, the two bottles of gin given by an Ashanti groom to his wife's kin (Fortes, 1950, p. 280) and the very heavy transfer of vital economic resources made to his wife's kin by a Nuer groom can usefully be compared as examples of the same institution.

But although we should not analyse a polythetic class as though it were a monothetic one, it is possible, and indeed necessary, to carry out a more limited analysis: that is, we may be able to distinguish, within a polythetic class, sub-classes of phenomena having important characteristics in common, and which may therefore be analysed as monothetic classes. Such sub-classes are more likely to be found among neighbouring peoples of a single ethnographic area, who have similar economies. It may well turn out, of course, that the peoples compared are less similar than it was at first thought, and that their institutions, initially classed as bridewealth, are significantly different, at least where their functions are concerned. But if so, this can be regarded as an advance. In this chapter, therefore, I shall describe and analyse bridewealth among the Mursi and compare it with bridewealth among some other East Africa herders, who are listed in the Table on page 76. By "bridewealth" in this ethnographic context I refer to the cattle and other stock which a man must transfer to the kin of a woman in order to establish a marriage with her; by "marriage" I mean that transaction by which a woman acquires the socially recognised status of a wife to the man in question, a status which obliges her to supply the man with various domestic, sexual and procreative services. I shall focus on the economic setting of bridewealth and shall try to relate differences in bridewealth payments to differences in the economic role of cattle in the chosen societies. Firstly, I shall outline the rules according to which Mursi bridewealth is paid and distributed, and give some idea of how these payments and distributions are made in practice.

II

Although I have no record of a Mursi bridewealth payment which reached the ideal total of thirty-eight head of cattle, it was clear, from those payments, the negotiations for which I witnessed, that grooms are expected to give to the limit of what they can afford. Since everything, therefore, depends on the groom's cattlewealth (meaning by this both the animals he actually possesses and those he can obtain from relatives and friends), it follows that actual bridewealth payments vary in amount. Many also turned out, on closer examination, to include symbolic substitutes for cattle, which are nevertheless treated as cattle in the final reckoning. Thus, a man who proudly told me that he had handed over 28 "cattle" to his wife's kin, turned out to have paid 22 cattle, two goats, each standing for one head of large stock, and a rifle, standing for four head of large stock, its exchange value. Although, because of this variation in amount and composition, it is difficult to say what is "normal"; a bridewealth payment which contained 20 head of large stock would be a very respectable one. The Mursi account for this falling short of the ideal by reference to their current poverty where cattle are concerned. They have access to veterinary services, and rinderpest epidemics appear to occur about every seven years. Then there are the more insidious inroads of bovine trypanosomiasis, which are apparently on the increase. The essential point is that the ideal payment is so high in relation to the present cattlewealth of the Mursi that virtually all grooms are forced, during negotiations, to pay as much as they can afford, almost certainly impoverishing themselves in the process.

All the bridewealth cattle should be handed over to the bride's close agnates before she begins to live with her husband, but this also did not seem to be a common practice at the time of my fieldwork. The precise constitution of the total bridewealth is, however, always decided before the bride joins her husband. There are no vague promises, well intentioned or otherwise, about cattle that will be given in the future, for if any animals are to be given later, each is carefully identified during the negotiations. Often, for example, the outstanding animals are calves that have not yet been weaned.

The groom, aided by his close agnates, is responsible for collecting and paying bridewealth, but he does not distribute it. That is, he hands it over, ideally *in toto*, to a close agnate of the bride (whom I shall assume to be her father) upon whom the task of distribution falls. In performing this task the bride's father is faced with various types of claim. The strongest, in terms of the sanctions available to the claimants, come from those male kin of the bride who are agnates of her mother, her two grandmothers, and her four great-grandmothers — in other words, the wife-givers of her father, grandfather and great-grandfather. These men are known as the *zuo a modain* ("people of the saliva") because, if their claims are not satisfactorily met, they are able, by virtue of their kin relationships to the bride, to curse her, thus either preventing her from having children or causing any children she does bear to die of a disease, the main symptom of which is said to be constant salivation. A further indication of the strength of these claims is that they are the only ones which are numerically specified — all other claims are residual. The genealogical relationships of these men to the bride, the number of bridewealth cattle due to each and the kin terms applied to them are shown in Fig. 1.

   This diagram corresponds to the way in which the Mursi themselves habitually formulate the rules, and it is a formulation which is implicit

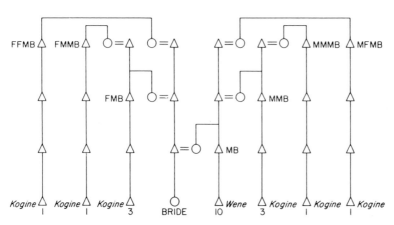

Fig 1: Ideal distribution of bridewealth
cattle among *zuo a modain*

in their "Omaha-type" kinship terminology. Thus, for example, male agnates of Ego's mother, of his mother's own and descending generations, are classed together (MB = MBS) as is the mother herself with mother's sister and mother's brother's daughter. The same goes for the agnates of Ego's two grandmothers, and four great-grandmothers.

Thus, for example, MMB = MMBS = MMBSS. The terminology therefore enables a set of rules which have complex ramifications, in practice, to be stated succinctly. This can be seen from the fact that, had I chosen to assume in the diagram that all bridewealth recipients were of the bride's father's generation, instead of her own, the kin categories used would have been the same. The diagram therefore shows categories of kin, and not individuals. The number of cattle to which, for example, an actual mother's brother of the bride is theoretically entitled will depend upon how many other men are related to her in the same way as himself, and upon their relative seniority, while he will have a stronger theoretical entitlement than any classificatory mother's brother (e.g. MFBS). Three further points need to be made about this diagram.

Firstly, it is clear that we have here a series of what Evans-Pritchard, writing of the Nuer, has called "deferred payments" (1951, p. 78). That is, a girl's bridewealth is distributed in recognition of seven previous marriages, those of her parents, her grandparents and her

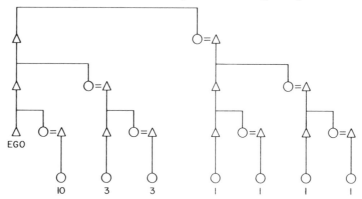

Fig 2: Non-patrilineal kinswomen whose
bridewealth a man has a right to share

great-grandparents. Thus, for example, the three cattle which are due to her MMB's agnatic descendants may be seen as a deferred payment for the marriage of her maternal grandmother. Each marriage, therefore, has what might be called a "time depth" of three generations, or conversely, the furthest a man needs to trace back his agnatic descent in order to claim a share in the bridewealth of a girl who is not patrilineally related to him is three generations (see Fig. 2).

Secondly, the rules of bridewealth distribution pick out eight lines of patrilineal descent, originating in the bride's four great-grandfathers, and in the brothers of her four great-grandmothers. The rules as much give rise to, as follow this patrilineal division which, although thought of as primary by the people, cannot therefore be appealed to, without circularity, as an explanation of the distribution. Indeed three generations above living adults is the limit of accurate descent reckoning, which is consistent with the fact that this is as far back as a man needs to go in order to establish a claim to the bridewealth of non-patrilineal kinswomen. The patrilines shown in Fig. 1, therefore, may be regarded as a function of the rules of bridewealth distribution. It is true that shallow agnatic descent groups, consisting of the descendants of a common grandfather or great-grandfather, do exist in Mursi society, and that the members of one of these descent groups think of themselves as having rights in each other's cattle. But almost all transactions in cattle have, directly or indirectly, to do with bridewealth, this being by far the most significant economic transaction in which any Mursi ever engages. Thus, what these descent groups actually incorporate are claims to the bridewealth cattle of patrilineal and other kinswomen. It would therefore also be circular to interpret the payment of bridewealth as compensating a group of agnates for the loss of a sister or daughter, when bridewealth is such an important factor in making them such a group in the first place.

Finally, the descent lines picked out in Fig. 1 can only be kept conceptually apart if marriage is prohibited between men and women who are already linked through bridewealth transactions: in other words, who fall within the range of third cousin. Thus the bride in the diagram cannot marry any agnatic descendant of her FFMB since these men, who were due 10 cattle from the bridewealth of her FFZ, and three from the bridewealth of her FZ, are still owed one from her own bridewealth. They have no entitlement, however, to a share in the bridewealth of her brother's daughter, which means that, in the fourth generation, the marriage of her father's paternal grandparents could be repeated. That is, a second and reciprocal affinal link could be created between the two descent lines. It would not, of course, be seen as a repetition by the Mursi, since the falling away of bridewealth debt equals the falling away of kinship. The rules of bridewealth distribution, then, define a range of kinship, and a series of patrilineal descent lines, by also defining degrees of prohibited marriage.

The actual distribution of bridewealth cattle among the *zuo a modain* is obviously affected by the total amount of bridewealth paid, which, as we have seen, never reaches the ideal of 38 large stock. A second factor which may need to be considered in accounting for an actual distribution is the way in which the bridewealth of an elder married sister of the bride was distributed. Thus, from one fairly sizeable bridewealth, consisting of 21 cattle and one goat, which was paid about ten years ago, the bride's MBs received only six cattle and one goat. This was explained not only by the less than ideal size of the bridewealth, but also by the fact that these relatives had taken their full share of ten cattle from the bridewealth of the bride's elder sister. On the other hand, the agnatic descendants of the bride's MMB received four cattle, one more than their due, and this was explained by the fact that they had received only six cattle from the bridewealth of the bride's mother, their classificatory ZD. Thirdly, it is very unlikely that each category of *zuo a modain* specified by the rules will be accounted for in any particular distribution. The categories most frequently unrepresented are, predictably, those of the agnatic kinsmen of the bride's four great-grandmothers, the usual explanation of this being that the people in question have "died out", although occasionally they are said to be living with a neighbouring group. At the level of the third ascending generation there is clearly a good deal of ambiguity which allows the bride's father more or less room for manoeuvre in deciding which claims need to be admitted.

The cattle which remain after the claims of the *zuo a modain* have been met are not all retained by the bride's father. He is expected to give at least one animal to a son of a female agnate of his own, his father's or his grandfather's generation, an own sister's son having the strongest claim, and he is also likely to be asked for one animal by a grandson or great-grandson of a female agnate — most probably a grandson of his FFZ. The remaining cattle are distributed among the close male agnates of the bride, although one of her married sisters may also be given an animal. It is by no means the case that the bride's father necessarily gets the lion's share of what is left over. Indeed, the Mursi say that brothers "take turns" in the bridewealth of each others' daughters, so that a man is likely to receive more cattle from the bride-wealth of a brother's daughter than he does from that of his own daughter. Finally, it is common for the bride's father to use what cattle he does retain from her bridewealth to pay off debts he has contracted in the past to non-kinsmen.

Obviously such factors as the size of the total payment and the number of claims he has to meet from his full and/or half brothers will affect the number of cattle a man can retain from his daughter's marriage. But, however high the initial payment, this will gradually be whittled away, from the bride's father's point of view, by further distributions. And it should be noted that, equipped as they are with the power of the curse, and having numerically specified rights, the *zuo a modain* do not appear to suffer disproportionately as a result of reduced bridewealth payments. On the contrary, they appear to do proportionately better than the other claimants, including the bride's close agnates. It will be noted that just *over* half the total should go to the *zuo a modain* and, although their share decreases with smaller totals, it does not do so as dramatically as that of the bride's agnates which, furthermore, may well be left outstanding at the time the bride starts to live with her husband. Thus, to the extent that the size of the payments is correlated with the overall cattle-wealth of the population, we can say that, as this overall wealth decreases, payments made by the groom become proportionately heavier (since these must now reach the limit of what he can afford) and distributions made by the bride's father must give greater precedence to non-agnates than to agnates.

In spite of the fact, therefore, that Mursi fathers commonly speak gleefully of the prospect of marrying off all their daughters because of the cattle they will then receive, it is difficult to attribute these high bridewealth payments to individual rapacity. It has already been argued that it would be circular to account for them in terms of compensation to a group of agnates for the loss of a sister or daughter and her progeny. It is now clear that such an explanation would also run up against the fact that the agnates of a bride can expect to receive at most only half of her bridewealth and then only when the overall cattle-wealth of the community is relatively high. Thirdly, and as will appear in the next section, any simple correlation between "the quantum of rights transferred" and size of bridewealth immediately founders when the bridewealth practices of other East African herders with patrilineal ideologies are inspected.

III

Both Gulliver (1955, p. 220) and Rigby (1969, pp. 225-226) have commented in passing on the fact that there is no positive correlation between per capita stock-wealth and the average size of bridewealth payments among East African herders. Neither, however, attempts a systematic explanation of the range of variation found, and Gulliver remarks that, "There is a pressing need for a classification and comparative study of the institutions grouped together under the blanket term "bridewealth" " (loc. cit.). Jacobs has pointed out that, so far from there being a positive correlation between stock-wealth and bridewealth, it would appear to be mainly among those herders for whom pastoralism is of secondary subsistence importance (measured by per capita stock holdings) that livestock "tends to be more important for purposes of social exchange", including bridewealth (1965, p. 149 and 1970, p. 36). This observation is crudely borne out by the Table below, in which three groups, the Mursi, the Nuer and the Gogo, stand out as making very heavy actual payments, relative to per capita stock holding, and as having a fixed notion of how many

TABLE:

Stockwealth and bridewealth in some East African herding societies

	Per capita holdings		Actual bridewealth		Ideal bridewealth	
	Large stock	Small stock	Large stock	Small stock	Large stock	Small stock
Mursi	1		15-20		38	
Nuer	1		20-30		40	
Gogo	1.25	1.23	15	10	20 +	15-20
Jie	3-4	4	50	129		
Turkana	3-4	10	47	88		
Samburu	11-12		6-8 large stock and continuing transfers			
Dassanetch	4	9-11	Continuing transfers of large and small stock			
Maasai	14		4	2	4	2

Sources: Nuer: Evans-Pritchard, 1940, 1951; Howell, 1954. Gogo: Rigby, 1969. Jie: Gulliver, 1955. Turkana: Gulliver, 1955. Samburu: Spencer, 1965. Dassanetch: Almagor, 1978. Maasai: Jacobs, 1965, 1970.

stock ought, ideally, to be handed over. In these three societies the amount of bridewealth is decided in advance of the marriage through negotiations between the kin of the groom and the kin of the bride, even if it is not handed over immediately, and the distribution of bride-wealth among the groom's affines is not his responsibility but that of the bride's close agnates. The Jie and Turkana also make relatively high payments, which are decided in advance of the marriage by negotiations, and which are distributed by the bride's agnates. By contrast, the Samburu and Maasai make fixed but purely nominal payments (again, in relation to their per capita stock holdings) of formal bridewealth. Among the Samburu, the groom is subject to continuing and indefinite demands for large stock from his affines, while, among the Maasai, he is expected to make small gifts and loans of stock to his prospective father-in-law before the formal bridewealth is handed over.[1] Among the Dassanetch, also, bridewealth consists of an indefinite number of large and small stock which a man transfers over many years, directly to his individual affines, there being, in this case, no fixed initial payment at all.

This purely tabular presentation of the facts, therefore, appears to indicate that formal bridewealth payments can be expected to be high where cattle play a relatively insignificant part in the total economy, and that, in other words, "obsession" with the social and ritual use of cattle is negatively correlated with their economic significance, as though people can afford such extra-economic indulgences precisely because they do not depend upon cattle for their livelihood. Before jumping to such a conclusion, however, one should bear in mind the limitations of this Table as a basis for generalising about the relationship between stock-wealth and the social and ritual use of livestock. Firstly, the figures presented give a false picture of numerical uniformity. For, especially among those groups with high per capita holdings, very great variations may occur in the stock-wealth of individuals (cf. Jacobs, 1965, p. 150, "herd size varies enormously between families due to fortuitous factors"). As for the figures given for negotiated bridewealth payments, these are either based on the ethnographer's impression of "usual" practice (Mursi and Nuer) or are averages worked out from a number of actual cases among which the

---

[1] It is not clear from Jacobs's article "Masai Marriage and Bridewealth" (1970) whether or not informal transfers of stock continue to be made by a man to his wife's kin after his marriage.

range of variation may be considerable (Turkana, Jie and Gogo). Secondly, the table oversimplifies the institution of bridewealth itself, treating it entirely as a matter of how many stock are handed over. Equally important, however, are the rules according to which transfers and distributions are made: whether, for example, the cattle to be handed over are determined in advance by negotiations, who has the right to receive them, and from whom. Thirdly, the bare statement of per capita holdings of stock for a number of societies does not allow a realistic assessment to be made of the relative importance of cattle or other stock in their economies. It is the implications of this third point which I now wish to develop.

A distinction needs to be made between at least two senses in which a subsistence source can be described as important, or significant, in a particular economy. The first concerns the relative size of the contribution it makes to the normal diet of the population, and the second concerns the contribution it makes to the overall viability of the economy. In the first of these senses cattle are certainly of "secondary" importance to the Mursi, Nuer and Gogo, but in the second sense they cannot possibly be described as such.

Here we come up against the fact that, like the term bridewealth, "pastoralist" is itself an "odd-job" word, the usefulness of which is that it can be applied to a very wide range of peoples, geographically, culturally and economically, and which it would therefore be pointless to try to define. It should not be surprising, therefore, that the classic case of a "pre-eminently pastoral people" (Evans-Pritchard, 1940, p. 16), the Nuer, turn out not to be pastoralists at all, if that word is taken to refer to people who subsist mainly on their herds. Although Evans-Pritchard points out that "they grow more millet than is commonly supposed", the full extent of Nuer dependence on fishing and cultivation does not emerge until we consider the implications of the fact that their "cattle probably do not greatly exceed the human population" (op. cit., p. 20). Recent research on the dietary needs and minimum herd size of pastoral populations in East Africa suggests that at least ten head of cattle per head of human population are necessary to provide an adequate daily subsistence based entirely on the consumption of meat, blood and milk.[1] It seems likely, then, that *at most* only

[1] This is a very rough estimate based on the publications of Leslie Brown (1973 and 1977) and Gudrun Dahl and Anders Hjort (1976). While it is useful to try to arrive at such a figure for minimum herd size, based on dietary requirements, it should be noted that the figure eventually arrived

20 per cent of the subsistence requirements of the Nuer can come from their herds, the remaining 80 or even 90 per cent being made up mainly from cultivation and fishing. But to conclude that cattle are therefore of secondary importance in the Nuer economy would clearly be inappropriate, in view of Evans-Pritchard's elegant demonstration of the way in which "the necessity of a mixed economy follows from the ecological equilibrium" (op. cit., p. 92). It is as evident from Evans-Pritchard's account of the Nuer that cattle are highly significant — indeed indispensable — in the contribution they make to the viability of this mixed economy, as it is that they are relatively insignificant in the contribution they make to the every-day food intake of the majority of the population.

Like the Nuer, the Mursi are transhumant herders and cultivators, who have approximately one head of cattle per head of human population. Although they live alongside a large river, the Omo, fishing is not as important for them as it is for the Nuer and they probably depend for about 80 per cent of their subsistence needs on the cultivation of sorghum. (Some fish are speared between approximately November and January, when the Omo is low and its waters clear, but this method of fishing is ruled out for the rest of the year by the speed of the current and by the fact that the river is then coloured a deep reddish brown by the products of soil erosion in the Ethiopian highlands). Two types of cultivation are practised by the Mursi, one using rain and the other using the flood waters of the Omo. Rainfall in Mursi country is both low, probably averaging around 500 millimetres annually, and, more to the point, unreliable as to timing, amount and location. The rains frequently fail altogether, causing the harvest to be totally lost. Flood cultivation, on the other hand, depends not on the erratic local rainfall but on the very heavy rains which fall over the Ethiopian highlands, since it is these rains which control the rise and fall of the Omo (Butzer, 1971, pp. 35-39). The river reaches its maximum level in August or early September, when it deposits layers of flood silt along its banks, and these flooded areas are planted, as the water level recedes, in October and November.

at must be very tentative because of the many factors involved which are difficult to quantify. These include the energy expenditure and calorific requirements of the human population, the quantity of milk available for human consumption and its food value, the proportion of adult females in the herd, the calving interval, the lactation period and stock losses due to drought and disease. All of these factors will vary, not only from one environment to another but also from one time of year to another in the same environment.

The amount of land flooded and therefore cultivable, varies from year
to year and is never extensive, no system of irrigation being used to
overcome the topography of the Omo which, in Mursi country, does
not meander markedly and is flanked, for the most part, by steep cliffs.
The amount of land potentially available for rain cultivation is effectively unlimited, but the dilemma here is that land has to be cleared for
planting before it is known whether there will be enough rain to make
successful cultivation possible. These two forms of cultivation therefore
complement each other, the one going some way towards making up
for the deficiencies of the other, but even when taken together they
could not, alone, provide the Mursi with an adequate and reliable
subsistence. This is mainly because the potentially more productive
rain cultivation is so unpredictable. It should also be noted that,
because of humidity and insect pests, grain cannot be stored for more
than a few months at a time, so that no significant long-term advantage can be taken of the occasional bumper crop.

It is only in the light of these facts that the true economic significance
of the cattle which the Mursi keep in the wooded grassland east of the
Omo can be appreciated. Despite their poverty in cattle — as they themselves see it — their herds are at least as vital to their subsistence, in the
long run, as are the two other main means of subsistence just outlined.
Cattle, which can of course be moved around in response to local vicissitudes of rainfall, not only complement cultivation through their milk,
blood and meat, but are also an essential standby in the event of crop
failure. For, in times of shortage, they can be sold for grain in the highlands, on either side of the Omo valley. According to Leslie Brown (1977),
"The sale of one mature steer . . . enables a pastoralist in Kenya to purchase enough grain to feed his entire family for half a year." (op. cit.,
p. 13). Even though this calculation does not necessarily apply exactly to
the Mursi, it does, I believe, give some idea how vitally important the
possession of just one such animal may be to a Mursi family, since the
sale of it could save them from complete destitution, if not from starvation, over a period of severe food shortage. Indeed, I was told during my
last field trip (1973-74), which came at the end of a three year drought
unprecedented in living memory, that those who had been worst affected,
in some cases starving to death, had been those without cattle to exchange
for grain in the highlands.[1]

---

[1] For a fuller description of Mursi ecology and, in particular, for an account of their response to
the recent drought, see Turton (1977).

IV

The economy of the Mursi, then, rests upon the integration of three separate subsistence resources, each one of which, although insufficient and precarious in itself, makes, when taken together with the other two, a vital contribution to subsistence. The same, of course, can be said of the Nuer, if fishing is substituted for flood cultivation. I shall now argue that it is by focusing on the economic significance of cattle in the societies listed in the Table that the greatest insight can be gained into the paradox which this Table seems to present us with: namely, that bridewealth payments are heaviest where per capita stock holdings are smallest. The essence of the argument is that, where cattle play the economic role that they do among the Mursi and Nuer, they cannot be spread too thinly about the population, and that the way in which bridewealth is paid in these societies works against the net accummulation of stock by particular individuals. Evans-Pritchard tells us that, among the Nuer "cattle are everywhere evenly distributed" and that "a man never possesses many more beasts than his byre will hold because, as soon as his herd is large enough he, or one of his family, marries" (1940, p. 20). Elsewhere he remarks that "a man who receives only one cow of the bridewealth has in it the promise of a herd" (1951, p. 89). It seems, however, that it is the same institution of bridewealth which also sets a limit to the realisation of this promise. Whatever the Nuer say, the real economic importance of possessing a single animal is probably that it contains the promise not so much of a herd as of several sacks of grain in the event of crop failure. Dyson-Hudson has noted a similar effect of bridewealth on herd size among the Karimojong, where "the cattle received as bridewealth by a family for its daughters do not seem to match up with those paid out by its sons" (1966, p. 51).[1] All this can be said of the Mursi. What I want to focus on here, though, is the particular signifi-cance, firstly of the advance determination of the amount of bride-wealth through negotiation; secondly, of there being a recognised total

[1] The Karamojong have between 2.3 and 5 cattle per head of population (Baker, 1968, p. 70), but the importance of cattle in their economy is similar to their importance in the economies of the Nuer and Mursi: "It is not possible in the conditions of rainfall reliability which prevail in Kara-moja, to base family security on grains and this is the critical importance of livestock for, in a year of drought, they are the difference between starvation and survival" (Baker, 1975, p. 190). I have not included the Karimojong in the Table on page 76 because of the lack of data on bridewealth in Dyson-Hudson's book.

towards which it is thought appropriate to strive; and, thirdly, of there being a number of rules specifying to whom and in what numbers the beasts should be distributed.

The determination in advance of the amount, and the edifice of rules within the framework of which this determination is made, helps to ensure that the institution of bridewealth is most effective in spreading cattle evenly about the population precisely when this is most necessary — namely when overall cattle-wealth is relatively low. It is true of course that there are always ambiguities and therefore opportunities for manoeuvre in any set of rules, and some of these I have already noted. The fact remains, however, that, before he can marry, a Mursi must sit down with his future wife's kin and agree to make a payment consisting of many times the per capita holding of stock, the bulk of which must be handed over immediately, while any animals left outstanding must nevertheless be precisely identified. Similarly, in order to ensure the fertility of his daughter, or the well-being of her children (and hence to ensure that her husband will not ask for the bridewealth to be returned), a man must distribute to a wide range of his matrilateral and patrilateral kin about half her total bridewealth, if it is a large one, and probably a good deal more than half if it is a small one. The significance of the ideal total — 38 for Mursi and 40 for the Nuer — seems to be precisely that it is an ideal. That is, since virtually no groom can meet it, virtually all have to impoverish themselves to get married, and this ensures that it will not be until a significant all-round increase in the cattle-wealth of the population as a whole has taken place that more than a very few men will be able to meet the ideal payment comfortably. If such an increase were to occur, and more and more grooms became able to satisfy their wife's kin without stretching their cattle resources to the limit, one presumes that significant differences in cattle-wealth would begin to occur, since the opportunity would now exist for net accumulation of stock (if, that is, the ideal were not revised upwards).

Of the other groups listed in the Table, the Gogo of central Tanzania (Rigby, 1969) seem to approach the Mursi-Nuer case most closely. The "basis" of Gogo subsistence "is primarily agriculture" and their economy "relies so heavily on the production of food crops, it may not properly be termed 'pastoral' ". The primary significance of livestock to the Gogo lies, according to Rigby, in the "rights and obligations" they define and express, and it is because of this "that at the level of kinship relationships and ideology Gogo society may easily be said to be a pastoral one". He nevertheless admits that "livestock are also of considerable economic significance, *even* from the point of view of subsistence" (op. cit., pp. 24-26; my emphasis). Indeed, it seems that cattle must be indispensable to the Gogo, and for the same reasons that they are indispensable to the Mursi and Nuer. For Ugogo is as unattractive from the point of view of cultivation as are Mursi- and Nuerland: rainfall averages about 500 millimetres a year, there are no permanent streams, and famines are periodic (op. cit., p. 13).

> The problem of obtaining . . . sufficient rain for the crops . . . is a constant one in Ugogo. The short and erratic, single rainy season each year has a profound effect upon the ecology of the area . . . Droughts are frequent and constitute one of the primary factors influencing residential mobility (op. cit., pp. 33-34).

In these conditions, livestock

> impinge upon the agricultural cycle at several important points: (a) the use of manure, (b) the exchange of livestock intermittently for grain in normal years, and (c) the use of livestock as an insurance against famine in bad years, enabling the Gogo to obtain food enough to have the strength to carry out cultivation in the following season (op. cit., p. 43).

Although putting it this way still emphasises the subsidiary role of cattle in a predominantly agricultural economy, there can be no doubt that their economic role here is essentially the same as it is for the Mursi and the Nuer.

As for bridewealth payments, these "constitute the largest single transaction in the Gogo exchange system" (op. cit., p. 225) and the size of individual payments varies with "the subsistence conditions extant at the time" (op. cit., p. 228) — that is, grooms pay as much as they can afford. The amount of bridewealth is fixed in advance of the marriage by hard bargaining between the kin of the groom and the kin of the bride, but it "is not a profit-making transaction for those concerned; even the father of the girl may be left with only a couple of head by the time the distribution is over" (op. cit., p. 227). Finally, a "great variety" (p. 232) of kin attempt to obtain a share in a girl's bridewealth and the distribution defines the effective range of kin relationship.

The Jie fit this pattern less well, mainly because they have three or four times as many cattle per head of population as the three examples so far considered, and they also keep a significant number of small stock. Although they do not state an ideal total for bridewealth, it is "an explicit tenet of Jie and Turkana law" that a bridewealth demand is based "quite consciously and directly on what the girl's people estimate that the others can give" (Gulliver, 1955, p. 236). The groom must "be prepared to surrender a very large proportion of his herd" (op. cit., p. 239). The figure given in the Table for actual payments is an average worked out by Gulliver from 48 transactions. It is a payment of the same order of magnitude, in relation to per capita holdings of cattle, as those so far considered for the Nuer, Mursi and Gogo. But what about the economic significance of cattle for the Jie? According to Gulliver agriculture plays "an equally important part with pastoralism" in their economy, which is ambiguous in terms of the distinction made earlier between two senses in which a subsistence source can be "important". It seems clear, however, that the Jie could not survive without their cattle, of which they nevertheless have too few to allow them a purely pastoral existence. Average rainfall in the settled, central area of Jieland is around 600 to 650 millimetres, and "is characterised over the years by a wide range of variation" (op. cit., p. 17).

In an article on another group of the Karimojong cluster, the Dodos, who are northern neighbours of the Jie, Deshler (1965, p. 158), a geographer, notes that "crop yields vary widely as a result of the erratic rainfall" and that "agriculture does not consistently produce food adequate to supply Dodos subsistence needs". He also estimates that, despite a four to five per capita holding of cattle in the more densely settled areas, cattle products make a "modest" contribution to food intake, probably less than a quarter. Deshler (1965, p. 167) concludes that

> the significant fact of Dodos subsistence is that annual food shortage is a severe problem . . . grain supplies in dry years are not adequate to see the tribe through the drought period; gathered products are scarce at this time of year and often are not storable. Livestock, largely cattle, are their one means of hedging against possible famine.

It seems unlikely that the same is not true of the Jie.

The Turkana are a difficult case because, although they are apparently "almost entirely dependent on their herds for food" (Gulliver, 1955, p. 239), they nevertheless make bridewealth payments of an order that puts them into the Mursi/Nuer league, a groom being expected, as in Jieland, "to surrender a very large proportion of his herd". This is puzzling, since the Turkana have little more stock per capita than the Jie, who depend, according to Gulliver, equally on cattle and agriculture. Part of the answer presumably lies in the differentiation which exists within the Turkana herds themselves. For, not only are they "particularly wealthy in small stock", but the figures shown against the Turkana in the Table for large stock (both per capita holdings and bridewealth) include both cattle and camels. Gulliver estimates that the Turkana have 80,000 camels, which equals his estimate of the human population. "Many families", he writes, "have only about half a dozen" camels, but, although they are few in number, (approximately one per capita), camels play a very important part in the Turkana economy. This is, firstly, because they are better suited than cattle to the environment of Turkanaland which consists, for the most part, of an arid plain, covered intermittently with semi-desert bush and shrub and receiving an annual average rainfall of between 300 and 350 millimetres. Since camels browse rather than graze, they are able to survive in this environment the year round, while cattle are strictly confined to grasslands, these being found only in the mountains, over about 12,000 metres elevation, and, during "fair" wet seasons, along the banks of water courses in the plains. Each dry season, in fact, the Turkana cattle "suffer badly" (Gulliver, 1955, p. 39). The second reason why camels, though few in number, must be very important to the Turkana is that they have a higher individual milk yield than cattle and a lactation period about three times as long — around eighteen instead of around six months. Brown (1977) therefore estimates that half as many camels as cattle per head of population are necessary to provide a purely pastoral subsistence, although he acknowledges that "we know far too little about camels, which are very important animals for nomads" (op. cit., p. 69). Although camels do not provide the Turkana with the major part of their daily subsistence, therefore they are an essential supplement to and standby for the two other subsistence resources, cattle and small stock.[1]

[1] In which case, the economic role of camels among the Turkana may be analogous to that of cattle among the Mursi, Nuer and Gogo. It is therefore interesting to note that in the only example of a Turkana bridewealth distribution provided by Gulliver (1955, p. 236) no fewer than thirty-three of the fifty-nine large stock involved were camels. It is true that Gulliver describes this as an "unusually large" number of camels, the groom in question and his close associates being all wealthy camel owners, but it at least seems likely that, as elements in bridewealth, camels carry more prestige than cattle or small stock. One wonders, therefore, whether camels do not, in fact, make up a disproportionately large part of more "usual" bridewealth payments, in which case such payments would help to prevent the uneven accumulation of this scarce but vital resource.

It nevertheless seems likely that, given the stock-wealth shown in the Table, the Turkana depend more heavily on non-pastoral sources of food than Gulliver's statement that they are "almost entirely dependent on their herds" would lead us to expect. If their three types of stock are converted into Standard Stock Units, according to Brown's formula (one SSU = 454 kg live-weight = two *adult* cattle = one camel = ten small stock)[1], it seems that they have about three SSU per head of population. (I assume here that they have three cattle, and therefore no more than two adult equivalents, one camel and ten small stock per capita). Again according to Brown, 3·5 to 4 SSU are needed to provide a purely pastoral subsistence in a "semi-desert" environment (1977, p. 38). If we bear in mind that Brown's figures for minimum herd size are probably too low (cf. Dahl and Hjort, 1976, pp. 69, 141, 148, 156-59, 227) and Deshler's observation, quoted above, about the contribution of cattle to Dodos subsistence, it seems that the Turkana studies by Gulliver must depend heavily, since they do not cultivate, on hunting, gathering and various forms of foraging and that, for this reason, they should not be categorized, along with the Samburu and Maasai, as pure pastoralists.

I come now to those groups in the Table among whom total bridewealth is not fixed by negotiations in advance of the marriage. Into this category come the Samburu, the Dassanetch and the Maasai. Among the first, an initial payment of eight large stock is made at the time of the marriage and Spencer calls this the "bridewealth", to distinguish it from the "marriage payments" which are made over subsequent years. This is misleading, comparatively, since in the event of divorce it is not only this initial payment which must be returned to the groom, but all the subsequent payments as well. Here I shall refer to the total amount of stock paid out by a man to his wife's kin as bridewealth, for the contrast I wish to draw is between situations in which this total is decided upon and handed over in advance, and situations in which it is known only retrospectively, after a lapse of many years. It is this contrast, rather than one between absolute numbers of stock transferred, which I think is important. For bridewealth payments are relatively light among the Samburu, precisely because they are spread over many years. The husband keeps the capital of his herd, and satisfied his affines out of its interest. It is clear that, in these circum-

---

[1] For a comparison of various conversion rates for standard livestock units, see Dahl and Hjort (1976, pp. 224-230).

stances, the payment of bridewealth is by no means a burden, but only a minor irritant, due to the "predatory visits" of one's affines. So too for the Dassanetch, among whom, "Transfer of bridewealth are spread over many years" and a groom is not impoverished "at the point of marriage" (Almagor, 1978, p. 194). Almagor gives an example in which a man transferred 35 cattle and 58 small stock over a period of 20 years, an annual average of 1·75 head of cattle and about 4 head of small stock a year (op. cit., p. 187). Although it is not clear whether a Maasai groom continues to make transfers of cattle to his affines during the years following his marriage, Jacobs (1970) does emphasise that the livestock exchanges which precede and accompany the actual marriage ceremony are relatively unimportant, and that "bridewealth payments for Maasai impose no real economic hardship". Indeed, "when compared with the four head of cattle and two sheep which constitute the formal bride-wealth, and the altogether modest gifts and loans of cattle which a prospective son-in-law makes to his prospective in-laws in the course of establishing good affinal relations, the economic costs of getting married for Maasai is more than compensated for by the purely economic gains of 'wedding gifts' " which a man receives as a consequence of marriage and which are normally in the order of fifteen to twenty head of cattle, and a slightly higher number of sheep and goats (op. cit., p. 34).

The Samburu and Maasai pay bridewealth in a resource which is not complementary to and a standby for other resources which account for the major part of daily food intake. As for the Dassanetch, although their per capita stock holding is only a third of that of the Samburu and Maasai, cattle and cultivation do not have, for them, the same relative significance as they do for the Mursi, Nuer and Gogo. This is, firstly, because, being able to cultivate extensive "flooded flats" in the Omo delta region, the bulk of their cultivation does not depend upon the erratic local rainfall. Secondly, their stock wealth is controlled by the huge ritual slaughters which take place annually, and which Almagor (op. cit.) sees as reducing pressure on their limited grazing areas.

It is obvious that a Samburu groom cannot afford to hand over the bulk of his cattle to his future wife's kin at his marriage, since he would then have no means of supporting her. It is on this point — his ability to support his wife — that the girl's kin must satisfy themselves before agreeing to the match. To convince them the groom must be able and willing to provide 15-50 cattle for his future wife's "allotted herd"

(Spencer, 1965, p. 54). If the Samburu initial payment of 6 to 8 large stock were much higher, it could have the effect, in times of stock shortage, of forcing grooms to stretch their stock resources to the limit, thus evening out stock holdings it is true, but also running the risk of spreading them so thinly that the average family herd might drop below a viable size. Obviously there must be some means of levelling out marked differences in cattle-wealth among the Samburu and similar peoples, and transfers to affines (whose predations will presumably bear more heavily the more wealthy the husband) are one way in which this is achieved. But this levelling cannot be allowed to continue indefinitely (as it must be allowed to continue among the Mursi, Nuer and Gogo). For if the cattle holdings of individual families are levelled out to below 35-40 head of large stock (five to six per capita) then, according to even the most optimistic calculations, (Brown, 1973), the purely pastoral economy will collapse.

So far I have been concerned with the size of the payment, its determination and when it is paid. I now consider briefly the way in which it is distributed. In all the groups mentioned, bridewealth may be said, in a general sense, to be widely distributed, mainly among the kin of the bride. But, if we consider who is responsible for the distribution, the groups fall again into two broad categories, which correspond to the categories already distinguished. On the one hand there are those like the Mursi, in which the groom pays but does not distribute the bridewealth, and on the other hand there are those, like the Samburu, in which the groom both pays and distributes it. From the point of view of the distributor, in the first category of groups he distributes his sister's or daughter's bridewealth among his kin, it being these very distributions which define the range of kin, while in the second category he distributes his wife's bridewealth among his affines. Since, in the context of exogamy, kinship persists while affinity is, so to speak, lost with the passage of every generation, it follows that social ties created by the direct transfer of cattle by an individual to his affines do not have the same permanence as those which are not created or initiated by an individual but which are presented to him as a set of options within the framework of kinship. In both cases transactions can be widely spread, from the point of view of the number and range of individual recipients. But in the latter case each transaction has both a history of earlier transactions and predictable implications for future transactions.

Because of this time depth one can say that marriage among the Nuer and Mursi is a way of creating very long-term debts — or perhaps better, of giving very long-term credit. Glickman, in a recent article on the Nuer (1971), has pointed out that this kind of indebtedness, or system of "deferred payments", has considerable advantages for individuals, not in terms of the ownership of property, but in terms of economic security in the long-term.[1] For, as we have seen, a man can hardly expect to make a substantial gain out of his daughter's bridewealth, even when the amount paid is relatively high. Among the Mursi certainly, although men talk as though their daughters are a great source of cattle-wealth, there is no doubt that of far greater economic significance are the cattle they are entitled to receive from the bridewealth of the daughters, granddaughters and great-grand-daughters of their own, their father's, their grandfather's and their great-grandfather's sisters (see Fig. 2). Among the other category of herders, where bridewealth transactions do not have this time depth, there seems to be a correspondingly greater emphasis on each man building up, over his lifetime, a network of stock associates, bond friends or whatever, in the creation of which ties he is relatively undetermined by the relationships of his own father. There is not, in other words, the same ineluctable dissipation of the livestock capital of individuals which is ensured by the other system. Groups of the second category cannot afford to run down their herds, while those of the first category cannot afford not to.

V

I have tried to distinguish in this chapter between two broad categories of East African herders. In the first, large stock are complementary to, and an indispensable standby for, other means of subsistence which, although unreliable in the long-term, provide the bulk of everyday food intake for the majority of the population. Bride-

[1] One measure of the extreme seriousness of the 1971-73 drought is that some men took back, by force, cattle they had given in bridewealth, thereby effectively divorcing themselves. Such men could not afford to wait for the benefits of reciprocity to work themselves out in the long term. Having lost confidence in the natural order, they had lost confidence in the social order as well (Turton, 1977, p. 190).

wealth among these peoples is high in relation to per capita stock holding, is fixed by negotiation in advance of the marriage, is paid in a lump sum and constitutes the major economic transaction in the society. Because of these features, bridewealth is here the main means whereby cattle are distributed evenly about the population, being spread ever more thinly the smaller the total cattle population becomes. For herders in the second category, among whom cattle do not have the particular economic significance that they have for those in the first, bridewealth is not fixed in advance by negotiations and is a relatively insignificant transaction both from the point of view of those who make the payments and from the point of view of the role of these payments in the distribution of livestock resources. Bridewealth here takes its place alongside many similar transactions in which men engage throughout their lives and which appear to be more significant than they are among herders of the first category.

Finally, a word of qualification should be added. There is no suggestion, either implicit or explicit, in the above argument that the two categories which have been distinguished are, or should be, exhaustive of the ethnographic data, even within the region of East Africa, let alone beyond it. This may be illustrated by referring briefly to the Arusha of northern Tanzania among whom per capita stock holding is less than one, and bridewealth consists of five head of cattle (Gulliver, 1963, pp. 14, 242). On the face of it this contradicts the thesis presented above according to which it would seem that the Arusha should conform more to the Mursi-Nuer-Gogo pattern than to that of the Maasai. In fact, no such problem arises, since the role of cattle in the Arusha economy is quite unlike their role in the economies of any of the groups listed in the Table on page 76. Not only do the Arusha depend overwhelmingly on agriculture for their subsistence, but their territory, lying at over 1200 metres above sea level on the southwestern slopes of Mt. Meru, is an agriculturally highly favoured one. It is true that, since 1930, the Arusha have had to cultivate the less favoured "peripheral lowlands", due to the establishment of a forest reserve higher up the mountain, but at the time of Gulliver's fieldwork (1957) nearly two-thirds of the population lived in the more favoured region, at an altitude of between 1200 and 1500 metres, and at an average density of more than one thousand per square mile. Here, the volcanic soils are fertile, surface water is plentiful and, above all, rainfall is both heavy and reliable (Gulliver, op. cit., p. 11). There can be no question therefore of cattle having the same significance for the Arusha as they have for the Nuer, Mursi and Gogo, and there is consequently no reason why the phenomena designated by the term bridewealth among these last three groups should be significantly similar, from an economic point of view, to the phenomena so designated among the Arusha.

Bibliography

Almagor, U. (1978). "Pastoral Partners". Manchester University Press, Manchester.

Baker, P. R. (1968). The distribution of cattle in Uganda. *East African Geographical Review*, **6**, 63-73.

Baker, P. R. (1975). 'Development' and the pastoral people of Karamoja: an example of the treatment of symptoms. *In* "Pastoral Societies in Tropical Africa" (Ed. T. Monod). Oxford University Press for the International African Institute, London.

Brown, L. H. (1973). "Conservation for Survival: Ethiopia's Choice". Haile Sellassie I University Press, Addis Ababa.

Brown, L. H. (1977). The ecology of man and domestic livestock. *In* "Rangeland Management and Ecology in East Africa" (Eds. D. J. Pratt and M. F. Gwynne). Hodder & Stoughton, London.

Butzer, K. W. (1971). "Recent History of an Ethiopian Delta: the Omo River and the Level of Lake Rudolf". Research Paper No. 136, Department of Geography, University of Chicago, Chicago.

Dahl, G. and Hjort, A. (1976). "Having Herds". Stockholm Studies in Social Anthropology No. 2, Department of Social Anthropology, University of Stockholm, Stockholm.

Deshler, W. W. (1965). Native cattle keeping in eastern Africa. *In* 'Man, Culture and Animals: The Role of Animals in Human Ecological Adjustment". (Eds. A. Leeds and A. P. Vayda). Publication No. 78, American Association for the Advancement of Science, Washington, D.C.

Dyson-Hudson, N. (1966). "Karamojong Politics". Oxford University Press, London.

Evans-Pritchard, E. E. (1940). "The Nuer: a Description of the Modes of Livlihood and Political Institutions of a Nilotic People". Clarendon Press, Oxford.

Evans-Pritchard, E. E. (1951). "Kinship and Marriage Among the Nuer". Clarendon Press, Oxford.

Fortes, M. (1950). Kinship and marriage among the Ashanti. *In* "African Systems of Kinship and Marriage" (Eds. A. R. Radcliffe-Brown and D. Forde). Oxford University Press for the International African Institute, London.

Glickman, M. (1971). Kinship and credit among the Nuer. *Africa*, **XLI**, 4, 306-319.

Goody, J. (1973). Bridewealth and dowry in Africa and Eurasia. *In* "Bridewealth and Dowry" (Eds. J. Goody and S. J. Tambiah). Cambridge Papers in Social Anthropology No. 7, Cambridge University Press, London.

Gulliver, P. H. (1955). "The Family Herds". Routledge & Kegan Paul, London.

Gulliver, P. H. (1963). "Social Control in an African Society". Routledge & Kegan Paul, London.

Howell, P. P. (1954). "A Manual of Nuer Law". Oxford University Press for the International African Institute, London.

Jacobs, A. H. (1965). African pastoralists: some general remarks. *Anthropological Quarterly*, **38**, 144-154.

Jacobs, A. H. (1970). Masai marriage and bridewealth. *Mila: a Biannual Newsletter of Cultural Research*, **1**, 1, 25-36. Cultural Division, I.D.S., University College, Nairobi.

Needham, R. (1971). Remarks on the analysis of kinship and marriage. *In* "Rethinking Kinship and Marriage" (Ed. R. Needham). Tavistock, London.

Needham, R. (1975). Polythetic classification: convergence and consequences. *Man* (N.S.), **10**, 349-389.

Rigby, P. (1969). "Cattle and Kinship Among the Gogo: a Semi-Pastoral Society of Central Tanzania". Cornell University Press, Ithaca and London.

Spencer, P. (1965). "The Samburu: a Study of Gerontocracy in a Nomadic Tribe". Routledge & Kegan Paul, London.

Turton, D. (1977). Response to drought: the Mursi of southwestern Ethiopia. *In* "Human Ecology in the Tropics" (Eds. J. P. Garlick and R. W. J. Keay). Routledge & Kegan Paul, London.

Acknowledgements

I have spent two periods of fieldwork among the Mursi. The first, in 1969-70, was financed by grants from the Social Science Research Council, the Central Research Fund of the University of London, the Tweedie Exploration Fellowship Committee of the University of Edinburgh and the Royal Geographical Society. The second, in 1973-74, was financed by a further grant from the Social Science Research Council. I am grateful to all of these bodies for their generous assistance. For their comments on an earlier draft of this essay I am grateful to Dr. Richard Werbner and Dr. Martin Southwold, the latter, in particular, for his help in the formulation of the definitional problem, contained in the opening paragraphs. The shortcomings which remain are, of course, my own responsibility.

4 Marriage, Exchange and the Meaning of Corporations in Eastern Indonesia *

R. H. BARNES

I

We have a way of thinking, inherited from Maine via Rivers and Radcliffe-Brown, that unilineal rules are particularly suited for establishing discrete corporations. Following Maine, Radcliffe-Brown (1952, p. 46) held that corporate organizations based on kinship, rather than on location, would have to be unilineal. Subsequent work on cognatic societies has shown otherwise, but the idea lingers on. In fact, even unilineal peoples sometimes resort to supplementary or alternative procedures for allocating children to corporations.

In eastern Indonesia, marriage exchanges often have this function. Sometimes (as among the cognatic Ngada) they are sufficient by themselves. In other cases, although a unilineal principle may be present, groups are defined by more than one consideration and membership depends as much upon payment of bridewealth as upon descent. Where unilineal descent, affinal alliance and marriage exchanges occur together, they all have an essential part in the constitution of corporations, but each of these features may be present or absent independently of the others. The knowledge that groups are made up by means of a unilineal rule of membership tells us nothing else about their nature or purpose, nor does it guarantee that descent is the most decisive factor.

I have elsewhere (1980) tried to show that for a society practising prescriptive alliance (Kédang) it is not a simple matter to identify units corporately involved in alliance, despite the corporate patrilineal clans of the Kédang. Our idea of "alliance groups" may well have more than one application in a particular culture, and not all of these applications will necessarily coincide with a conventionally delimited corporation.

In this chapter, I should like to take up Sir Edmund Leach's suggestion (1957, p. 54) that "we think again about the relationship between 'corporateness' and 'descent' ". As in the case of alliance groups, we will have to be prepared to discriminate different kinds of corporations for different purposes. But we may also need to recognize that descent, locality, marriage prestations, and any other matters determining composition, will each have a different relative importance in different contexts. Perhaps we should try to develop a structural interpretation of corporations. Such an approach, taking its guide from Evans-Pritchard's "The Nuer", would be designed for those societies where descent is not present or else is not the only principle of social organization, and it would be intended to provide a necessary supplement to what Dumont (1961, pp. 24-25) has called "the structural theory of kinship".

II

No more than "descent" or "affinity" are such expressions as "bride-wealth" or "marriage prestations" absolute technical terms (see Leach 1961, p. 27). Some declaration is necessary, therefore, about my own vocabulary. Any particular piece of jargon I might adopt to characterize such sets of gifts or payments is likely to be in some way deficient. Even a choice between "payments" or "prestations" may imply some theoretical prejudgement. Does behind the one lurk a conviction that women are given out for commercial purchase, and behind the other an assumption that marriage is accompanied by disinterested gifts?

"Bride-wealth" was proposed by Evans-Pritchard (1931) as a term which would avoid the suggestion of purchase, while nevertheless stressing the economic value of the goods transmitted, and he seems to have been anticipated by several decades in his selection of this word by Dutch anthropologists using "bruidschat" (see van Straten, 1927). Reports from as early as the seventeenth century had shown that the implication of outright buying and selling of women was at variance with African attitudes (Torday, 1929); and the Dutch had often made the same observation in Indonesia.

Evans-Pritchard's express declaration that, "Bride-wealth has everywhere an economic value" (1934, p. 172), has not prevented anthropologists from interpreting his new term as a euphemism, disguising an economic institution (Gray, 1960). This misunderstanding depends, of course, upon equating economy with commerce. It may be though that we would do well in the future to speak of marriage or alliance "alienations", in the sense in which Rousseau (1973, p. 169) uses the word: "To alienate is to give or to sell". This designation would be justified by a view, more or less similar to Rousseau's, of society as a structured order of alienation.[1] The real difficulty with "bridewealth" is that it cannot be applied to situations where groom-wealth is exchanged in return for a man (cf. Goody, 1973, p. 6); and it is not well suited as a general term for Asian systems of reciprocal and opposed cycles of prestations associated with alliance (Needham, 1962, p. 95).

All of the societies I will be considering (except Ngada and the eastern Tetun) have explicit ideas about the use of marriage to establish alliances between collectivities, even those without prescriptive social classifications. For all of them marriage takes its place in a system of what Mauss called "total prestations". It is possible in special cases for the sequence of reciprocal gifts to be completed when the union is first established; but the normal pattern is a "constant redocumentation by payments throughout marriage" (Evans-Pritchard, 1934, p. 174). As Onvlee (1949, p. 457) observes for East Sumba, the exchange of gifts is not limited to marriage. Marriage is only one of the occasions, an important one, to realize, strengthen or continue the link between the two sides of Sumbanese social reality, that between wife-givers and wife-takers. In the background of this cardinal social distinction, as Onvlee shows us, lies a cosmological principle, the opposition of male to female.

In all cases to be examined in this paper, the gifts associated with marriage fade into a pattern of mutual assistance and services and are continued by exchanges, often extensive, in connection with later

---

[1] The clauses of the social contract, according to Rousseau (1973, p. 174), "may be reduced to one — the total alienation of each associate, together with all his rights, to the total community". It is another question, of course, whether the metaphor of a social contract has any bearing on a given set of institutions.

events like funerals or the birth and naming of children. If they are removed from this context, they will be misunderstood. So even expressions like "marriage payments" or "marriage prestations", which look neutral enough, bring with them an arbitrary and potentially misleading restriction in so far as they suggest that the exchanges are only concerned with marriage. In those societies where the sociological institutions express an idea of alliance, it may prove expedient to adopt a phrase coined by Dumont for a somewhat narrower application (1957, p. 32), namely "alliance prestations".

In the following, where it is appropriate and where social features may be explained in terms of alliance, I will speak of "alliance prestations" for the global set of exchanges beginning with betrothal or marriage and continuing throughout the duration of the tie which it initiates. "Marriage prestations" may be retained for those segments of the set of exchanges which are most directly connected with the union itself, and may refer to the goods given by either the wife's relatives or the husband's. Taking advantage of what Sahlins (1972, p. 182) calls the great lesson of "total prestation" — that the economic and moral orders are not distinguished where the relations between persons have not yet been organized on the basis of commercial exchange — I will retain "marriage payments" as a convenient synonym for "marriage prestations". "Payment" in this case does not imply commercial purchase, which can be otherwise clearly indicated when it is needed. "Bridewealth" indicates the marriage prestations given by the husband's relatives to the wife.

III

It has often been held that bridewealth is particularly associated with patrilineality, whereas it is absent or is replaced by brideservice in matrilineal communities. Wilken (1883, pp. 26-28) speculated that bridewealth (*bruidschat*) originated in those societies which were shifting from an original matriarchy toward patriarchy. Bridewealth, in its origin, would not have been a purchase, but a settlement for the offence caused by abduction of the bride. When patriarchical societies later had firmly established themselves, bridewealth became a true purchase.

Ethnographers working on Timor have described shifts from

patrilineal to matrilineal arrangements associated with the presence or absence of bridewealth among the Atoni (Schulte Nordholt, 1971, pp. 116-118), the Buna' (Berthe, 1961), the western Tetun (Vroklage, 1952a, p. 304; 1952b, p. 140), and the eastern Tetun (Hicks, 1975). Schulte Nordholt (p. 132) has advanced the generalization that, "Depending on whether marriages in Timor are more or less frequently and permanently uxorilocal or patrilocal, descent will be more or less matrilineal or patrilineal respectively"; and residence is usually decided, on Timor, by marriage exchanges. Hicks (p. 56) even speaks of matrimonial compensation acting as a selector between two possible regimes: patrilateral filiation, virilocal residence or matrilateral filiation, uxorilocal residence.

Not all Indonesian systems, however, fit Wilken's hypothesis associating agnatic kinship with bridewealth, descent through women with its absence. Wilken himself notes that endogamous, cognatic groups in Indonesia often use bridewealth where, in his view, it does not constitute a purchase. Van Straten (1927, pp. 1-2) raises the same point in criticizing the idea that the true form of bridewealth is found in patrilineal societies as an indemnification for the loss of a daughter. And Fischer observes (1932, pp. 66-67) that bridewealth is often found where marriage is matrilocal and where there is no loss of manpower for the wife's family.

Indeed, even on Timor there are a number of considerations which argue against a general association of the presence or absence of prestations with particular rules of descent. For one thing, among the eastern Tetun (Hicks, 1975, p. 58) and the Atoni (Cunningham, 1967b, p. 5), where children are sometimes affiliated to their mother's descent group, all clans and lineages are theoretically patrilineal. In some Atoni areas, even full payment of bridewealth does not entail assigning all children to their father's lineage, while in other areas there is no bridewealth at all, but descent is predominantly patrilineal and most marriages virilocal (Schulte Nordholt, 1971, p. 120). On Flores, the cognatic Ngada make extensive use of marriage gifts, whereas some sections of the Lamaholot, who are strictly patrilineal and eventually virilocal, do not. The Ngada hold a special interest because, although they are cognatic, they are organised in an elaborate system of exclusive, segmentary, corporate descent groups.

IV

From the eastern Indonesian peoples to be reviewed, we can con-clude that cognation does permit the establishment of discrete corporations, while unilineal rules may not in every society be suf-ficient. Both circumstances controvert a common understanding of kinship which we owe ultimately to Maine.

It is just as well, perhaps, that we look again at his explanation of the primitive corporation. Prior to political association on the basis of local contiguity, Maine asserted, kinship in blood was the only grounds for political union (Maine, 1861, p. 129). Kinship, however, is determined by the question of authority. It should not be possible for a person to be subject to two distinct *Patriae Potestates*. Therefore, the family and higher order corporations must limit membership to agnates. In this way, it is possible to avoid conflict of laws in the domestic forum (Maine, pp. 149-50).

One trend in anthropology has followed Maine, and later Weber (1947), in placing especial weight on the question of authority (e.g. Fortes, 1953, p. 32). I think though that this view is usually quite misleading. For present purposes, we can get further by considering another matter, what Maine called the distinctive characteristic of corporations, i.e. that they never die. What appears to be a sociological certainty turns out for Indonesians to be an aspiration which can too easily fail. Some cultures, not unexpectedly, allow a variety of ways to ensure perpetuation, and in some cases they result in alternative forms of social organization within the same society. If we invert Maine's view of corporations, and recognize that they are always concerned to avoid dying, we will see these facts in an entirely new light. Those societies which restrict themselves to exclusive unilineal institutions may be the most difficult to explain.

I have selected seven societies which show different ways corpor-ations may approach the problems of their definition and contin-uation. Four of these are on Timor, the eastern Tetun, the Ema, the Buna' and the Atoni. The Ngada are on central Flores, and the Lamaholot and Kédang are to be found in the Solor Archipelago.

The first two I wish to consider, the Ema and the Buna', have descent groups which are very directly delimited by a system of asym-metrical affinal alliance. Among the Ema, descent groups are patri-lineal, and the system of descent and alliance is governed by a corresponding social classification, defining a single form of organisation. Adoption is a privilege associated with alliance, and even here children are not inevitably allotted to their father's patrilineage. In contrast, Buna' descent groups are not at all unilineal, and alliance pertains to only one of two possible organizational procedures.

1. The Ema

The Ema of Marobo have been well described by Brigitte Clamagirand (1975).[1] Like all of the other peoples they are sedentary agriculturalists. They are situated in north-central Timor on either side of the boundary which separates former Portugese Timor from Indonesian Timor. Mme Clamagirand's study pertains to the 45,000 Ema on the formerly Portugese side. They speak an Austronesian language, are organized into villages and chiefdoms, are divided into patrilineal clans and lineages, maintain asymmetric matrilateral alliance relations between lineages, and order these alliances in terms of a social classification of asymmetric prescriptive alliance.

The Ema distinguish between senior and junior lineages of their descent groups. The patrimony for each clan is retained in the main clan ceremonial house, where the clan performs descent group rituals, and which symbolizes the unity of the descent group. An elder of the senior lineage resides here, while the younger or secondary lineages live in houses usually located outside the village. Each clan maintains a traditional set of ties with a multiplicity of wife-givers and wife-takers, whereby one line of wife-givers and one of wife-takers are singled out as the founding allies of the clan. Junior lineages may not contract marriages at variance with the pattern of alliances for the descent group as a whole. In the case of schism, when a lineage separates itself from its original clan and sets itself up independently, this departing line will signal its new status not only by erecting its own ceremonial house, but by rupturing the established pattern of alliances as well. To this end, its leader may, for example, select his wife from among the former wife-takers and thereby convert that line into his own foundation wife-givers.

The Ema employ two distinct and alternative schedules of marriage prestations, each of which results in a different status for the wife and

[1] Mme Clamagirand has kindly granted me permission to use the following information from her thesis.

her children. The more common, so called "small price", consisting of only two stages, allows divorce and the division of goods and children corresponding to the relative responsibility of the two parties for the separation. Payment of the first stage of this schedule (a buffalo and a golden or silver disk for which two decorated cloths are returned) brings a shift to virilocal residence. Completion of this form of payment entails patrilineal descent for the children, but the woman, if widowed, may return to her natal lineage. The more expensive "large price" makes divorce and the return of the widow impossible and brings with it the complete integration of the woman into her husband's lineage. The woman is ceremonially separated from her ancestors, as a way of demonstrating that her lineage no longer has any claims whatsoever on her children. A son of this marriage is now fully integrated into his father's lineage and may for the first time touch the sacred objects of the lineage without danger to his life. In this form of marriage, the woman may bring with her a dowry consisting of clothing and jewellery and possibly a field.

Mme Clamagirand observes that prestations cycling from takers to givers permit the counter transmission of life, by virtue of women returned in the opposite direction. Prestations are made not only to wife-givers, but also to wife-givers of wife-givers, since the young woman has received her own life from her mother's natal lineage. The gifts associated with alliance are not exhausted by the "large" or "small" price. Certain payments are made to wife-givers when they reconstruct their clan ceremonial building, and there is an elaborate sequence of prestations accompanying funerary ceremonies.

Lineages in danger of dying out may resort to adoption in order to continue their line, and this procedure is more readily available to wealthy and high status lineages than to others. A lineage may resort to adoption even when it has a sufficient number of male children of its own. A child may be acquired either from wife-givers or from wife-takers. In either event, only a very small payment is required (a bracelet and a woven cloth). The lineage which gives the child away hopes thereby to enhance its status and to reinforce the ties of alliance between the two groups.

A lineage which lacks sons may also assure its continuation by retaining a daughter and finding a husband to live with her. Children born to the union will then belong to their mother's patrilineage. A child bears the name of the lineage upon which it depends, and, if at its birth its family is residing uxorilocally, it belongs to its mother's lineage until a part of the marriage gifts has been paid.

We may observe the following points in summary. For the Ema, the set of alliances of both kinds are part of the permanent structure of the clans themselves. Mme Clamagirand found that with almost no exception marriage corresponds correctly to the rules. A two-way transmission of gifts accompanies the circulation and exchange of the material and mystical aspects of life. Alternative patterns of payment exist, and they result in differing degrees of integration of women and their children into the patrilineages of the men. Payment may be made immediately or occur in stages; and a son may in the end complete the payments for his mother in order to remove all attachment to her lineage and to gain full access to the ritual community of his father's clan. Divorce is rare when children have been born; and it is not at all possible when the more expensive schedule has been completed. Despite a patrilineal structure and preponderantly virilocal pattern of residence, marriage payments may, in some cases either be dispensed with or simply not forthcoming, and children will then be attached via their mother to her patrilineage. Even under normal circumstances of payment, children will not always end up in their father's lineage, since one or more of a set of siblings may be adopted by an allied lineage after a small prestation. So although there are clearly defined patrilineages corporately involved in a strict pattern of alliances, the rule of descent is not sufficient in itself to determine membership.

2. *The Buna'*

The neighbours of the Ema to the south are the Buna', who also live on either side of the border between the two halves of Timor; they number some 65,000. They have recently been described in a series of studies by Louis Berthe and Claudine Friedberg (Berthe). Like the Ema, they are hierarchically stratified, organized into villages and chiefdoms, and maintain named, exogamous, corporate descent groups. Unlike the Ema, they speak a non-Austronesian language (Berthe, 1959, p. 362; Schulte Nordholt, 1971, p. 26), have a non-prescriptive terminology (Berthe, 1961, pp. 20-22), and their descent groups are not constituted by patrilineal descent.

Political power in this society is based not on ownership of land, but on control of the sacred patrimony of the large-scale descent group.

The lineages which retain these objects are, according to Berthe, nobles, while the junior lineages of the clan are commoners (1961, p. 7). Each lineage keeps up a distinct pattern of alliances and is defined to a certain extent by them (p. 8). It is advantageous to have as many allies as possible and to have a greater number of takers than givers. The more powerful lineages are successful in pursuing this aim (p. 16). The Buna' distinguish among their allies of each type according to the relative duration of the tie. To this end they employ a sequence of five terms which are identical with the birth order designations for children (Berthe, 1970, pp. 711-12). Lineages are marked by a strong degree of solidarity, in which members through adoption or descendants of freed slaves are on an equal footing with those born into the lineage. The accent is on continuity, rather than upon filiation (p. 713). Indeed, according to the nature of the marriage, natal members may be affiliated through either male or female links, with the latter possibility apparently predominating.

The Buna' possesses two forms of marriage. One variety entails the exchange of two complementary and oriented sequences of gifts and brings with it patrilocal residence and the affiliation of children to their father's descent group. This type is also associated with a preference for marriage with the matrilateral cross-cousin and with asymmetrical alliance. The direction of exchange between wife-givers and wife-takers may not be reversed by this kind of union (Berthe, 1961, pp. 7-10). Alliance ties once established by such marriages are irrevocable, even when they have not subsequently been renewed and refreshed (Berthe, 1970, p. 713).

A woman married in this way becomes a member of her husband's descent group. Though she may later separate herself from her husband, she may not divorce him in law (Berthe, 1961, p. 17). Gifts given by the husband's lineage to that of the wife are regarded as masculine, while those returned are feminine; and a rigorous disjunction is maintained between them. A gift is also made to wife-givers of wife-givers. The Buna' have a separate term for alliance prestations and do not employ the word for commercial purchase. It generally takes a considerable time for payment to be completed, and the duration of this period is given no attention; but a wealthy lineage may complete its obligations immediately. The stages of the exchanges are clearly determined, but the value of each may vary considerably; for the wife-givers attempt to acquire as much as possible. The counter-gifts include a dowry of sacred objects, jewellery, utensils, palm trees, seeds and a field (Berthe, 1961, p. 10-15).

Despite the structural importance of this first variety of marriage, the Buna' do not often practise it. More common is the second version which is accompanied by a substantial but much reduced bridewealth, and in which the husband takes up residence in his wife's home. There he assumes a subordinate position without becoming a member, works on the fields, and is spoken of as a visitor. A man may marry more than one woman in this way, living alternatively in the house of each wife. Divorce is possible and uncomplicated. The woman need not be chosen from a wife-giving line, but may come from any group other than the husband's own lineage by birth or adoption. Marriage with a woman from a wife-taking line is disapproved, but is nevertheless possible and does occur (Berthe, 1961, p. 25). If the woman does not come from a traditional ally, the marriage brings with it a fragile alliance between the two groups which is ruptured by the death of one of the spouses. Children belong to their mother's lineage; but some of them are often adopted by the father, a procedure which is especially easy when the two groups have traditional ties (Berthe, 1961, pp. 17-19). Among the Buna' of the district of Mau-gatal, the first form of marriage is never practised. As a consequence residence is always matrilocal and children are always affiliated to their mother's group. The accompanying prestations from the husband's lineage are much smaller than elsewhere, but the penalty for divorce is extremely high.

There is a form of adoption closely associated with traditional alliance ties and which entails the exchange of very nearly the same sequence of prestations as are to be found in the first, more elaborate marriage variety. Although adoption is permitted only between allied groups, children may be taken from either wife-givers or wife-takers. In the latter case, the prestations are smaller in number and value. It is apparently even possible to initiate an alliance by means of adoption.[1] The more frequent practice in any case is to take one or more children from the wife-givers. As in the case of the wife, the children become full legal members of the adopting lineage and they have the same rights of inheritance as do the members born into it; they may not,

---

[1] There seems to be a contradiction in Berthe's report that adoption may be used, like marriage, to initiate an alliance and that, on the other hand, adoption is permitted only between allied groups: but this contradiction is only superficial. Adoption is used either to establish an alliance or to continue one, and it is not otherwise practised.

however, marry into their own natal group (Berthe, 1961, pp. 16-17).

As with the Ema, among the Buna', the set of alliances are part of the permanent structure of descent groups, in this case of lineages rather than clans. Adoption of children is a normal accompaniment of an alliance relationship; and it may acquire a similar role as marriage in initiating and renewing such ties. Nevertheless alliance seems to take on a basic organizational importance without being the exclusive or even preponderant mode. Any given corporate lineage will be made up and defined by a multiplicity of alternative procedures. Buna' lineages are not even ideologically patrilineal. Affiliation is determined for the most part, but not for everyone, by marriage exchanges. Even where residence is uxorilocal and affiliation matrilateral, some amount of bridewealth is given, and the same is true in Mau-gatal, where descent seems to be normally matrilineal. This payment appears to have the result, if not the purpose, of facilitating the father's adoption of some of his own children.

Among the Ema alternative schedules of prestations determine the degree to which the wife and her children are attached to the husband's patrilineage and clan. Among the Buna' two alternative forms of marriage, associated with a greater or lesser bridewealth, allocate the woman and children to one or the other of two different descent groups. In both societies, adoption is closely associated with alliance and allows siblings to be distributed among different lineages. The Eastern Tetun, to which we now turn, have no (or only a residual) notion of alliance. Two sets of exchanges relating to two separate marriages are necessary to give a man membership in a patrilineage. Men and women may, as a recognized procedure, be denied membership in a descent group; and a man may even be accorded a partial membership in his wife's lineage.

3. The Eastern Tetun

David Hicks (1975) has recently published a description of marriage prestations among the eastern Tetun of Caraubalo princedom, a population who speak a dialect of Tetun, an Austronesian language, and who are situated well into former Portugese Timor and separated from the main body of the Tetun further to the west (see also Hicks, 1976). Caraubalo clans and lineages are theoretically patrilineal (as opposed to the matrilineal western Tetun). The eastern Tetun have a non-prescriptive form of social classification and no longer practise asymmetric alliance. All property, except personal objects given by a mother to her daughter, is conveyed through the male line. The most important right transmitted for a son is his potential membership in his father's lineage. A woman is (with certain exceptions) necessarily a member of a lineage, but a man may be deprived of this status. A man may or may not become his father's legal agnate, but he has nothing himself to say about the matter.

Prior to his own marriage a young man has the right to reside with his father and to be clothed and fed by him, and he may be regarded as a candidate for membership in his father's lineage. He may be expected to provide aid and assistance to this lineage, but he has no claims on it. In return he can only hope that the lineage will provide him eventually with the means of making prestations so that he may marry. A young man, even if he is rich, is forbidden to supply these gifts, as they may come only from his father's lineage, who thereby signal their willingness to incorporate him into the group. A bachelor past thirty will never become a member of a clan or lineage. Marriage is an agnatic rite of passage, bringing with it lineage rights and full social position for the groom.

The most common form of marriage involves prestations, results in patrilocal residence, and establishes membership for a daughter in her father's patrilineage and potential membership in this lineage for a son. According to Hicks, this institution is centered on the two contracting lineages, rather than upon the young man and woman. A second form is a purely individual arrangement with the sanction or approval of the community. Children born of such a union will have no lineage membership whatsoever. Of more sociological interest is the final alternative.

A young man whose marriage has not been made possible by his father's agnates, and who has thus been denied lineage membership, may seek to acquire a wife without making marriage gifts. Until the birth of his first child he must live in the house of his father-in-law, where he must provide domestic service and is considered a dependent member of her lineage. With the birth of a child he may erect a separate dwelling on the property of this group, but may live elsewhere. His children will be affiliated to his wife's lineage, where their line will take a subordinate role and be excluded from political functions in the interior of the group.

Matrimonial compensation, according to Hicks (1975), acts as a selector between two regimes, patrifiliation and patrilocal residence or matrifiliation and uxorilocal residence. Following Berthe (1961) and Vroklage (1952a), he suggests that it will work this way generally on Timor. It is worth noting at this point that among the eastern Tetun, it is possible for men, and in some cases women, to have no lineage membership at all, which is not true for the Ema and Buna'. Children of unions in which there are no prestations exchanged do not attain unrestricted membership of their mother's line, as they do among the Buna'. Lineages are in fact much more thoroughly patrilineal in their constitution, although they may contain subordinate lines attached through female links. A man's lineal membership is secured only when exchanges have been completed in connection with his father's marriage and when prestations have been made available for his own. A man may acquire a degree of membership in his wife's lineage in the absence of bridewealth.

The last Timor example, the Atoni, shows variation in almost every point so far considered; in addition, some Atoni regions permit simultaneous membership in two descent groups.

4. *The Atoni*

The western part of Timor is occupied by the Atoni, 600,000 agriculturalists distributed among eleven princedoms, and speaking an Austronesian language. Atoni relationship terminology is symmetric prescriptive (see Cunningham, 1967a, pp. 54-57; Fischer, 1957, pp. 22-24), but the Atoni make supplementary distinctions between wife-givers and wife-takers, and avoid the direct exchange of genealogically close relatives (Schulte Nordholt, 1971, pp. 106, 109; Cunningham, 1967b, p. 4). Children ideally belong to the father's descent group, but only in Amfoan are Atoni thoroughly patrilineal. Elsewhere there is considerable variation in practice; and in some regions residence is preponderantly uxorilocal and filiation matrilateral.

The basis of Atoni society, according to Schulte Nordholt (1971, p. 92), is the exogamous, territorially localized descent group or lineage which forms part of a clan. Members of such groups share corporately in the responsibilities of providing alliance and marriage prestations, and the properties involved are held by the descent group and inherited by its members (Cunningham, 1967b, pp. 2, 4). Such lineages maintain established affinal alliances among themselves. Complete payment of bridewealth brings with it patrilocal residence, patrifiliation for children and ceremonial initiation of the wife into her husband's lineage. The amount of the prestation is determined by what had been previously given for the woman's own mother. It will be less if the woman is taken from a previously allied group and correspondingly higher and the object of protracted negotiations when it is with a new lineage. The Atoni prefer to maintain alliance ties and a long term pattern of direct exchange. Such an alliance can be renewed by a single marriage. There is though regional variation in the degree of interest shown in continuing such marriage ties. Alliance exchanges are made at each subsequent ceremony connected with the life cycle (Schulte Nordholt, 1971, pp. 92-116; Cunningham, 1967b, p. 2-5).

If there is no bridewealth, children join their mother's descent group. But in some regions even when such exchanges have been completed children may be recruited into the mother's natal lineage, and sometimes into other affinally related groups. Children may be demanded by the mother's agnates. Cunningham (1967b, p. 6) reports of Soba village, Amarasi, that 15 per cent of children and 20 per cent of married adults had been brought in by this means. Again, the frequency of recruitment varies according to region and lineage. In some areas, at least, it is regarded a normal aspect of affinal ties. Children brought into the lineage in this way are spoken of as "female people" and take up a subordinate position in daily and ceremonial affairs within the lineage, although their own children may acquire membership within it. Cunningham distinguishes between recruitment in this fashion and adoption.[1] The latter requires negotiation and compensation but brings unrestricted rights for the child in the adopting lineage. A recruit must contribute to the bridewealth of his mother's lineage and may in turn be helped by her agnates, but he inherits property only at their discretion. His own descendants will retain the same subordinate status. It is possible for several or even all segments of a lineage to have been attached in the past in this manner; so precedence and relative claims to rights are decided by reference to the distance back to the female link. Recruited members, thus, acquire

---

[1] Cunningham (1965) describes yet another procedure, in which children are loaned for a limited number of years to families in other lineages. Borrowing of children operates along different social ties than affinal alliance or affiliation to the mother's descent group, and it involves no shift in their lineage membership; nor does it lead to exchange of formal prestations.

qualified rights in their mother's lineage, but do not lose rights and obligations in that of their father, to which they must also contribute in matters of bridewealth and whose marriage alliances govern their own marriage choices. Such a person may live with his father's agnates prior to his own marriage, and he may even take a wife from the main agnatic line of his mother's lineage. "Female" and "male" houses of a lineage are each exogamous and may be linked to each other by marriage ties. The external pattern of affinal alliance may in this way be continued within the descent group.

Schulte Nordholt (1971, p. 116) speaks of a "remarkable series of differences which form a scale of gradation from a purely patrilineal and patrilocal to a chiefly matrilineal and purely matrilocal system". At one end of the scale is Amfoan on the north coast; here all children are incorporated into their father's lineage (p. 117). Recruitment of children to the mother's lineage does not occur. Descent is strictly patrilineal, and there is great stress on regulation of marriage and the transfer of women and goods over a long period. Bridewealth is higher here than anywhere else in Atoni territory; frequently sons must fulfill their father's payments. Unlike other princedoms, it is permitted, where the wealth is available, for a lineage in Amfoan to complete the last stage of payment called "skull" before the couple are old or are dead. The Amfoan say a woman has little redress once skull has been paid, and other Atoni, who reserve this payment accuse Amfoan of selling their daughters (Cunningham, 1967b, pp. 5, 10-11).

In Molo princedom, bridewealth is lower but varies with social status, and a considerable portion of it may be acquitted by brideservice. Marriage remains uxorilocal longer. The first children are therefore born into the wife's lineage and acquire its name. The husband retains membership in his own lineage, but he is temporarily adopted into his wife's clan and admitted into its ceremonial centre. Bridewealth payments must be completed in order for his lineage to establish a claim on any of his children. Schulte Nordholt speaks here of a shift in which the practice of brideservice tips the balance away from an agnatic system towards uxorilocal marriage and partially matrilineal descent. Nevertheless, descent is mainly patrilineal and residence patrilocal. Unlike Amarasi as described by Cunningham, here a boy taken into his mother's lineage may not marry a girl in it; he is instead wholly integrated into it and may under certain circumstances attain leadership in it (Schulte Nordholt, 1971, pp. 117, 118).

A similar pattern obtains in Insana where, even when bridewealth has been completely paid, one child is retained by the mother's line (p. 120).

Anas of Amanatun provides the extreme of the Atoni shift from agnation: here residence is permanently uxorilocal; there is no bridewealth. Descent and inheritance is matrilineal, although the husband's lineage has a right to one of the children of the marriage (Middelkoop, 1931, pp. 284-85; Schulte Nordholt, 1971, p. 122).

There is then very roughly a shift from the relatively strict patrilineal arrangement in the north-west toward the preponderantly matrilineal arrangement in the south-east. This shift corresponds, again roughly, with a transfer away from reliance on the full payment of bridewealth. Again marriage payments appear to act as a "selector", as Hicks (1975) calls it, between two regimes; but completion of prestations does not everywhere finally determine the affiliation of each of the children.

One Atoni region deviates from the general association between the form of affiliation and the presence or absence of marriage gifts. In Noemuti, no bridewealth is given at all, but residence is usually patrilocal and descent is predominantly patrilineal, although some children will belong to the mother's lineage.

Some of the contrasts that we observed between the eastern Tetun and the Buna' recur within the Atoni. In some districts attachment to the mother's descent group brings with it subordinate status, in others full membership. In Amarasi it seems that children recruited to the mother's lineage have membership in two different groups at the same time. Furthermore, marriage and alliance exchanges relate not only to the transfer and incorporation of wives and children, but in some cases husbands as well. In Molo it would appear that a man holds a kind of membership in his wife's group and in his own at the same time, whereas in Amanatun he is more firmly attached to his wife's group.

According to Schulte Nordholt (1971, p. 137), in the Atoni view, a lineage consists of a number of living souls, called *smanaf* or vital force. When a woman is given out, the lineage loses not only her *smanaf* but future lives as well. In return they may expect prestations, such as buffalo, silver coins or silver, capable either of reproduction or embodying a permanent value which can in turn be exchanged for life. Brideservice is part of the same set of ideas, for the rice and corn which the husband produces is also regarded as *smanaf*. Surely the recruitment of children, in both directions, can be understood in the same terms. Schulte Nordholt observes that where the husband is integrated into his wife's lineage, the husband's lineage is thought to be contributing *smanaf* and may expect the return of one or more children.

5. *The Ngada*

The Ngada of central Flores conveniently exhibit a further shift away from unilineal descent, while at the same time they retain a number of features which are interestingly comparable with those that have been reviewed from Timor. The Ngada are a class-stratified society numbering about 40,000 practising sedentary agriculture and some industrial arts. They speak an Austronesian language, have a cognatic system of social classification and a segmentary system of corporate descent groups; and they practise no form of affinal alliance.

The Ngada are divided into some one hundred clans containing up to several thousand members. Each such clan is identified with a particular locality, marked by a clan house which is the ritual centre for the clan and is inhabited by the clan head. Large clans are further segmented into groups likewise marked by a ritual house and leader, and these segments are composed of several extended families. Membership in the clan, clan segment, and family may be acquired through either male or female ties. Membership in a household, and consequently descent, residence, and the inheritance of property and name, depends entirely upon whether the father has paid full bridewealth for his wife. If so, the children acquire rights in their father's group, otherwise they are members of their mother's. The Ngada are strongly endogamous and prefer marriage within the same clan segment (Arndt, 1954, pp. 18-19, 167-169; Barnes, 1972).

The greater part of the marriage gift goes to the bride's mother's brother, and another portion goes to her parents. Responsibility for providing it rests with the groom's own parents and other close relatives. In certain cases responsibility lies with his entire descent group. It is not usual for the complete set of prestations ever to be fully paid, but even in those regions where it is common for the family to remain with the wife's relatives, two or three stages are usually given. If the greater portion of it is given then the woman may be brought into the husband's group.

Arndt interprets bridewealth as constituting a true purchase, although an expensive payment insures a high status for the woman.

Where it is given in full, the woman becomes herself a member of her husband's descent group and belongs to it, in Arndt's interpretation, almost like a piece of property. She must observe his clan food restrictions and the other practices of his descent group. In some regions an extra payment is required in order to free the woman and her children from all restrictions and ritual institutions of her natal clan. She may not then return to her original home if she is widowed. Divorce is rare when bridewealth has been paid, more frequent otherwise (Arndt, 1954, pp. 69-70). All children belong to their father's group.

Bridewealth requires substantial return gifts. A woman may be reminded that she has been purchased, and she may complain that she is treated like a slave, but her husband and his relatives may never tell her that they regard her as being a slave. Should they do so, she may flee to her parents, and her husband would be obliged to pay them a heavy penalty.

Frequently a woman's parents prefer not to accept bridewealth, even when the groom is capable of providing it. Rather they wish to retain their daughter as a means of ensuring support for their own old age and in order to secure the labour of her husband. If no bridewealth is given or only a small portion, the husband moves into his wife's home but does not acquire membership in her group and takes no part in its ceremonial restrictions or rituals. He has the position only of a worker and provider of children, which belong then to his wife's family. If the smaller portion of the marriage prestation is given, the husband's family may request and be given a child. When nothing has been paid, the husband acquires no right of possession, and he fills an exceptionally unpleasant position in his wife's household; but if the first three stages are paid he can at least build a separate house in the fields and move there with his wife and children, where he will be relatively free from the importunities of his affines. Children are then divided between the two groups by prior agreement and in proportion to the amount of bridewealth which has been handed over.

In certain cases, when a man has proven himself incapable of delivering any part of the required prestation, the woman's family may demand that he be completely integrated into their descent group. Formerly, a lineage which had no fertile male members might actually seek out a man or indeed several who were willing to be taken into their line in this way and to completely separate themselves from their natal group. Such a move is regarded as a severe loss by the husband's lineage and an important gain by the wife's. Under such circumstances, a true groomwealth is given to the groom's descent group (Arndt, 1954, pp. 42-6, 50-58, 69-70).

Ngada have then large-scale corporate descent groups in which membership is determined solely by the system of marriage prestations. There is no institution of unilineal descent. Clans and lineages may derive from male or female ancestors, and their members will be attached through male or female links. There appears, however, to be no such thing as dual or overlapping membership; so the prestations permit the retention of discrete boundaries between corporations. Women, children, and even men are exchanged. Arndt speaks of bridewealth as the basis of the whole of Ngada marriage and family law.

The Lamaholot offer a thorough contrast to the Ngada.

6. *The Lamaholot*

The Lamaholot are a predominantly agricultural people located on the eastern end of Flores, on Solor, Adonara, and most of Lembata. It would appear from the writings of Arndt (1940) and Vatter (1932) that there is a great amount of variation in the social arrangements on these four islands. Nevertheless, such information as is available indicates that the Lamaholot everywhere have a system of patrilineal descent groups and an emphasis on asymmetric affinal alliance. The social classification on each of the islands is asymmetric prescriptive (Barnes, 1977).

Our best available information concerns the village of Wailolong in the district of Ili Mandiri on Flores. Here clans are identified with separate wards of the village and divided into named lineages. These lineages are related to each other by a strict system of rules for the exchange of women, determined by a principle of asymmetric alliance. Information recorded by Kennedy shows that marriages accord with the schedule of rules in well over eighty per cent of cases (Kennedy n.d.; Barnes, 1977). Clans here own fields communally, and a clan elder determines annually which fields are to be cultivated and allots them to the individual families (Arndt, 1951, pp. 140-42; Ouwehand, 1950, pp. 59-61).

Marriage prestations in Wailolong formerly consisted in elephant tusks, for which locally dyed and woven sarongs were returned. Today, other items, such as rice or cement, are substituted for the tusks; but the return gifts have remained the same. Payment may take several generations to complete. Where it has not yet been paid, residence may be matrilocal, but according to Kennedy it will be so in only about half of the cases. Brideservice is *not* an institutionalized practice. A man may choose to live with his father-in-law and to work for him, but he retains the privileges of his own lineage and his children trace descent patrilineally. In the long run, however, marriage gifts must be completed. If tusks are not available, then a daughter may be pledged in return. But Kennedy reports explicitly that this daughter does not become a member of her mother's lineage, nor does she live apart from her parents. All that is involved is that bridewealth which is eventually received for her goes directly to her mother's lineage; so this arrangement merely reinforces a pattern already present to the nature of alliance.[1] It appears that in the past, if not today, the amount was predetermined by that given for the woman's mother and reflected to some extent class distinctions. Most marriages in Wailolong are within the village, and payment of bridewealth is largely a book-keeping procedure, involving little material expense, since bridewealth circulates among the same lineages. Marriage outside the established ties requires higher marriage payment.

Wailolong may be said to be, in practice as well as in ideology, exclusively patrilineal regarding descent group make-up and strict in observing the obligatory pattern of alliance between corporate lineages. Marriage payments must be given, either actually or through a ceremonial means of cancelling debts against each other, for all unions. Divorce is not allowed, and adoption does not seem to be practiced. In the past most marriages were arranged by the parents.[2]

Elsewhere among the Lamaholot, in so far as information is available, there are a number of shifts away from the Wailolong model. Clans and lineages are of lesser importance in some parts of Adonara, and they do not everywhere observe the same obligatory pattern of alliance among lineages. Furthermore, they do not everywhere hold land corporately. However, in only one other region do we

---

[1] Arndt (1940, p. 19) mentions that where bridewealth is lacking, a sister may be given in marriage to the wife-giving clan. This procedure violates the marriage rule, and no other information is available on it.

[2] These matters and the relevant sources have been reviewed in Barnes (1977 and 1978).

have information in sufficient quantity to allow comparison. In Lewotobi in the Lobetobi district of Flores, exogamous patrilineages practise a pattern of asymmetric affinal alliance, but they do not, for the most part, own and regulate the use of land (Vatter, 1932, p. 145; Ouwehand, 1950, pp. 65-67). Marriage does not usually entail the exchange of gifts, but leads rather to a period of brideservice and residence with the wife's family. With the birth of children, the couple move into their own house and requirements of service are reduced, though not abolished. The agreed period of service varies between one and seven years and depends on the social position of the woman. There is no question of a later payment of bridewealth. The man remains a member of his own lineage, but if he is unable to maintain his family in a separate house, his children may belong to their mother's group. Otherwise, however, children belong to their father's patrilineage. Bridewealth is usually employed only when the man comes from outside the Lobetobi district and prefers not to enter into brideservice.

The use of brideservice is nowhere else so extensively developed and may here have been introduced by Portugese missionaries during the period of their first contact in the sixteenth and seventeenth centuries. However that may be, brideservice does not here normally entail permanent uxorilocal residence and matrifiliation (Ouwehand, 1950, pp. 61-71; Vatter, 1932, p. 152).

7. The Kédang

My last example are the Kédang, whom I have already described in several works (see Barnes, 1974, 1980). They number 25,000, speak an Austronesian language, are divided into patrilineal clans, have an asymmetric prescriptive social classification and an asymmetric pattern of affinal alliance, and are located at the eastern end of the island of Lembata.

Clans do not hold land; their members are not necessarily all resident in the same village, though they will maintain contact with the village where the clan is located, and there are no named lineages within the clans. Nevertheless, clans play a role in village government and have elders invested with authority in the clan, and a ceremonial house, located, in most cases, in the village religious centre. The clan acquires most of its meaning and even organization through its external relations with other clans, and it is possible to say that the chief activity of the clan and the feature which most clearly gives it corporate organization is the holding and exchange of alliance prestations.

There is an extensive schedule of alliance prestations, which are never given at once and which are usually completed late in the life of the couple or after their deaths. Tusks and gongs are provided to wife-givers, and sarongs are returned. Responsibility for supplying bride-wealth lies not with the man, but with his clan as a whole. Exchanges are easiest to arrange and tend to equilibrium within the village where, as in Wailolong, the Kédang prefer to set up merely ceremonial cycles which cancel a sequence of debts in a circle. Outside the village, at least, a marriage establishes an entirely new tie; the schedule of pre-stations, the value of each and the worth of the actual objects given are the subject of difficult and protracted negotiation and lead to considerable expense (Barnes, 1974, pp. 282-94). Formerly, the amount was until recently determined by that received for the mother of the bride.

Except in the case of unmarried mothers the exchanges are eventually always completed and children always belong to their father's patrilineage. Residence, however, is not an issue for the Kédang and the couple may establish a house of their own soon, or it seems even immediately, after beginning the union; and the location of the house may be anywhere they choose, often at fields many miles away from the village. There is no custom of brideservice; nor are children ever adopted.[1] Divorce, however, is relatively easy to arrange and not infrequent if no children have been born. Marriages are not usually arranged by the parents, but are the outcome in most cases of the preferences of the two young people.

Kédang interestingly resembles Wailolong among the Lamaholot in its strict patrilineality, its matrilateral prescription and pattern of alliance, and its exclusive reliance upon marriage gifts, rather than service. However, the differences are also marked regarding the questions of divorce, arranged marriage, and land-ownership. In addition, the Kédang do not share the Wailolong pattern of fixed

[1] There are a certain number of unwed mothers in Kédang, whose children are wards of the mother's patrilineage. They occupy, in the Kédang view, an anomalous position, for they confuse the pattern of alliance exchanges. Such children are often incorporated, with their consent, into other clans, but this transfer requires full payment of bridewealth for their mother (see Barnes, 1974, pp. 262-3).

alliances among corporate lineages. In comparison with Wailolong, Kédang clans have very reduced corporate functions; and it is all the more striking that it is in fact the regulation of alliance exchanges which most clearly gives them corporate identity.

V

Let me return now to the specific issue with which I began this chapter, namely whether there is an analytically essential connection between unilineal principles and corporate descent groups. Sir Edmund Leach has argued very forcefully (1962) that we should follow Rivers (1924, p. 86) in restricting the phrase "descent group" to *unilineal* institutions where membership is "determined permanently and without option by the circumstances of birth". In such a society, groups are discrete and do not overlap, an individual belongs to only one segment, about which he has no option, and his freedom of choice in exploiting social ties is confined to links of filiation of affinity. Leach also mentions that societies on Timor (and the Sepik River of New Guinea) do not entirely fit River's presuppositions and that these facts have tempted anthropologists to abandon River's contentions. Nevertheless, Leach holds (at least regarding Samoa) that, where "descent does not in itself specify who is or who is not a member of any particular group, it is . . . misleading to describe the operative corporations as 'descent groups' ".

Whether we follow Leach or choose some other definition will depend upon the relative advantages of the alternatives and thus to some degree upon our particular interests. In this controversy, my own preference would be to use the phrase "descent group" more broadly, for the reasons put forward by Forde (1963) and Firth (1963): specifically that the aim of establishing discrete corporations may be achieved by allowing descent to operate in combination with other factors.

In effect Leach wishes to treat descent as a form of obligation, and there are reasons, given the emphasis he places on the absence of choice, to compare his position to the related issue of categorical injunctions in marriage alliance. The principal difference is that he is talking about actual people in actual groups and not about the location of relatives in a social classification. If the anthropologist's main concern is the study of collective categories, there are advantages in distinguishing, in the way Needham has done (1973a, pp. 174-76, 179), between societies with terminologically enjoined marriage relationships and those without.

The same interest might justify treating descent in an analogous fashion, for, as Needham (1973b, p. 111) has argued, in lineal societies there will be at least a limited correspondence between the symbolic and social orders. It remains a question though whether "obligation" has the same interpretation when referring to unilineal features of relationship terminologies as it does in connection with marriage prescriptions.

But these considerations are not those advanced by Leach, and in any event they are inapplicable where the investigation is not directed toward classification; in particular they have no bearing when the first interest is in groups. The sociological circumstances of the Flores and Timor area do not well match River's recommendations. If we follow them we may be distracted inappropriately into thinking that these societies themselves are deviant. But the problem only results from adhering to a particular terminological tradition. Groups are organizations of individuals around some purpose. They might be permanent or ephemeral, actual or potential, manifest or latent, separate or overlapping, corporate or non-corporate. Membership in them may be optional or enjoined, and their functions may be single or multiple. More than one kind of collectivity can usually be found in a given society; and although they may have some common features (say, rule of recruitment), their shared elements will not mean that they have the same sociological standing.

The functions associated with corporations vary considerably; and there is no clear comparative tie between their functions and the principles which constitute the groups. It is not altogether clear, indeed, why descent groups *should* maintain exclusive corporate boundaries. The Lamaholot of Wailolong practise strict patrilineal descent in a region where land is limited and tightly regulated. Societies of this kind might suggest that the answer lies in the control of some scarce resource, such as land or labour. But in Wailolong it is the clan which corporately owns land, whereas named lineages are the alliance groups responsible for the provision of marriage gifts. Other Lamaholot districts and the Kédang are just as patrilineal as Wailolong but do not link descent groups to the possession of fields. Elsewhere corporate involvement in the control of the soil occurs where descent is not unilineal.

If we ask what Indonesians usually refer to in accounting for their institutions, we will find quite often that they are most concerned with retaining the objects used in alliance exchanges and with ensuring the means to provide for the continuation of descent lines. In determining membership marriage payments may allocate from one family to another not only children, but also wives, and in some cases even husbands. Such payments can be used to establish an exclusive connection, but they may just as well leave an individual with membership and obligations in two locations. Where unilineal descent is employed as an ideological principle (among the Atoni) dual membership is sometimes possible; and on the other hand dual membership need not be the practical consequence of a cognatic system.

In the somewhat unrepresentative sample I have selected, strictly unilineal descent groups are rather rare. In addition, alliance, which is uniformly thought to provide the substance for a group's existence, is not everywhere conceived as the exclusive transfer of life through offspring from one line to another. On the contrary, among the Ema, the Atoni and the Buna', it is often treated as a mutual undertaking to secure life and continuity for *both* parties. Here, alliance easily leads to distributing children between the mother's and the father's line, and in one case (Buna') this transfer of children has the same value in expressing the tie of alliance as does the exchange of wives.

Two factors may help in understanding, if not in accounting for, this variation. The first is that in a given locality, the different matters which require corporate activity may be expected to call forth collective association at different structural levels. It is a commonplace that the exogamous group is often larger than the alliance group. In the same way, the ownership of different kinds of property, not excluding rights in human beings, need not pertain to a single structural level, nor to the presence of an identifiable figure of authority.

The second consideration has to do with the transfer of real material value. It is frequently observed that bridewealth is more expensive in Indonesia when marriage initiates a new tie or is outside the community (see e.g. Fischer, 1935, p. 368). Cunningham (1966, p. 17) reports that the Atoni value marriage within a restricted local region and within established alliances. The further outside of this circle one marries the higher the bridewealth. "Bridewealth is considered to be evidence of the man's ability to provide and secure help from his agnates, a guarantee for good treatment of the wife, and a replacement for help which the daughter and son-in-law could not provide in case of virilocal residence in a distant place." Leach (1951, p. 52) has proposed the hypothesis that, "A substantial bridewealth consisting of objects of symbolic and ritual value only probably goes with high rank and equality of status." High rank is not everywhere necessary, as is shown in Kédang; but it does seem likely that such exchange will show a purely ceremonial aspect where it is possible to be certain of the eventual return of the material equivalent. Circumstances often limit this security to ties within the community or to the established pattern of alliances. Where this security can be assured, it may make little material difference whether the exchanges are ever actually completed or whether there are any marriage payments at all.

Alliance and marriage exchanges in Indonesia unite what we would call spiritual and economic aspects, and marriage itself brings with it elements both of competition and of mutuality. The risks involved are matters of public comment; and they are not only material. In Kédang, the active participation of wife-givers during a funeral is essential for transferring the deceased to the land of the dead, and they are quite prepared to withhold these services if the wife-takers have defaulted in alliance debts or have otherwise been remiss in their duties.

Marriage payments are not to be fully understood without reference to the relative distinction between the internal and external contexts and to the degree of exposure to loss. The objects used in marriage exchanges, whether they be gold or silver coins, elephant tusks or gongs, are often items which have been brought in through trade and which derive prestige from this foreign origin. None of the societies in eastern Indonesia have ever been genuinely isolated; all have had continuous contact with foreign traders. In the past, slaves were one of the prime means of purchase of these foreign objects, and it is this fact which lends an especial point to the frequent Indonesian denial that they sell women or treat them like slaves. It is not that Indonesians were unfamiliar with commercial transactions, but that these occurred at the margins of society and did not take the form of enduring contracts. The common and spontaneous denial that bridewealth constitutes commercial purchase is not the result of ignorance of that form of transaction. It derives rather from the uncomfortable similarity between exchanging a slave for bridewealth and bridewealth for a wife.

The pattern of flow in these exchanges, as well as their content, is open to historical change. It may happen that the number of stages and alternatives to payment are subject to quicker transformation by communal agreement or fashion than are rules of descent. But

decisions about the make-up and responsibility for bridewealth cannot
be made independently of decisions about the make-up and nature of
corporations. Very few communities seem to leave these matters entirely to individual preference. Nevertheless, it is possible that there
has been in some locations, where bridewealth has been introduced
from the outside, a development from individual toward corporate
responsibility. Lineages often seem to work like joint stock formations
for providing these goods; and in Kédang at present the clans seem to
have retained hardly any other function. Local uniformity, however,
requires some concerted communal effort to produce; and it is to be
expected that there will be variation from district to district not only in
the degree to which marriage prestations are a corporate rather than
an individual concern, but also in whether they are regulated by a
single means or by alternative procedures. Since such payments have
much to do with the nature of corporations, it is conceivable, though
impossible to prove at the moment, that they might be closely involved
in a causal sequence leading to changes in rules of descent. But the
variety of ethnographic arrangements make it appear unlikely that the
causal pattern will be quite the same in each particular locality. Nor
should a single configuration even be expected once it is realized that
groups, descent and rules of exchange are in some degree defined
reciprocally.

Let us in future make our interpretation of collective associations
more supple. We are told, after all, very little by being informed that a
society has corporate unilineal descent groups. In the past we have
tended to fix upon them because their stability seemed to make
analysis easier. There is no reason though why they should not alter
their purpose and composition as context shifts. Nor need it be the case
that it is always the permanent groupings which do the major work of
society. A long and careful analysis is required in each particular study
to disclose the implications of corporate action; and in Indonesia we
are likely to be led well away from the ideas about descent and
corporations which have been handed down to us from Maine.

Bibliography

Arndt, P. (1940). "Soziale Verhältnisse auf Ost-Flores, Adonara und Solor". Anthropos, Inter-
    nationale Sammlung Ethnologischer Monographien, vol. 4. Aschendorffsche Verlagsbuch-
    handlung, Münster i. W.
Arndt, P. (1951). "Religion auf Ostflores, Adonara und Solor". Studia Instituti Anthropos,
    vol. 1. Missionsdruckerei St Gabriel, Wien-Mödling.

Arndt, P . (1954). "Gesellschaftliche Verhältnisse der Ngadha". Studia Instituti Anthropos, vol. 8. Missiondruckerei St. Gabriel, Wien-Mödling.

Barnes, R. H. (1972). "Ngada". In "Ethnic Groups in Insular Southeast Asia" (Ed. Frank M. LeBar). Human Relations Area Files Press, New Haven.

Barnes, R. H. (1974). "Kédang: a Study of the Collective Thought of an Eastern Indonesian People" (with Foreword by R. Needham). Clarendon Press, Oxford.

Barnes, R. H. (1977). Alliance and categories in Wailolong, east Flores. Sociologus, 27, 2, 133-157

Barnes, R. H. (1978). Injunction and illusion: segmentation and choice in prescriptive systems. Anthropology, 2, 1, 19-30.

Barnes, R. H. (1980). Concordance, structure and variation: considerations of alliance in Kédang. In "The Flow of Life" (Ed. James J. Fox). Harvard University Press, Cambridge, Mass.

Berthe, Louis (1959). Sur quelques distique Buna'. Bijdragen tot de Taal-Land- en Volkenkunde, 115, 336-371.

Berthe, Louis (1961). Le mariage par achat et la captation des gendres dans une société semi-féodale: les Bunaq de Timor central. L'Homme, 1, 3, 5-31.

Berthe, Louis (1970). Parenté, pouvoir et mode de production. Eléments pour une typologie des Sociétés agricoles de l'Indonésie. In "Echanges et Communications" (Eds. Jean Pouillon and Pierre Maranda), vol. 2. Mouton, The Hague.

Clamagirand, Brigitte (1975). Marobo: organisation sociale et rites d'une communauté ema de Timor. Thèse de Doctorat de 3 Cycle (Ethnologie), Ecole Pratique des Hautes Etudes, Université René Descartes (unpublished).

Cunningham, Clark E. (1965). Atoni borrowing of children: an aspect of mediation. In "Proceedings of the American Ethnological Society" (Ed. M. E. Spiro). Annual Spring Meeting, 1964.

Cunningham, Clark E. (1966). Categories of descent groups in a Timor village. Oceania, 37, 13-21.

Cunningham, Clark E. (1967a). Atoni kin categories and conventional behaviour. Bijdragen tot de Taal-, Land- en Volkenkunde, 123, 1, 53-70.

Cunningham, Clark E. (1967b). Recruitment to Atoni descent groups. Anthropological Quarterly, 40, 1-12.

Dumont, Louis (1957). "Hierarchy and Marriage Alliance in South Indian Kinship". Occasional Papers No. 12 of the Royal Anthropological Institute, London.

Dumont, Louis (1961). Descent, filiation and affinity. Man, 61, No. 11.

Evans-Pritchard, E. E. (1931). An alternative term for brideprice. Man, 31, No. 42.

Evans-Pritchard, E. E. (1934). Social character of bridewealth with special reference to the Azande. Man, 34, No. 194.

Evans-Pritchard, E. E. (1940). "The Nuer: a Description of the Modes of Livelihood and Political Institutions of a Nilotic People". Clarendon Press, Oxford.

Firth, Raymond (1963). Bilateral descent groups: an operational viewpoint. In "Studies in Kinship and Marriage" (Ed. I. Shapera). Occasional Paper No. 16 of the Royal Anthropological Institute, London.

Fischer, H. Th. (1932). Der magische Charakter des Brautpreises. Der Weltkreis, 3, 65-68.

Fischer, H. Th. (1935). De annverwantschap bij enige volken van de Nederlands-Indische archipel. Mensch en Maatschappij, 11, 285-297, 365-378.

Fischer, H. Th. (1957). Some notes on kinship systems and relationship terms of Sumba, Manggarai and South Timor. Internationales Archiv für Ethnographie, 48, 1, 1-31.

Forde, C. Daryll (1963). On some further unconsidered aspects of descent. Man, 63, No. 9.

Fortes, M. (1953). The structure of unilineal descent groups. American Anthropologist, 55, 17-41.

Goody, J. (1973). Bridewealth and dowry in Africa and Eurasia. In "Bridewealth and Dowry" (Eds J. Goody and S. J. Tambiah). Cambridge University Press, London.

Gray, R. F. (1960). Sonjo bride-price and the question of African 'wife purchase'. American Anthropologist, 62, 32-57.

Hicks, D. (1975). La compensation matrimoniale chez les Tetun. L'Homme, 15, 55-65.

Hicks, D. (1976). "Tetum Ghosts and Kin: Fieldwork in an Indonesian Community". Mayfield, Palo Alto.

Kennedy, Raymond (n.d.). "Field Notes on Indonesia: Flores 1949-1950" (Ed. Harold C. Conklin). Human Relations Area Files, New Haven.

Leach, E. (1951). The structural implications of matrilateral cross-cousin marriage. *Journal of the Royal Anthropological Institute*, 81, 23-55.

Leach, E. (1957). Aspects of bridewealth and marriage stability among the Kachin and Lakher. *Man*, 57, No. 59.

Leach, E. (1961). Rethinking anthropology. In "Rethinking Anthropology". London School of Economics Monographs on Social Anthropology No. 22. Athlone Press, London.

Leach, E. (1962). On certain unconsidered aspects of double descent systems. *Man*, 62, No. 214.

Maine, Henry Sumner (1861). "Ancient Law". John Murray, London.

Middelkoop, P. (1931). Gegevens over het Timoreesche Adat-huwelijk. *Bijdragen tot de Taal-, Land- en Volkenkunde*, 88, 239-286.

Needham, R. (1962). "Structure and Sentiment". University of Chicago Press, Chicago.

Needham, R. (1973a). Prescription. *Oceania*, 43, 3, 166-181.

Needham, R. (1973b). The left hand of the Mugwe. *In* "Right and Left: Essays on Dual Symbolic Classification". University of Chicago Press, Chicago.

Onvlee, L. (1949). Naar Aanleiding van de Stuwdam in Mangili: opmerkingen over de sociale structuur van Oost-Sumba. *Bijdragen tot de Taal-, Land- en Volkenkunde*, 105, 445-459.

Ouwehand, C. (1950). Aantekeningen over volksordening en grondenrecht op Oost-Flores. *Indonesia*, 4, 54-71.

Radcliffe-Brown, A. R. (1952). "Structure and Function in Primitive Societies". Cohen & West, London.

Rivers, W. H. R. (1924). "Social Organization". (Ed. W. J. Perry). Kegan Paul, Trench Trubner, London.

Rousseau, Jean-Jacques (1762). "The Social Contract and Discourses" (translated by G. D. H. Cole). Dent (1973), London.

Sahlins, Marshall (1972). "Stone Age Economics". Aldine, Chicago.

Schulte Nordholt, H. G. (1971). "The Political System of the Atoni of Timor". Nijhoff, The Hague.

Straten, L. B. van (1927). "De Indonesische Bruidschat". Noorduyn, Gorinchem.

Torday, E. (1929). Bride-price, dower or settlement. *Man*, 29, No. 3.

Vatter, Ernst (1932). "Ata Kiwan, unbekannte Bergvolker im Tropischen Holland". Bibliographisches Institut, Leipzig.

Vroklage, B. A. G. (1952a). Bride price or dower. *Anthropos*, 47, 133-146.

Vroklage, B. A. G. (1952b). "Ethnographie der Belu in Zentral-Timor", 3 vols. Brill, Leiden.

Weber, Max (1947). "The Theory of Social and Economic Organization". Free Press, Glencoe.

Wilken, G. A. (1883). "Over de Verwantschap en het Huwelijks — en erfrecht bij de Volken van den Indischen Archipel". Brill, Leiden.

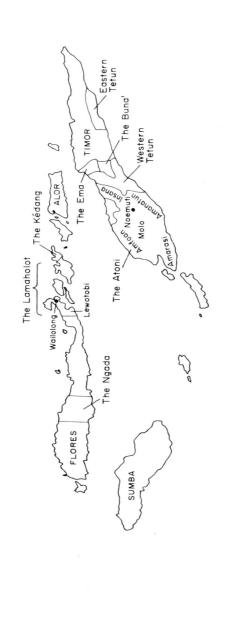

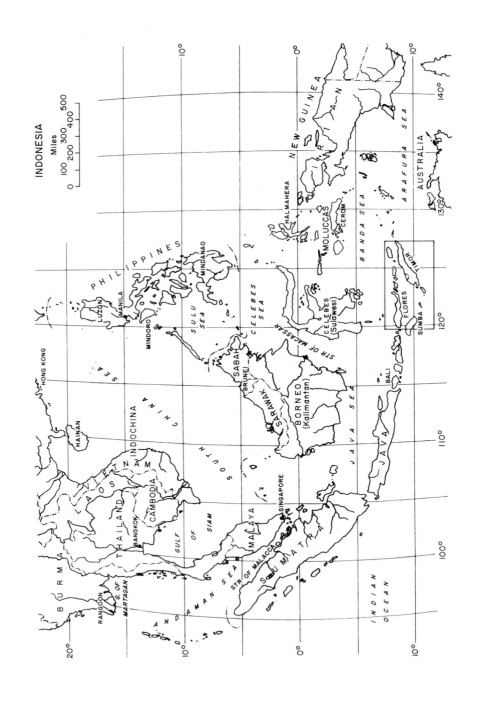

5 Aspects of Bedouin Bridewealth among Camel Herders in Cyrenaica[1]

EMRYS PETERS

Bridewealth, coupled with exogamy, has long been viewed as a means of bringing together otherwise unconnected lineage segments or clans. The overall effect of these separate alliances is seen as "knitting the whole system together".[2] Several assumptions are contained in this view. First, it assumes that the political separation of segments in a lineage system would be so complete that groups would be left virtually isolated. Second, it is primarily marriage, and the property transfer it entails as bridewealth, that can interlace these groups, by the kinship it creates: in some societies, kinship appears to be so urgent a necessity that even affinity passes for it. Many who would vehemently deny the mystique which, allegedly, Fortes (1949) bestows on kinship, ascribe to it in this context, with a curious twist of logic, a binding force which would probably make Fortes himself demur. Third, despite the immediate effect attributed to exogamous marriage, and its extension through delayed transfers of bridewealth, the affinal relationship it creates must be short-lived, for, when this becomes transmuted into

---

[1] The ethnography in this article is based on research among some southern sections of the Awaqir and Bara'asa tribes, and some of the sections of the Magharba tribes in the southwest of the country. Although research was carried out among the trading Zuaiya tribe at their trans-Saharan terminus near Ajadabiya, it is so different from other Cyrenaican tribes that this data is excluded.

I have used the present tense as a convenience. The data is derived from research undertaken during the years 1948-50.

[2] Leach (1976, p. 67). Fox (1967, Ch. VII) elaborates this view; and, of course, Levi-Strauss (1949) devotes a stout volume to it. In addition to these three arbitrarily chosen contributors there have been many others.

kinship, it ceases. The power of the link, that is to say, resides almost exclusively in affinity, since each and every marriage must be exogamous and connect otherwise autonomous peoples. Fourth, to give the link strength the wife must be incorporated into the receiving lineage. Gluckman (1950) attached such importance to this that the stability of marriage in African societies, in his view, was based on the extent to which wives were incorporated, the bridewealth being the main instrument in this, with other forms of marriage (levirate, sororate and so on) serving as corroboration.[1] Fifth, since exogamy with bridewealth knots, binds or cements "the whole system", then exogamous marriages need to be dispersed to the maximum extent — and it is worth noting that precisely the same metaphors are used to explain the function of bridewealth among Arabs, who marry their first or other patrilateral parallel cousins.[2] Bridewealth is thus spread like a blanket over the whole population, since the number of clans is always limited. Sixth, although exogamy is accompanied by other marriage rules (which, if taken together, would appear to make the task of finding a marriage partner difficult or impossible), precedence is given to exogamy, certainly in explaining bridewealth. In the effect on marriage patterns, it is suggested that this is unwarranted precedence, because the accompanying rules relating to marriage prohibitions of certain kin are equally important, and in some cases the latter might be more selective, in practice at least. Seventh, stress is placed upon exogamy because anthropologists give it its full jural force as an implacable rule; peoples practising it might view it differently, not only as one rule among many, but as a rule of thumb possessing considerable mutability. Finally, the assumption is made that exogamous marriage interconnects people throughout all the clans in a maze of cross-cutting ties, whereas a few well chosen links with otherwise unrelated groups would be much more effective. Why should a particular lineage need to have links into all clans, and, indeed, into most of their segments?

[1] Lewis (1962, pp. 41, 43) effectively demolishes this argument. It might be worth recording that I asked Gluckman whether he thought that, when Nuer married, they drew strange women from long distances into their local communities and provided for their incorporation into it. He replied that he was sure of this. A few days later I asked Evans-Pritchard where Nuer got their brides; his answer was that they married women they knew from the general area in which they lived.

[2] The offenders, with regard to writers on Arabs, are legion. It would be unfair to single out anyone; save for Marx (1967), it is difficult to cite anyone who has *not* used parallel cousin marriage to add a bit of cement to the system. Writers on non-Arab peoples, who peddle this view, are equally numerous.

While assumptions of this sort are regularly made, the details of particular cases lead to quite other views of exogamy. Thus, although Nuer clans and lineages are exogamous,[1] the prohibition on marriage to daughters of clansmen applies with equal force to all kin of any kind,[2] even if the relationship is through a third person.[3] Yet, a Nuer is able to establish kinship with any other Nuer he meets at any time during his life, anywhere in Nuerland.[4] Obviously, if the rules, taken together, were applied, Nuer would be unable to marry. Evans-Pritchard is careful to qualify these rules — or, to be more precise, to add other rules — in the statement that different ranges of kinship are recognised for different purposes, and that known kinship links can be ignored as easily as tenuous ones can be made crucial, as suits the circumstances.[5] Even the boundaries of clans and lineages are not inviolable, and if there is ambiguity about a particular case of marriage, it can be resolved by ritually splitting a gourd: clan exogamy is "not unalterable".[6]

There is no suggestion in this that the rules matter so little that they are vulnerable to whimsical alteration. The suggestion is that any of the rules are of importance in circumstances where their application is required. Clan exogamy ceases to be a bar when people decide that the agnatic relationship is too distant, or when they reach a local consensus about restricting the span of a clan. Similarly, kinship can be adjudged to be too distant to impose a bar on a marriage. In short, particular cases require to be negotiated by taking account of all the rules — a wholly different matter to manipulating the rules to suit individual convenience.

This does not mean the absence of an exogamous unit among the Nuer. Represented in a village is an agnatic core, with a gathering of

---

[1] Evans-Pritchard (1940, p. 225): "A man may not marry into his clan and, *a fortiori*, into his lineage".

[2] Evans-Pritchard (1951, p. 30) mentions six categories of kin among whom marriage is prohibited and confirms this on p. 34.

[3] Evans-Pritchard (1951, p. 8). In this context he is discussing *mar*, kin. He includes in this category a person related "through a third person who is in different ways related both to himself and the other person". I assume that when he refers to marriage bars between kin, persons thus indirectly related are included.

[4] Evans-Pritchard (1951, p. 8). I assume that he does not mean that consanguinity can be demonstrated. He adds the rider: "For all social obligation of a personal kind is defined in terms of kinship". The kinship he is speaking of here is not of blood, but of idiom, a manner of speaking — a most important point with regard to the view of exogamy I offer.

[5] Indeed, a bar can be evoked just to rebuff an undesirable suitor.

[6] Evans-Pritchard (1951, p. 30). He also refers to the ambiguities in the field of kinship.

cognates around them. The people residing in them are drawn together by tribal "bulls",[1] including the agnatic core of which the "bull" is the leading member, some of his affines and matrilateral relatives.[2] Among these co-residents kinship is close, possibly according to the degree of consanguinity, certainly in a general social sense. It is this effective kinship which composes the local community into a *de facto* exogamous unit;[3] that is to say, the rules of thumb which prohibit marriage between clan members and kin are subject to rules relating to propinquity. Consanguinity and residence both count; members of a local agnatic core come under the ban of exogamy, whether the agnatic connection be close or relatively distant; and kinship further excludes marriage, however it is traced, directly or indirectly, or through affinity. What makes exogamy (with regard to clan origin or kinship) effective is co-residence.

It is characteristic of the Nuer that they move about a great deal. Seasonal variations in climate, vegetation and water compels annual transhumance from the wet season villages, above the floods, to pastures, as the waters recede, and thence to water holes or streams during the winter drought. During these moves people from different villages spend time together, in small camps at the beginning of the drought; and, in winter, kinsmen of different villages may spend the season together in a large camp. Apart from these seasonal moves, Nuer also change their village residence.[4] All Nuer aim to become "bulls" — to be able to lead a local community — having as followers a few agnates, maternal relatives and affines; and in furtherance of this aim brothers and cousins part company.[5] The manner in which village communities split is patterned. Nuclei of kin form, and congregate to occupy different sections of a village.[6] These same people marry outside the bounds of their village to people in neighbouring villages, so that kin in the latter aggregate to a kin nucleus in the former. When

---

[1] Evans-Pritchard (1951, p. 27). These "bulls" are not necessarily real aristocrats, but they are accorded this status when they become bulls.

[2] Evans-Pritchard (1951, p. 9). Here, he gives ethnographic evidence on "bulls" and the composition of the localities in which they are dominant. See also pp. 16, 23 and 58 for further evidence.

[3] Evans-Pritchard (1951, pp. 35, 47). Although rules are not based on locality, they are so composed that marriage is excluded within them.

[4] Evans-Pritchard (1951, p. 24): ". . . they change from year to year and from season to season inasmuch as Nuer frequently change their place of residence". On p. 28 he refers to the freedom with which Nuer change their residence and the ease with which they attach themselves to new neighbours.

[5] Evans-Pritchard (1951, p. 2). Village splits are due to rivalries. See also pp. 20, 24 and 28.

[6] Evans-Pritchard (1951, p. 2). This is most notable in larger villages, but it appears to be common.

a "bull" emerges, he takes with him his local nucleus and the aggregated kin from elsewhere, thus constituting a new residential unit of pre-determined and effective kin, exogamous from the outset, but enjoying a new freedom to marry in the neighbourhood because of the shift in residence. Effective kinship is intense among the people of this newly constituted residential unit, bridewealth cannot be passed between them, and in its absence they have become exogamous.

Bridewealth, even where a rule of exogamy exists, does not act as a palliative gift or compensation for the acquisition of rights in the daughters of enemies, despite the abundant proverbial wisdom often quoted to this effect. "Enemy" is perhaps, an inappropriate translation anyway, since words of this kind have a plurality of meanings; the reference is more likely to be to lineage discreteness only, and lineage relations never subsume all relationships anywhere. Furthermore, most marriages are not alliances in any meaningful sense of the word, although a few are. Since people marry people with whom they are familiar already, as inhabitants of a common area, or with whom they have some kinds of relationship, then bridewealth must serve to alter pre-existing relationships or to create a specific set of new ones. The bedouin case might assist in identifying the different kinds of relationships which bridewealth regulates.

The Nuer case is used for comparative purposes for four reasons. First, it is well documented:[1] Evans-Pritchard began writing about bridewealth in 1931, published what has remained an important article on the subject in 1934, and continued his interest in a number of subsequent publications. His writings were also the source of many later ideas. Second, the bedouin and the Nuer bear superficial resemblance: they are both transhumant pastoralists, they are arranged in corporate groups, they possess elaborate lineage structures, and, although culturally quite disparate, some of the details of their behaviour, the sentiments they express about various matters — marriage among them — are, at least at first flush, uncannily alike. Comparable in general in many ways, the Nuer stand in sharp contrast to the bedouin in that they observe a form of exogamy, and this would seem to be critical in assessing the significance of bridewealth. Third, both employ the same general type of bridewealth. The only similarity between the many forms of property

---

[1] In saying this I am not suggesting that there are no other good accounts: Harris (1962), La Fontaine (1962), and Lewis (1962) are all admirable — a vintage year in sooth!

transfers at marriage, about which anthropologists write, is the English word "bridewealth". There is little point in attempting to give an analytically specific definition of this descriptive term here, but it is necessary to limit its meaning to those transfers in which several categories of kin of both spouses are involved, thus distinguishing it from transfers made between the two spouses only, or with the assistance of their parents, or varieties of these. The differences are so fundamental that to lump them all together under the same term is confusing, and misleading when comparison is attempted. Those, like Fox,[1] who deprecate the inclusion of details of the collection and distribution of bridewealth, are clearly ignorant of the basic fact that it is not just one thing but a bundle of parts, and that a particular bundle is characterised by these details. Omission of the latter is bound to lead to a reductionist argument. Hence the absurdity of the stance taken when bridewealth is reduced to a simple device for forging an alliance. Fourth, there is no well documented Arab case available for comparative purposes.

The bedouin of Cyrenaica are neither exogamous nor endogamous. The bars to marriage can be stated under three sets of general rules.

1. *Consanguinity.* Anyone on ego's descent line, in the ascending or descending generations, is excluded. Siblings of the father and mother are also debarred, a relationship which causes most difficulty because siblings sometimes range in age from about twenty to over sixty years, with the result that, not uncommonly, uncles and aunts are of the same age or younger than nieces and nephews. Reared in the camps in the social context of first cousinship, the danger of breaching the ban on sexual relationships between such relatives is evident, and it is stressed by bedouin, and subject to dire penalty.

These are the main bars to marriage:[2] they define the range of incest as well. Sexual intercourse with grandparents is dismissed as laughable, with parents it is regarded as unbelievable. It is admitted as a possibility with the siblings of parents, between siblings, and with the children of siblings; and for these reasons feelings of horror, disgust and outrage are expressed in talking about its taking place with any

---

[1] Fox (1967, p. 233): ". . . this kind of thing has been called 'the right foreleg of the ox' school of anthropology". It is just as well that there are some who know the difference between one end and the other.

[2] Fyzee (1949, Ch. II) gives a good summary account of formal marriage laws.

of these three categories of kin. Represented diagrammatically, for a male, the simplicity of the arrangements become evident at once.

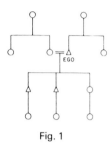

Fig. 1

An extension of this range of bars is that marriage with lineage collaterals of the same generation as the parents should not occur. It does, because not only are genealogical and age generations confused, but there is also such marked ambiguity that sometimes it cannot be resolved. In effect, unless there is known close consanguinity, the rule has no force. Indeed, the records show that it sometimes occurs where it is known, as in the instance of a man marrying his grandfather's brother's daughter. The same can be said of the general rule that a man should not marry a woman older than himself, since their time reckoning is inadequate for this purpose: unless there happens to be certainty about the order of birth, an estimation based on general appearance suffices to settle this issue. Women marry men who are both older than them and who might also be of one or two generations up from them. Some sense of the complexities of separating generations and ages can be gained from a small segment of an actual genealogy, of part of a camp (see Fig. 2).

2. *Affinity.* A man is prohibited from marrying any woman in his wife's own descent line; that is, her mother, grandmother, daughter or granddaughter. Also applicable is the rule that a man should not have two wives simultaneously who, had they been of different sexes, would have been unable to marry — two sisters, for example. In Hanafi law[1] this is regarded as irregular, but not sufficient cause

[1] The Turks (who colonised Cyrenaica until 1913) follow the Hanafi school of Islamic law and the Sanusi, to whose religious order the bedouin belonged, follow the Maliki school. The bedouin were unversed in either.

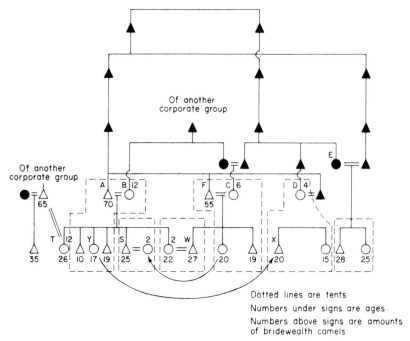

Of another
corporate group

Of another
corporate group

Of another
corporate group

E

Dotted lines are tents
Numbers under signs are ages
Numbers above signs are amounts
of bridewealth camels

Fig. 2

to make a marriage null and void. Most bedouin regard this with repugnance, but it is known, although of infrequent occurrence. Some view sororal marriage with distaste also, but this form is common.

3. *Other bars.* Children who have been suckled by the same woman cannot marry. This foster relationship is known as *riḍā'*. The bar is strictly observed by the bedouin, for, as they see it, such infant nourishing puts people in a sibling relationship. A wet nurse is usually a relative, and, unless her own child is a still birth or dies young, her natural child and foster child share her milk. Fosterage affects two or three pairs in practically all corporate groups, and has the effect of reducing, slightly, the available number of spouses. The effect is more if the wet nurse is of another corporation, since the possible spouses here are much more limited in number.

After divorce or death of a husband a period of sexual continence, known as *'iddat*, must be observed by a wife. The concern here is with paternity, and, consequently, if a woman is not known to be pregnant already, three menses must pass before she is free to re-marry. In the event of pregnancy, conventions are recognised for the rearing of children.

After a triple divorce, re-marriage is not permitted until the wife has been married to another man, divorced, and then observed the period of *'iddat*. Much is made of this in some Arab countries, and a "young donkey" is used to perform the service of freeing the wife from the bar. Among the bedouin, although they maintain that the rule must be obeyed, the divorce pronouncement is used so frequently that it is much of a manner of speaking, used to bring pressure on someone, or to let off steam, or as a threat.

Men are permitted a maximum of four wives simultaneously, but a woman — a rule that rarely receives mention — is allowed only one husband at a time.[1]

These three general categories of rules cover all marriage bars as the bedouin know them. Disagreement about the appropriateness of a possible match sometimes occurs, but the instances of this are very few, to do with the kind of ambiguities cited earlier, or, at most, with irregularities. Compared with reports about other peoples, bedouin (and other Arabs for that matter) devote little attention to problems arising out of the rules when they discuss marriage, perhaps because they are so straightforward and so few, and permit a great range of choice. Unlike Jewish law,[2] Islamic law does not permit marriage between relatives as closely consanguineous as nephews and nieces, but the closeness of permitted degrees is not exhausted by the statement that they can marry a first cousin on either side — that is the four first cousins, a fact which requires to be stated because of the overwhelming primacy given, in the literature, to marriage with the father's brother's daughter. Indeed, in the majority of cases, relatedness other than first cousinship pre-exists first parallel cousin marriage. Thus, for example, a favoured marriage is a first parallel cousin marriage between the son and daughter of two full brothers who had themselves married first parallel cousins, as shown in Fig. 3. Almost invariably, these three kinds of marriages are described as first patrilineal parallel cousin

[1] Religious bars also exist, but they are irrelevant since all bedouin are Sunni Muslims.
[2] Epstein (1942, p. 274). Attempts to reform this law began some time ago.

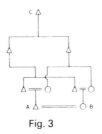

Fig. 3

marriages, as if this is the only relationship.[1] The majority of first
patrilineal cousin marriages contain a plurality of connections: A and
B are related as first patrilineal parallel cousins, as first maternal parallel cousins, as children of their fathers' sisters-in-law, as children of
their mothers' brothers-in-law, as children of grandfathers who are
brothers; they have common paternal and maternal grandparents, and
they are both great-grandchildren of C. These seven different modes of
relationship are, by no means, the maximum possible number, but
they will suffice to substantiate the point that cousin marriage among
Arabs is a much more complicated matter than is generally assumed,
particularly when people are well aware of these plural connections,
and regularly use them to account for details of their behaviour.

This tendency to expunge the complexities in Arab marriage by
reducing it to cousin marriage is only possible if women are omitted
from consideration. The expression "first patrilateral parallel cousin
marriage" refers to three men, and the one woman included as a wife is
there only to complete the diagram, so to speak. The importance of
including all the components that enter into marriages, which
subsequently affect behaviour, can be made clear with reference to the
data in Fig. 2. The six tents shown are situated very closely together,
in a large camp of which they are a part. The people in them had lived
in exile in Egypt together, along with some of the people shown as
dead, and others who are not shown. They went off together, and
returned to their homeland as a group.[2] Since A is the shaikh (leader)
of the corporate group of which the inhabitants of the six tents are a
part, it would appear that his ability to hold the group together, as a
small nucleus of his power, rests on his command of close agnates, their
wives and children, his wealth in animals providing him with the

---

[1] I suspect this results from the use of questionnaires.
[2] These people, along with many others, were forced to leave their territories during the wars with
the Italians from 1911 to 1931. This group left in the late twenties, returning in 1944.

additional economic assets to exercise his power. The agnates, shown in the diagram, are not all his nearest, and his hold over those who are not shown is much more tenuous. In this statement there is no intention of diminishing the significance of agnation as a force for drawing men together, but it is imperative to note, also, that there is a selector at work, which discriminates among men who are equals (*aswā'n*) to persuade some to stand together through all kinds of vicissitudes. Some of these agnates, to be sure, are poor: other agnates are equally poor and equally close, or closer, patrilineally. The shaikh is well off: other agnates were as well, or better off. It is the thread running through women which pulls the men of the six tents to knot them securely together, a fact recognised by all: hence the parallel cousin marriages in the succeeding generation, with the addition of a proposed marriage between X and Y, and possibly another similar one or two, still to come. The eldest of these women (B) is the wife of the shaikh. She is mother's sister to C, the first parallel cousin of D, and sister's sister-in-law to E, who was father's sister to C and D; although now dead, she lived for twenty years, as a widow with two young children, with this little group, sure of its mens' help in herding her few animals, and of their generosity in giving her gifts of wool, meat, clarified butter, and barley. A basic element in the shaikh's structure of power is this group of faithfully devoted followers. Without the linkages between them, and through them between men, it would not be possible to account for his full brother's constant co-operation, much less that of any of the other people. Yet women are disinherited both as daughters and wives. Thus disabled, it might appear that they could not expect to exert more than a mild form of pressure on men, petticoat influence at best. Their positions in Fig. 2, however, make it abundantly clear that they are part of a pattern of relationships, which rests not on fortuitous friendship or anything as casual as that, but on selection of spouses by men and women together. Their strength, their ability to insist on a meaningful say in affairs, lies in bridewealth.

A few more examples are given here to illustrate the closeness of spouses, which appears in many marriages, but which is concealed when they are designated merely as parallel cousin marriages, and to provide a more realistic context for bridewealth.

In Fig. 4a, a father (A) and son (B) marry a mother (C) and her daughter (D). The children of B and D marry the children of their

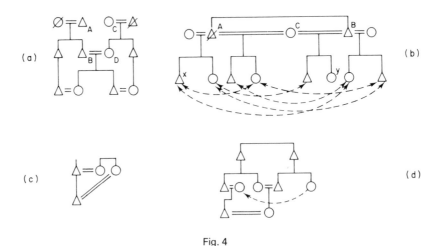

Fig. 4

brothers, one of these marriages being to a first parallel cousin, and the other to a cross cousin. All four spouses are also the grand children of A and C. There are fourteen forms of affinity shown in the diagram. The total number of relationships is formidable.

In Fig. 4b, two brothers, A and B, marry wives who are themselves closely related, and who are closely related to their husbands. Both beget children by these wives. The elder brother A marries a second wife C, begets children by her, but pre-deceases her. His brother B marries his sister-in-law in a leviratic union, and begets children by her. Among the four sets of children of these two men and three women, six first parallel cousin marriages are possible, although only four can be realised, and they are realised in practice. These marrying pairs are related in a variety of other ways, and in the following generation the relationships become even more intricate.

The marriages shown in Fig. 4, c and d are included as variants of the same theme.

Stress has been given, thus far, to the closeness of kinship in marriage. The closeness, however, is not consistently within a limited patrilineal range, for many of the more crucial marriages are to women of other corporations, that of the woman T in Fig. 2 being a good example. At the heart of the agnatic group, therefore, there are always women possessing connections with other women and men, some of them the daughters of agnates, others from outside it but linked to women inside it as matrilateral relatives of one sort or another. Apart from this, there is a consistent tendency, once a link with another corporation has been established, to replicate the original marriage with a succession of cross cousin marriages in the same generation or the following ones. When these sorts of marriages are reciprocated, as they are so often, then the interconnections become as intricate as those resulting from marriages within the corporate group. Occasionally marriages occur between people whose homelands lie far apart, with a 100 miles or more between them: one went right across country, from the southwest to the Aulad'Ali tribe in Egypt. These are major alliances between two important corporate groups, and once made appear to have the durability to last for two or three generations.

Obviously there is no question of this marriage pattern approaching an endogamous condition. The fiction that Arabs "marry endo-gamously" has been perpetrated by many anthropologists.[1] Marriage is permitted within the patrilineage, but there is no rule which prescribes it, and marriage outside it is also permitted. Statistically the corporate lineage group is not an endogamous unit either. Preference is expressed for the father's brother's daughter, and a man can force his claim to her, although this would be conceded to only one of several brothers. Preference is also expressed for the mother's brother's daughter, who, the bedouin say, "is sweeter than milk", and, in physical conditions where the water is brackish, this is sweetness indeed, but she cannot be claimed in marriage by the sister's son. The only motive for viewing parallel cousin marriage as a problem of endogamy is the wish to simplify it by focusing the attention on men, and defining the marriage universe so widely and imprecisely that the majority of marriages are bound to be to parallel cousins of one sort or another, despite the fact that consanguinity between the spouses cannot be demonstrated;[2] and by thoughtlessly casting aside the other relationships between spouses, sometimes when one of these is the nearest in terms of degrees. Such perversity robs bedouin marriage of its considerable interest, and the bridewealth associated with it is denuded of its full meaning to be explained as an insignificant amount, or not given.

---

[1] There are so many offenders, in this respect, that it would be absurd to give specific references. The sloppiness of thought implied by the use of the term endogamy to refer to Arab marriage leads to serious errors.

[2] This stems from the habit of confusing agnation and patrilineality, I suspect.

There are three conditions to be satisfied for a legal marriage, irrespective of the closeness of consanguinity between the spouses: consent of the spouses, a statement giving the amount of the bridewealth, and the contract witnessed.[1] Consent is assumed by those who initiate the process, the fathers of the spouses if they are alive, or, if the former are dead, their guardians. More trouble originates in guardianship. A boy, when he matures to manhood and demands his inheritance, might be told that it has been expended on his rearing, or that he must wait. If he insists on bridewealth for marriage, his guardian (his father's brother or next nearest agnate) might comply, but the amount of wealth he releases might be small, depriving the ward of choice, since it is the guardian who conducts the negotiations.

The witnessed statement of the amount of the bridewealth constitutes the marriage contract, but it is only a part of the bridewealth process. Prior to this the contracting parties will have been known to each other, either because of existing kinship, common residence, or propinquity. When approaches are seriously being considered, occasions are found for mutual entertainment, whether the parents reside in the same camp and are agnates, or live in camps set apart by some distance and are of different corporate groups. These preliminaries, during which soundings are taken to ascertain the exact amount and details of the wealth required, are the first sign of the changes in the relationships which marriage is to bring about; for entertainment is not proffered to those with whom casual relationships already exist and are to remain unaltered, or to those with whom relationships are not desired. If things go well, several of these reciprocal exchanges of hospitality are likely, especially if the bridewealth is likely to be large, while all the time negotiations are afoot, without the principals (the fathers of the future spouses) mentioning the mater of the marriage they have in mind. This process ended, the scene is now set for the formal public negotiations to take place.

The bride and groom do not enter into these negotiations, nor in those that follow, and only become the principals when they are brought together on the first day of the nuptials. During the preliminaries, both are told who the spouse is to be, and if the bride vehemently objects — and it is the bride, not the groom, who most usually raises objections — every endeavour is made to reconcile her to the decision

---

[1] Witnesses are required by Sunni Law, but not by Shi'ite law, although in practice Shi'ites use them as well.

her parents have made. If she remains obdurate severe measures might be taken against her, although the threat of spinsterhood, and the commiserable status it implies, is enough to move her to acceptance. She would be left without the support of bridewealth to sustain her for life, and without a son to care for her as she ages. For a woman, while she can reasonably be almost certain of marriage, cannot demand it. She has to receive a proposal (*talab*), whereas a man has the right to demand that his corporate group provides him with the wherewithal to marry (if he is bereft of animal wealth himself), and with it he is able to initiate a proposal. A woman is free to object but must yield; a man is not permitted the indulgence of obstructing his father's plans, yet marriage for him is certain. Both come under the father's authority, but with different effects. The father can delay the right of a son to marry, since it is he who is ultimately answerable for the bridewealth; if a daughter is adamant in her refusal she may not be given another chance to marry.

The appropriation of choice by the parental generation does not mean that parents act only in their own interests. When A in Fig. 2 arranged to marry his eldest daughter to an important shaikh for a large bridewealth, self-interest was not his motive. He was too advanced in age to be swayed, in his choice, by material gain or status. He was a shaikh of some renown, but since the days when his own marriage proved to be politically rewarding — and fructive to boot — circumstances had so changed that an immediate renewal of this link in the next generation had been rendered unnecessary. Consequently, he sought a different external connection for his son, S, through his eldest daughter, T, which provided this son with an important ally as a brother-in-law. T was disconsolate when told who her husband was to be, and prayed that her first cousin, W, would assert his right to demand her for himself. This was unacceptable to her father, who had refused this demand only a year earlier. She (T) had been reared in her mother's image, a confident and distinguished personality, something of a *grande dame*, fit to be the wife of a shaikh. This was the rub; everyone knew that the most threatening challenger to S's succession to the shaikhship, in the next generation, was his first cousin, W, and to have agreed to this parallel cousin marriage would have been to improve the latter's chances markedly. In giving T as a wife to a shaikh of another corporation, A was not only sure that his son would enjoy the benefits of an important political connection, but that his sister had the strength of personality to dominate it. The shaikh's concern was to provide a structure of power, while he was still alive, for his eldest son, as a kind of inheritance, much as townspeople attempt to give children a preferential start in life with a good education or a trade.

The first formal move towards marriage is the arranged appearance, in the bride's camp, of a delegation from the groom's camp. The groom's father accompanies these men, but says nothing during the negotiations. The delegation consists of four or five men, as a rule, the most important of whom is the man who is to do most of the talking, a mother's brother of the groom if one is available, or, if not, a close friend. This spokesman is the sponsor, or guarantor (sometimes referred to as the *kafīl*). The father's brother, although present, is not used in this role, because he and the father are unlikely to have divided their inheritance of animals at this stage in their lives, and since the negotiations turn on the amount of this wealth to be trans-ferred it is better to exclude both of them. Brothers who have yet to agree to the division of their inherited wealth are said to be of the "one cooking pot" (*ḥalla waḥida*). Although such temporary arrangements might resemble a form of joint ownership, it must be made clear that animals are individually owned, and that this "joint ownership" obtains only while solutions to inheritance problems are still pending. But while this is so, there is sufficient ambiguity about property relations to merit the exclusion of both the father and his brother.

Witnessed statements concerning the amount of bridewealth must be made in advance of marriage taking place, no matter how close the relationship of the spouses. Before the formality of negotiation and witnessing begins, a number of animals known as the *sīaq* (from the verb *sāqa*, to drive or to herd cattle) are given "to the bride's tent". Contributions to the *sīaq* come from several kinds of relatives, among whom the father's brother (unless he is the bride's father) and the mother's brother are counted, but otherwise the precise category of kin is of no consequence. The number and kind of animals varies. The largest recorded was fifteen sheep. A camel was delivered as *sīaq* at one of these meetings. The more usual number ranges between three and seven, sometimes made up entirely of sheep, sometimes a mixture of sheep and goats, and some three goats only if a man is poor. At least one of the animals of the *sīaq* is likely to be slaughtered for the feast, provided by the bride's father for the delegation, to mark the successful conclusion of the contract. The rest are distributed among kin, whose specific relationships, as described, are to the bride and not to the parents, brother or guardian. The mother's brother almost invariably gets one, and so does the father's brother, unless he happens to be the groom's father. Otherwise, the exact kinship category of the recipients is unimportant. People are free to choose according to their own assessments of the needs of others, their friendship with them, and whatever personal considerations they think should influence them: thus the wife of S in Fig. 2 gave to her mother, "her mother's first cousin's tent" (D), and "to the tent of the children of" E; two of the animals she retained for herself, branding them with her mother's brother's sign.[1]

The significance of the *siāq* is not to be dismissed as an inconsequential part of the bridewealth process. Until these animals are delivered, the formal negotiations cannot commence. At their conclusion, by way of celebrating the institution of new relationships or of putting existing ones on a new footing, the slaughter for the commensal meal is one of these animals. It would be too much of a diversion to enter into a discussion of the significance of animal sacrifice among the bedouin here, but it is necessary to note two points about the slaughter of a *siāq* animal. When a man gives or slaughters an animal "from his own wealth", it is a surrogate for a life, his life, which is in the blood of the animal, and, in this sense, what he gives is, vicariously, part of himself. The receiver is said to be in debt to the giver, and it is a debt which cannot be "redeemed" until an appropriate occasion occurs later on: to return a slaughter without cause for doing so would be gross insult in normal circumstances; its return, the redemption of the debt, in the correct context, is meritorious, enabling further relationships to proceed in a spirit of amity. At the commensal meal, however, the slaughtered animal is one that is given and received, thereby making both men giver and receiver at the same time, a permitted haste of return indicating the urgent desire that both parties should become instantly enmeshed in their new relationships. Although the whole of the *siāq* is only slaughtered at the celebrations if both parties are rich, it is thought to be a generous act, bringing people closer, and specially propitious for the marriage and the other relationships which are to stem from it. The one camel *siāq*, mentioned

---

[1] With this mark, the animals are distinguished from those of her father-in-law and husband. If she used her father's or brother's mark, the animals could be claimed by either of them, or if the spouse's fathers had not divided their inheritance then the possibility of ambiguity in the rights to animals is serious. The mother's brother cannot lay claim to the animals either, because his mark, which they bear, is added to that of the husband's. Both marks on the same animal leave little scope to dispute rights to it.

earlier, was slaughtered at the celebrations, but this was a marriage between a shaikh and the daughter of a shaikh; it was considered magnanimous, befitting a shaikh of some standing.

The *sīāq* represents the first transfer of wealth between the parties. It is not included in the contract, and the amount given is the giver's estimation, based on information he has gathered, of the number of people to whom the receiver wishes to give an animal. The fact that the *sīāq* is not a contractual obligation makes it all the more important. It is always confidently anticipated, but it is regarded as wealth which can be witheld or varied in amount, and, to this extent, it is a measure of the relationships into which the giver wishes to enter: the higher the amount given, the greater the number of animals slaughtered for the celebrations (if the giver's expression of his intentions are to be reciprocated), and the more people partaking of the commensal meal, itself an act rich with meaning. It is also the first public commitment to proceed with a marriage, binding in the sense that should anything baneful happen between the negotiations and the nuptials, or during the nuptials, it is returnable in full — the bride's father has to take the risks that his daughter is a virgin, that she is not frigid, nor sexually malformed.

The choice people exercise in deciding to contribute to the *sīāq*, and in its distribution, means that, in advance of a marriage taking place, contributors and recipients are singled out, from potentially much larger numbers, for more intimate involvement. These are the effective affines through whom future relationships are expected to pass. The spouses, it must be stressed, have yet to meet. Although the principals at the negotiations can be said to be representing the bride and groom, the *sīāq* is delivered before negotiations start, and their meeting is expressly intended to configure or reconfigure relationships. Later, affinity will be claimed by a vastly larger number of people on both sides, but for the first difficult year or so of the new marriage, it is this select group of people who will bear the responsibility for all going well. The delivery of the *sīāq* is the occasion, *par excellence*, for getting to grips with affinity, and, for this reason, it is distinctively different from any of the succeeding arrangements.

The negotiations take on a set form. First, the delegation's spokesman calls out the name of the bride's father who feigns not to hear; there follows a repetition of this. At the third calling, "he hears" and responds. The spokesman then asks for the daughter, and the conventional reply is given: "Welcome, if you have camels". The number demanded in the first instance is several camels in excess of expectations. This is reduced according to accepted conventions. A shaikh of standing begins by requesting that two camels are removed from the total for his sake, and the request is promptly granted. A second shaikh requests a like reduction, and this is granted with equal promptitude. Then a "client of the goodness" asks for another one to be taken off, and this too is conceded with alacrity. Finally the spokesman requests a last reduction, in favour of the gathering — a gathering of men, particularly if one or two shaikhs are included in it, confers honour on the host — and this cannot be denied. Although this apparent bargaining is strictly conventional, it is not without meaning. Each time a shaikh asks for a reduction in an amount of wealth to be transferred, whether it be bridewealth or blood money, he incurs debts. They are not held against him in the manner of a debit accounting, but as concessions which require concessions in return. Hence, the shaikh must be a person who can be approached by the bride's father at some future date, a shaikh within a structure of alliances between corporate groups; but he must also be of a stature to be able to accept debts of this sort with aplomb — a shaikh from among the "small fry" would be quite unacceptable for the job. Part of the measure of a shaikh's puissance is the frequency of calls made on him for such purposes. Likewise, the "client of the goodness" must be one thought genuinely to possess *baraka* (blessing), and not one with dubious credentials.

Moreover, once the formalities have ended all the men present rise, kiss each other on the head, and go out into the open, to "read" the *Fātiḥa* (the opening sura of the Koran), palms of the hands upturned, much as they do when blood money negotiations are terminated. The women herald the end to the agreement by the excitable trilling of tongues, which they reserve for an action which can be said to be something of a triumph, or to urge a person forward in a hazardous undertaking. The kissing of heads, followed by the *Fātiḥa*, has a singular significance, without which the bedouin do not accept an agreement to be binding; a peace brought about by the intervention of government officials, concluded in an office, is thought to be no more than an expediency, lacking the compulsive force of moral authority, to be kept only for as long as it suits both parties. The kissing of heads, and repeating the *Fātiḥa*, endows an agreement with this authority, and thus makes it lasting.

Prominent in the formalities, and the subject of the genuine negotiations which precede them, are the animals which are to constitute
that part of the bridewealth known as the ṣāḥiba.[1] The word has
several meanings, but the connotation it carries in this context is that
of master or owner, although neither of these words express its precise
meaning. Insistently, the bedouin affirm that a woman's "bone"
belongs to her natal corporate group, and that if she is killed in homi-
cide the blood money goes, not to her husband, but to its members.
(Anthropologists see this as evidence that she is not fully incorporated
into her husband's lineage). In practice, the matter is not as simple as
this. If the bridewealth has "died" (by which the bedouin mean that
the marriage has endured to the point where bridewealth arrangements are no longer an issue), the blood money might be given to the
wife's father, but only for him to transfer it to the husband. If the
marriage is only two or three years old, and only one payment of
bridewealth has been made, the wife's father must compensate the
husband for the loss of bridewealth, and argument about the rights of
the wife's children is likely to ensue. The most satisfactory settlement is
that the wife's sister (or her father's brother's daughter) is given in
sororal marriage, with an agreed ṣāḥiba equivalent to the dead sister's,
with the difference that none of it will actually be given to the father.
What is certain is that both bridewealth and blood money will not
accumulate on one side. Neither, it is said, have baraka in them. They
are for disposal, not for keeping. Bridewealth should be kept until
given for another marriage, and the best thing to do with blood money
is to use it as bridewealth at the earliest opportunity. Replacement of a
human being is not a matter of material assessment, but of using
material goods to beget another. That is to say, the issue is never one of
a fracas over animals, or of the degree of incorporation into a family or
group, but in establishing who has what rights over women and men at
particular stages in their lives. Indeed, the issue of incorporation is
irrelevant since almost half of the women marry men of their own
corporate groups.[2]

If there is any substance to the definition "owner" given to the word
ṣāḥiba, it is that the husband acquires certain limited rights in his wife.

---

[1] The word hulwān is used among cow herders in the northern plateau areas, and it is known
throughout the country. The word mahr, common in other Arab countries, is not used among
the bedouin.
[2] Since this article is not meant to be an analysis of marriage patterns, this statement is given only
as a guide. The incidence varies from group to group.

No one but a husband has the right of sexual enjoyment in her, and her procreative powers are his. This gives him the liberty to allow another man sexual congress with her if he deems it necessary, but any issue she bears is his — "The boy for the bed" (*al-walad li'l farsh*), as the saying goes.[1] A woman, in other words, can be accused of adultery if caught in *flagrante delicto*; and unless her husband is in connivance with her, she risks her life — I recorded several cases of husbands, who had suffered cuckoldry, killing their unfaithful wives. By the same token, a wife has a right to sexual enjoyment and to pregnancy, and if it is demonstrated that the husband fails to satisfy her on either count, she can demand that he makes arrangements to provide her with this satisfaction, or that he frees her. Just as a woman must needs be sexually normal, so, too, sexual deficiency in a man is good cause for his wife to seek separation from him. Whereas sexual abnormality in a woman leads to a summary termination of a marriage — there is a virginity test on the first day of the nuptials, and consummation takes place that night — the consequences for a man need not necessarily be as severe: as owner of her sexual and procreative powers he can solicit the aid of another man, but if a woman is sexually abnormal she cannot provide a substitute woman. Further, while a wife's issue jurally belong to her husband, and remain under his authority for his lifetime, a woman has the right to rear her children, strictly until they have been properly weaned, and, in practice, long afterwards;[2] and she also has the right to live with them, if their father leaves them, or after they have reached maturity. In short, a wife has a right to motherhood, in its procreative and social senses. Complementarily a husband has the right to expect it of her. The rights of the *ṣāḥiba* are not exclusively the husband's. They are distributed between both spouses to form the symbiosis which is the very minimum requirement in any marriage.

The camels (often used as a generic term for animals, enabling camels to be compounded for sheep, goats or some of all three) are never given immediately, nor, when a transfer is made, are they all given at one time. The terms of reference in the agreement are: "We will put 'so many' in front of you (*qadamak*), and leave 'so many' in case of *'aib* or *ghaib*." The word *'aib* is given very many nuances of

---

[1] There is little point in discussing these rights at length, since so much has been written about them already. Fortes (1962; 1969, pp. 18-84) gives admirable summaries of the issues involved in these rights — and of issues relating to bridewealth in general.

[2] Weaning can be delayed for several years. The bedouin believe that a long period of breast-feeding produces strong males.

meaning; here, it is intended as the shame brought upon a husband if his wife flaunts her sexuality persistently, or has sexual congress with another man, so that she is publicly thought of as an adultress or is one in practice, and makes a cuckold of her husband. The word *ghaib* means absence, either through death or desertion. None of the bridewealth is given for about a year; "in front of you" is taken to mean after the next lambing or next harvest, but, in any case, after sufficient time has elapsed to determine whether the union is fertile. The initial *sīāq* is in respect of affinity (*nasab*. An affine is called a *nasīb*. The same root can also be used in a generic sense to refer to affinal and cognatic connections between groups.). The *ṣāḥiba* is tied to parenthood.

Women are proud to boast that the *ṣāḥiba* is "on their backs". All of it will not come their way, since that which is "put in front of you" (the fathers) is soon expended on another marriage. People implore God to give them boys. But without girls the boys might well be unable to marry, particularly boys of the poorer families. Women do not gain materially from bridewealth. The giving of bridewealth is a process whereby relatively small numbers of animals are circulated among large numbers of people, leaving in their trails no appreciable amounts of individual gains in animals, but huge accumulations of relationships. As far as a woman is concerned a portion of these relationships are contained in the rights she acquires over her husband, her father, and the brother who marries with her bridewealth; for it is the promise of bridewealth for a daughter which prompts the father to make an acceptable promise of bridewealth to get his son a bride. If a husband does not bring a trinket or a dress length for his wife, after returning from a visit to town, she can demand such things of him: her bride-wealth gives her just cause for doing so. If her husband abuses her in any way, she has the right to return to her father or brother, who can demand justice. The word *ḥaqq* is frequently used for this, and it has an abundance of related meanings. In this context, the word *inṣāf* is preferred. It is used to refer to the wealth a wife receives as "justice". Depending on the seriousness of the complaint, the *inṣāf* varies from one to about five sheep or goats. Let it be clear: the *inṣāf* is not a gift; it is a claim to the husband's property which is made against the wife's bridewealth; and it goes to her, the animals of which are then branded with the personal sign of her mother's brother, so that there will be no fear of them being merged into her husband's or father-in-law's flocks (but if the wife is a first maternal cross cousin she uses her father's sign). There comes a time, however, when a woman finds the company of neighbours so congenial that she will not leave it, especially after her children have survived the perils of infancy and have grown into maturity, when it matters little if her husband abandons her for a young wife — he does not divorce her after the menopause: "he throws her off his back". At about this time even the most dogged among fathers will have relinquished all hope of receiving any more bridewealth. Instead, the father insists that the portion reserved to meet the contingencies of adultery, death or desertion is now put "in front of her", and on these animals a wife again brands her mother's brother's personal sign. The brand does not give her complete ownership of the animals; it does separate her rights in them from those previously held by her husband, and thereafter, she is free to will them (together with any of the *sīāq* or *insāf* animals) to her sons, as she wishes.

There is point in delaying the transfer of bridewealth. The initial amount is usually only a portion of the total contracted amount, and this is stated at the formal negotiations. It is not transferred until the wife is pregnant, or preferably after childbirth; the rest is left. While it is still unpaid the husband can expect formal but unannounced visits from his immediate affines, when he is expected to display his generosity. At first, when the son-in-law sees or hears that his father-in-law is approaching his tent, he skedaddles to hide in another tent, or to his sister's husband (in the hope of getting something from him), because he knows full well the purpose of the visit. After some years have passed, and the marriage is prospering, relationships move to another stage at which affines meet each other more as equals, and a spirit of give and take grows between them. Nevertheless, the contract remains, to be evoked whenever trouble arises between the spouses. Its importance, however, lies in the fact that it is allowed to remain unfulfilled. Completed to the letter it would act to sever relationships. Left over as a debt, bridewealth incites people to indulge in continuously changing relationships.

Included in the *sāhiba* is a detailed list of items the bride is to receive, and which, when they are given to her, are called the *kiswa*. They can all be seen at any wedding as the bride, riding high in a canopy on the hump of a camel, is taken to her wedding tent. All she wears, boots, cummerbund, dress, silver bracelets and so on will all have been given her as part of her *kiswa*. Draped over the canopy are the hand woven carpets for her tent, and a straw mat (*dīs*), in a roll slung in front of the canopy, and, hanging over the side, a few pots and pans. All part of the wedding gaiety it would seem, but no less important for that: the groom pays the cost of all the clothes his wife wears to her wedding, and he must continue to clothe her henceforward; the straw mat they will lie on together and any children born on it are theirs, since no other woman has the right to lie on the mat, not even another wife of the husband; the carpets are provided to start married life, and thereafter the husband must provide wool to make others; the wife must cook for her husband — it is her right to do so — but he must buy the utensils. These details of the *kiswa*, so carefully listed during the bridewealth negotiations, are not intended merely to give the young couple a start; they define rights and responsibilites for both for the rest of their life together. Such is the importance attached to the *kiswa* that the nuptials cannot begin until every item has been brought, and delivered to the bride.

There is still the bride's mother. She gets nothing specifically earmarked for her until the bride becomes a wife. As soon as possible after the nuptials are over, the husband and wife along with the husband's mother, sister and sister-in-law, pay their first visit to the wife's mother, taking with them one or two sheep or goats, one of which will be slaughtered, the intention of which is "to steal the affinity". Months later, certainly if the wife is now pregnant, the mother will receive her due, *ḥaqq al-ḥalīb* (right of the milk) or *suwār al-ḥalīb* (silver bracelets of the milk). In practice, it is unlikely that a husband, however well off, would be so rash as to buy his mother-in-law a pair of very heavy bracelets (they weight about ½ kilo), but if his relationship with his wife is thriving he might give up to about five sheep — animals which are again given a mother's brother's brand, and disposed of among her sons as she wills.

In giving these details pertaining to the woman's rights that are caught up in bridewealth it is not the intention to overstress them, but such emphasis is placed on rights accruing to men in bridewealth, in the literature on Arabs, that an attempt to restore the balance is necessary. Women are not being irrational or unrealistic when they reiterate the statement that the bridewealth is on their "backs", and add that it goes to their fathers. What they mean is that authority over the bridewealth is held by the father, but the rights which are derived from it are carried by the wife. They last until the bridewealth is "dead", by which time they have become defunct or the spouses have entered the stage of connubial companionship for the rest of their lives. Unless this were the case bridewealth associated with father's brother's daughter's marriage would not make sense.

In one way or another a considerable amount of property is needed to make a marriage, and the details already given are ample evidence of this. During the nuptials, the consumption of food is prodigious. Whatever a man's status, the number of guests is always high. About a hundred people assemble on the first day of the nuptials, and a score or so are present on each of the remaining six days. The guests at an important marriage are considerably in excess of these numbers. Five to ten sheep or goats are likely to be slaughtered during the week's festivities; some 100 kilos of flour, 50 kilos of rice, 25 kilos of sugar, 5 kilos of tea, and 100 gallons of water are used. This represents a modest estimate of the average consumption for an ordinary wedding, the sort of entertainment provided by the owner of five to ten camels and about 100 sheep. For a man of these means, the expenditure represents roughly a third or more of his total wealth. For a man of poorer means the proportion is likely to be much higher. When a shaikh marries the expenditure is likely to be double the amount of most other marriages, although the proportion might not be as high. Clearly, this scale of expenditure would be an intolerable burden for most individuals. During the festivities the guests themselves bring animals, sugar and tea, each group of men from a camp bringing one animal between them, or a few kilos of sugar, as they judge to be fitting. Men from the groom's camp are also likely to contribute. All in all, the groom's father — or the groom himself — is likely to gather more wealth than he dispenses during the nuptials, and if he is a shaikh he will probably gain a substantial number of animals. Direct contributions are also made to the bridewealth, and both father's and mother's brothers are picked out as those who are most obliged to give. Others contribute as well, but it would be wrong to categorise them in specific kinship terms. Agnates do not contribute because they are agnates, no more than do matrilateral relatives. Agnates, matrilateral relatives and affines might contribute, not because they fall into these kinship categories, but because they are differentiated from the other people of all three categories, as a result of a history of relationships which have brought them closer together to form a distinct nucleus of more effective kin. They are self selecting because they are caught in such an entanglement of any or all of these three types of relationships, with the bride or the groom, or both, that they are susceptible to as many pressures to give as there are strands in their relatedness.

The upshot of all this is that the number of people directly involved in any marriage is high, and the crowds at the festivities are eloquent testimony of a wider involvement. The number directly implicated varies considerably depending on the particular circumstances. It is known to rise to as high as fifty, if men and women are counted; it would be an odd sort of marriage if it dropped to under a dozen, especially if the bride were a maiden. These people help for one prime reason: to promote the success of the marriage. They are always available to advise — gratuitously and abundantly, very often — and to assist in all sorts of ways. They are intimately concerned because their contribution has made new, or renewed old, relationships. It is they who make personal enquiries about the wife's condition, who watch every detail of the spouses' behaviour, and so on. It is not the material value of the animal given as a contribution that they have in mind; uppermost in their minds are their social relationships, for which a breach in the marriage would be disruptive. Assuming sexual compatability between the spouses, the fertility of both, and a minimum of social compatability, there is no reason why any bedouin marriage should not endure. The demands on the spouses of a marriage are few and they are not onerous. They can be met by the vast majority because the foundation of marriage lies in a stable social environment. This stability is the major contribution made by those directly implicated, the animals given serving as emblem of their intentions. A more general context of stability is created by the guests at the festivities. They come, kith and kin from round about, with their gifts, to join in the jollifications, and to display their public pleasure with the match that has been made. At dusk, when the young men dance in a crescent formation, led by a virgin, they clap until their hands become very sore. Unless they do this, they will not, they say, get a bride. They know full well that hand claps, however vigorous the effort, will never fetch a bride: they also know that without the support of others they cannot hope to marry and remain wedded. From the outset, a marriage is ringed around with two defences, an inner one of intimates, the contributors to the bridewealth, and an outer one of friends, the wedding guests. Bridewealth, *per se*, has little to do with marriage stability. Marriages which carry a bridewealth of five sheep are as stable as those carrying twenty camels. Animals, as material goods, do not hold human beings together. Despite the arguments, in the literature, pertaining to the amount of wealth transferred and the difficulty or ease with which it can be retrieved, when spouses are determined to part, they are not thwarted by considerations of this kind. The animals are there as symbolic of the nature of social relationships. Marital stability is rooted in the moral context created by a community, symbolically expressed through the animals which change hands at the several stages on the way to a union.

The number of animals promised as bridewealth is not the same for all marriages. The range is considerable, as it is among most peoples,[1] despite the predilections of some authors to iron out the differences, to arrive at high bridewealth here and low there, ascribing these unwarranted evaluations to societies as it suits their arguments.[2] Among the bedouin, it can drop as low as about five sheep, and soar as high as twenty camels.[3] But the range in the number of animals delivered to the fathers of brides is much less than this. For example, if the promised number is twelve camels, the number handed over after a year of the marriage has elapsed is four; if it is six camels, the number handed over is likely to be three; if it is five sheep, the probable number a father gets is three or four. This does not mean, however, that the wife's rights contract correspondingly. "The camels on her back" is the total number promised at the formal negotiations, and it is this total which symbolises her rights, not the number required by her father to set in motion arrangements for marrying off one of his sons. Nevertheless, the discrepancies in the total amounts would appear to affect the rights of wives in a like order of magnitude, since there is a close correspondence between the bridewealth and the rights a wife derives from it. Some wives, it would seem, are provided with a greater store of rights than others. Why should there be this apparent discrimination among women?

The saying is that a woman's contract should be the same as her mother's (*shart hā kaif shart umm hā*. As well as meaning contract, the word *shart* also means crevice, and is used indecently, in this

---

[1] Nuer bridewealth is negotiable (Evans-Pritchard, 1951, p. 83). It is also negotiable in many other societies: see Lewis (1962, p. 39 ff.).

[2] Most of those who participated in the arguments, which appeared mainly in *Man*, concerning the relation of the amount of bridewealth to marriage stability, were guilty of this kind of gross evaluation of amounts.

[3] As a guide for conversion, about six sheep would buy a grown camel, in the market. Nowadays the value of sheep is relatively higher.

context, to mean vagina). Like all proverbial wisdom it tells only part of the truth. A father always attempts to get a promise of bridewealth for one of his daughters, at least equal to the amount promised for his wife, particularly if her bridewealth had been big, say, eight camels or more. In Fig. 2, the shaikh A delayed his eldest daughter's marriage until he received an offer equivalent to her mother's: twelve camels. His stature would have suffered had he accepted less: his ability to command bridewealth is a test of his power. His second daughter was married soon after the eldest, with a bridewealth of only two camels. His eldest son, heir to the shaikhship at that,[1] married a wife who was promised only two camels — telling evidence to show that the direct status effect of the amount is attached to the wife, and to throw into relief the pivotal position a wife occupies in affinal relations. A man's status is affected indirectly by the control he commands over affinal links; therefore, it is largely fortuitous whether the bridewealth promised for the wife of a leader is big or small. An upstart shaikh, exulting in his new found status, endeavours to command a big bridewealth, if not in his own marriage then through one of his kinsmen or kinswomen.

Status differences affect bridewealth in other ways. Daughters of clients are married to freeborn men for very little bridewealth, but clients who marry daughters of freeborn men have to promise large amounts. Both rules apply to grafts, co-residents who are nothing more than neighbours, and shepherds from elsewhere. In a rough and ready fashion, status sought means promising a large amount, status granted the opposite. Actual arrangements are subject to the contingencies of the circumstances: a wealthy client would not give his daughter to a freeborn nonentity for five sheep; whether a shepherd would promise much or little would depend entirely on the particulars of his relationship with the girl's father and his agnates, and so on. In one way or another, status considerations impinge on all bridewealth arrangements, but in ways too complicated to allow a list to be drawn up showing the appropriate bridewealth for each status. Bridewealth and status do not necessarily match. Were this so, then an important element in the power structures of individuals would be permanently fixed, frustrating any shifts in power, and relegating those without it to persistent deprivation. But power does shift; some men without it succeed in capturing it, and some of those possessing it fall into

[1] He has since come to be acknowledged as the shaikh of his corporate group.

decline. A detailed listing of each arrangement does not reveal much about power, for what matters most is not their serial order but their configurations, and the command of these configurations by individuals.

The suggestion advanced here is that the seeming differentiation of women by bridewealth is not attributable to a single cause, such as status, but to the kind of social relationships already in being or desired. Very many of these are encapsulated in property, and before proceeding with the argument it is necessary to point to some of its characteristics. As a preamble, it must be stressed that women are implicated in property, however circuitously. They may be denied the right to inherit such property, but this does not leave them bereft of all relationships there are in it; it is flimflam to say otherwise. Apart from their claims to bridewealth, they critically affect the use to which corporate resources are put.[1]

Land and water are owned by males collectively. Corporate property is available for use as a right by all adult male members of a group, and because they are equals in this respect, they cannot transfer their rights to others *qua* their status as agnates. Agnation does not provide for preferential access to corporate resources, and were it the only means of control, any unexpendable shares would revert to the common pool without much gain to anyone: individuals would not be able to grow much more, nor increase the size of their flocks and herds with this trivial additional access to resources, and little reliance could be placed on it in any event. Affinity and all forms of matrilateral kinship, however, are recognised as legitimate grounds for temporarily relinquishing — and, conversely, for gaining — rights in resources. In this way, an agnate can give the use of his right to another agnate, as long as they are otherwise related. Poor agnates can be valued affines. A shaikh who controls a number of such links is able to expand his flocks and herds, and enlarge his grain store appreciably. There would be little point to this expansion if the continuity of additional supplies rested entirely on local resources. It is a characteristic of the bedouin economy, due to the vagaries of the rainfall, that insufficient rain might fall, in a season, to fill the well or to permit ploughing. To maintain sizeable flocks and herds, or increase them, it is imperative to have access to the natural resources of other corporations, in order to

---

[1] Peters (1977). This matter is dealt with in more detail there. Also, other types of property transfers at marriage are discussed.

make good local deficiencies as they occur. Affinity and matrilateral kinship open the way to the resources of agnates in other corporate groups. The term for affinity, *nasab*, is applied to all affines, whether they are within the corporate group or member of others, irrespective of generational differences, a usage consistent with their behaviour as equals. Generations are not merged in the term (and its derivations) used for matrilateral relatives, but it is used to cover them all, whether they are of the same corporate group or of others. As a result of selected marriages within a corporate group and connections to others outside — links which, moreover, are both replicated — corporate groups come to be differentiated internally, forming two or more kinship clusters, and demarcating the lines of division, if and when the pressure on resources rises to an intolerable level.[1]

Animal property is individually owned, in that there is an individual proprietor. The bedouin make much of a form of ownership of livestock, which they refer to as the *ḥalla waḥida*, mentioned earlier. The small group based on this kind of ownership does not last for more than two generations; more often it breaks up after brothers have married. Its interest here, is that while it lasts, there is much more likelihood of first parallel cousin marriage occurring than when brothers have divided their inheritance. In Fig. 2, the shaikh, A, was the proprietor of all the animals in which the occupants of all six tents, shown in the diagram, had claims. Before arranging the marriage of his eldest daughter for a large bridewealth, he consulted his nephew, W, who agreed to the match on condition that he should be given the second daughter. Previously, the shaikh's eldest son, S, was confidently expected by his kinsmen to marry the daughter of a shaikh of another corporation. As soon as the shaikh's nephew, W, demanded the second daughter, he arranged for this nephew's sister to marry his eldest son. One other first parallel cousin marriage had been agreed, and there was talk of one more. If the latter were consummated, the number of first parallel cousin marriages would have reached the maximum for this small group. Equally interesting is that not one of the five seniors of the group married a first parallel cousin.

[1] I do not, as Khuri (1970, p. 604) claims, attribute lineage proliferation to parallel cousin marriage: on the contrary I stress (Peters, 1960) that lineages split when the relation between the carrying capacity of the resources and the population living off them becomes seriously imbalanced. When split occurs the seceding groups are composed of cognatic kin, linked partly by parallel cousin marriage, mostly by matrilateral marriages, and their external marriage links assisting in the process of severance.

In discussing the two major types of property, the outline of the marriage pattern has emerged. To give it more sharpness the main directions of the links are now summarily given. Highly selective first parallel cousin marriage occurs when there is a connection in the ascending generation other than the sibling link, giving genealogically localised spots of intensity, interspersed with its partial or complete absence. Selective marriages with parallel cousins, other than the first, are numerically more common and the majority of these are between people related in other ways, as matrilateral parallel cousins, as cross cousins of both types, or as affines. Marriages into other corporations are roughly equal to internal marriages, but they are restricted to a limited number of groups.

Variations in bridewealth, while they do not match the marriage pattern, are consistent with it. In most corporate groups, there is general agreement as to what the bridewealth should be. One such group gave it as "two female camels and a pair of silver bracelets" (nāqatain wa suwār), for the daughters of agnates; another as four camels. Differences arise because a new link with agnates, previously known to be related patrilineally only, commands a higher bridewealth than a renewal, other things being equal. The number of animals given is more of a maximum than a fixed amount, many falling below it. There is also a general consensus that an initial marriage link with another corporation requires a large bridewealth of ten or more camels, and records confirm this. If it is followed by another marriage, the bridewealth drops by about a third, until, after a succession of reciprocal marriages has erected a kinship structure to span the two groups, the amount declines further until it becomes like the bridewealth of corporate parallel cousin marriage.

Property relations, marriage patterns, and variations in bridewealth are of a piece. In many instances, first patrilineal parallel cousin marriage is open competition for property. A man who thought he had been denied his proper inheritance by his guardian, his father's brother, demanded the latter's daughter in marriage, and deliberately defaulted on the bridewealth (naqs al-ḥaqq, lit. defective justice). Another man, a weakling shaikh, spoke of such marriage as tha'r, vengeance, albeit after he had suffered the indignity of his brother's son entering his tent and throwing his toga over his daughter — a conventional way of asserting the right forcefully; still enraged, after some time had elapsed, he swore he would compel his son to do the

same. Further, it is common for a man to remain demure while prep-
arations for the marriage of his first paternal parallel cousin are afoot,
only to appear in high dudgeon as the nuptials are about to begin,
and to deny (ḥajara) anyone's right to the bride except his own. It is
known in advance that this disturbance might arise, and provision is
made to buy off the recalcitrant cousin with some garments and a few
sheep.

All first paternal parallel cousin marriages are not as hostile as these.
In Fig. 2, the brothers A and F concurred in the marriages arranged
between their children. Nor is it true to say that such marriages are
invariably rooted in gain, greed or competition. They are often evidence of the will to co-operate, to allow one brother to rise above the
other, or because women want their chosen children to remain with
them. Hence the exchange marriage (tabādul), shown in Fig. 2, in
which the men received nothing; but bridewealth was promised for
both wives, giving them their separate rights in the common property
— since exchange marriage is illegal in Islam, the elder brother "put
five extra sheep on his son's wife, but they will never be given to her
father nor his brother".

In first or any other parallel cousin marriages the redistribution of
property between men is of small amounts, or none at all. But then
bridewealth is small, and men get only a part of it anyway. It gives
women rights, through property, in their relationships with men,
and puts men on a new footing with one another. Women and men
also have rights in each other as members of the same corporate group.
The alteration in their relationships is an addition of a new component
to these. And if the marriage breaks, the other relationships endure.
The bridewealth is small to match the dimension of change. By the
same token, where there has been neither affinity nor kinship before, a
commensurately greater number of animals must be proffered. A large
bridewealth is earnest that the people involved wish their relationships
to grow to the richness of the wealth put into it. Only when there are
no relationships is there no bridewealth — save where relationships are
those of chronic enmity.

The stress given to bridewealth, in this chapter, has been on its
power to generate relationships, between men and women separately
and collectively. There is little else available for the purpose. The
relationships are essential. Men meet in the pastures, or when they go
in search of straying animals, or go to market. They need access to the

resources of other groups, and the means must readily be available when it arises. The economy does not coerce groups to co-operate on a permanent basis. Each corporate group has the labour force to tend its animals and grow a crop. The products, however, are uniform throughout the land, and few in kind — barley, wool, milk products and meat. These cannot be used for regularised exchanges between people, since between groups they are not required on an ordered basis. But the need for maintaining production is regular, and it necessitates that men are free to call on others to provide them with the basic resources of production, at short notice and in unpredictable quantities. Affinity and kinship create the context in which these needs can be met. Marriage within a corporate group resolves the problems arising from the equal rights to resources, which frustrates some people who might suffer deficiencies, and others who have assets they cannot use. Marriage into other corporate groups resolves the problem of giving stability to the local economy. The prime mover, in this type of environment, is the right of access to the resources of others, and only by marriage can it be achieved and securely held. This is not to say that precedence is not given to affinity, and the relationships which issue from it, in other conditions, where various forms of differentiation might be marked; but it is suggested that the precedence given to social relationships, *per se*, among the bedouin, is intimately related not so much to the paucity of the economy, but to the recurring fluctuations in usable resources.

With parallel cousin marriage among the bedouin, and exogamy among the Nuer, both put into their perspectives, the two cases have been brought within the bounds of comparability. Evident differences exist, and the temptation is to put them down to major cultural dis-similarities between the two. The bedouin are Muslims, and, as such, they perforce include a statement about property transference in their marriage contracts. There would be more point to this declaration if property arrangements in marriage were uniform throughout Islam. They are not. On the contrary, the variety of these arrangements is impressive. It is not suggested that cultural differences are of no importance for comparative purposes, but to evoke them when confronted with the slightest difficulties, particularly in the general terms of a religious culture which subsumes a vast disparity of social conditions, is bound to be abortive. Data on Arabs is rarely used for comparison by specialists in other cultures.[1] This is unfortunate, since they afford such useful test cases for many hypotheses.

If maps were available showing the distribution of actual marriages for the bedouin and the Nuer, it is probable that the patterns would show similarities, especially with regard to the dispersal of connections. The reasons for the kind of dispersal, if not completely consistent in both cases, would be well within the bounds of comparability. But whatever comparisons might emerge, the fact remains that there is an exogamous group among the Nuer, while, among the bedouin, there is only a limited incest group. Or, to put the matter in question form, why do Nuer stop marrying as kinship intensifies in a locality, while the bedouin regard this kind of intensification as good reason for augmenting it? Part of the answer might lie in those very external links which make the marriage pattern of the Nuer comparable to that of the bedouin. If these have to be widely spread to deal with the contingencies of meeting with unrelated people, as a regular feature of their lives, it may well be that so much of their marriage capital, so to speak, has to be dispersed in this fashion that it would be a waste of a valuable asset to expend it within a local community. This, in turn, raises several issues, the most immediate, obviously, relating to the differences in the form of pastoralism. The bedouin occupy areas they call their homelands. They are notoriously foot loose within them, some tribal sections moving considerable distances seasonally. They are not compelled, however, to move into other territories, and join the groups occupying them. Their moves into other territories are temporary, mainly for two or three weeks of ploughing, and of a similar duration for harvesting. The Nuer, it would appear, not only mix with diverse people in their seasonal movements, but they leave one local group to join another with ease; local communities split up and the nuclei fuse with others to form new ones, without the constraint of residential or descent rules to give the composition of territorial units much stability. But these differing modes of pastoralism raise further issues related to economic differences. In Nuerland,

---

[1] Levi-Strauss (1949) in his massive writings on marriage neglects data on Arabs almost entirely. Were he to take it into account he would have to revise some of his hypotheses. Goody (1973; 1976, pp. 32, 104-110) suggests that the plough and dowry go together, and are spread throughout Eurasia. The other combination suggested is that hoe agriculture and bridewealth go together throughout Africa. Into which of these combinations do the people who are spread from Morocco to Iran fall? Among them are many communities which practise some form of bridewealth, and where the plough has long been used. Pitt-Rivers (1977) is one of the few non-Arab specialists to give data on Arabs his serious attention.

there is a greater evenness in the distribution of resources, there is greater differentiation in them, they occur in greater abundance, and there is greater reliability about them than there is in the land of the bedouin. These factors, taken together, obviously affect inheritance. Land is not vested in a corporation of agnates as securely among the Nuer as it is among the bedouin. Animal wealth is attached to individuals among the bedouin, despite the common ownership in which animals are sometimes held; among the Nuer, it would appear that herds of cattle are not divided into individual lots. Division of animal wealth on an individual basis, among the bedouin, makes bridewealth transactions intelligible. Among the Nuer, bridewealth transactions among kin, who own herds in common, might be practically impossible.

Acknowledgements

My wife and I worked together during the whole fieldwork period. Without her, much of the information presented would not have been gathered.

I wish to thank Dr. D. Turton for the many conversations we have enjoyed on some of the issues treated in this article.

Bibliography

Aswad, B. (1971). "Property Control and Social Strategies among Settlers on a Middle Eastern Plain". University of Michigan, Ann Arbor.
Barth, F. (1954). Father's brother's daughter's marriage in Kurdistan. *Southwestern Journal of Anthropology*, 10, 164-171.
Barth, F. (1973). Descent and marriage reconsidered. *In* "The Character of Kinship" (Ed. J. Goody). Cambridge University Press, London.
Cunnison, I. (1966). "Baggara Arabs". Clarendon Press, Oxford.
Epstein, L. M. (1942). "Marriage Laws in the Bible and the Talmud". Harvard University Press, Cambridge, Mass.
Evans-Pritchard, E. E. (1931). An alternative term for 'bride-price'. *Man*, 34, 36-39.
Evans-Pritchard, E. E. (1934). Social character of bridewealth with special reference to the Azande. *Man*, 34 194, 172-175.
Evans-Pritchard, E. E. (1940). "The Nuer". Clarendon Press, Oxford.
Evans-Pritchard, E. E. (1947). Bridewealth among the Nuer. *African Studies*. 6, 4, 81-88.
Evans-Pritchard, E. E. (1951). "Kinship and Marriage Among the Nuer". Clarendon Press, Oxford.
Fortes, M. (1949). "The Web of Kinship Among the Tallensi". Oxford University Press, London.

Fortes, M. (1962). Introduction. *In* "Marriage in Tribal Societies" (Ed. M. Fortes). Cambridge University Press, London.

Fortes, M. (1969). "Kinship and the Social Order". Routledge & Kegan Paul, London.

Fox, R. (1967). "Kinship and Marriage". Penguin Books, Harmondsworth.

Fyzee, A. A. A. (1949). "Outline of Muhammad Law". Oxford University Press, London.

Gluckman, M. (1950). Kinship and marriage among the Lozi of Northern Rhodesia and the Zulu of Natal. *In* "African Systems of Kinship and Marriage" (Eds. A. R. Radcliffe-Brown and D. Forde). Oxford University Press, London.

Goody, J. (1976). "Production and Reproduction". Cambridge University Press, London.

Goody, J. and Tambiah, S. J. (1973). "Bridewealth and Dowry". Cambridge University Press, London.

Granquist, H. (1931). "Marriage Conditions in a Palestinian Village", 2 vols. Societas Scientiarum Fennica, Helsingfors.

Harris, G. (1962). Taita bridewealth and affinal relationships. *In* "Marriage in Tribal Societies" (Ed. M. Fortes). Cambridge University Press, London.

Khuri, F. (1970). Parallel cousin marriage reconsidered. *Man* (N.S.), 4, 597-618.

La Fontaine, J. S. (1962). Gisu marriage and affinal relations. *In* "Marriage in Tribal Societies" (Ed. M. Fortes). Cambridge University Press, London.

Leach, E. R. (1957). Aspects of bridewealth and marriage stability among the Kachin and Lakher. *Man*, 57, 59.

Leach, E. R. (1976). "Culture and Communication". Cambridge University Press, London.

Levi-Strauss, C. (1949). "The Elementary Structures of Kinship". Eyre & Spottiswoode, London.

Lewis, I. M. (1962). "Marriage and the Family in Northern Somaliland". East African Institute of Social Research, East African Studies No. 15, Kampala.

Maher, V. (1974). "Women and Property in Morocco". Cambridge University Press, London.

Marx, E. (1967). "Bedouin of the Negev". Manchester University Press, Manchester.

Murphy, R. F. and Kasdan, L. (1959). The structure of parallel cousin marriage. *American Anthropologist*, 61, 17-29.

Peters, E. L. (1960). The proliferation of segments in the lineage of the Bedouin of Cyrenaica. *Journal of the Royal Anthropological Institute*, 90, 29-53.

Peters, E. L. (1963). Aspects of rank and status among Muslims in a Lebanese village. *In* "Mediterranean Countrymen" (Ed. J. Pitt-Rivers). Mouton, Paris.

Peters, E. L. (1965). Aspects of the family among the Bedouin of Cyrenaica. *In* "Comparative Family Systems" (Ed. M. F. Nimkoff). Houghton Mifflin, Boston.

Peters, E. L. (1976). Aspects of affinity in a Lebanese Maronite village. *In* "Mediterranean Family Structures" (Ed. J. G. Peristiany). Cambridge University Press, London.

Peters, E. L. (1978). The status of women in four Arab communities. *In* "Muslim Women" (Eds. N. Keddie and L. Beck). Harvard University Press, Cambridge, Mass.

Peters, S. M. (1952). A study of the bedouin (Cyrenaican) bait. B. Litt. thesis, Oxford University.

Pitt-Rivers, J. (1977). "The Fate of Shechem or the Politics of Sex". Cambridge University Press, London.

Rosenfeld, H. (1957). An analysis of marriage statistics for a Moslem and Christian Arab village. *International Archives of Ethnography*, 48, 1, 32-62.

Rosenfeld, H. (1958). Processes of structural change within the arab village extended family. *American Anthropologist*, 60, 6, 1127-1139.

Rosenfeld, H. (1960). On determinants of the status of Arab village women. *Man*, 60, 95, 1-5.

6 Bridewealth and the Control of Ambiguity in a Tswana Chiefdom

JOHN COMAROFF

I

In this chapter I intend to question an established orthodoxy pertaining to the study of marriage and its associated prestations. Loosely termed the "jural approach", this orthodoxy holds that "jural analysis . . . is a necessary preliminary to the understanding of [their] institutional concomitants and structural consequences" (Kuper, 1970, p. 466). For, whatever the problems attendant upon its universal definition or the interpretation of its structural implications, the conjugal process is seen ultimately to consist in the generation and exchange of recognised rights (Fortes, 1962, p. 3 ff.), notwithstanding their variability in comparative terms (Leach, 1955, *passim*). This common ground has frequently been noted; as Kuper (loc. cit.) states:

> Modern social anthropology has stressed the jural approach, whose starting point is the dictum that 'marriage is a bundle of rights'. Marriage is generally reduced, for purposes of anthropological analysis, to the transfer of a set of rights in a woman and the creation of new linked social statuses.

Even Needham (1971, p. 31), who has argued that the term covers too diverse a phenomenal field to constitute a single heuristic class, concedes that, minimally at least, "marriage" involves a *"contractual union of sexual statuses"* (my italics). There is, in short, no need to labour the conceptual debt owed, in this regard, to the discipline of western jurisprudence (cf. Roberts, 1977). This is especially marked in the attribution of meaning to marriage payments;[1] for example, while there is a growing literature on the economics — and, to a lesser extent, the semiotics — of bridewealth transfers, it is their jural aspect which has been accorded the status of "first principles". Thus generations of students have been nurtured on the truism that such movements of cattle, cash or whatever must initially be comprehended in terms of the reciprocal passage of legally sanctioned rights (see, e.g. Mitchell, 1963, p. 32).

There are, in particular, two related tenets which underpin the jural approach and which are of direct relevance to the present analysis. First, it is generally taken for granted that a clear *emic* distinction is made between approved and disapproved forms of mating; once the appropriate procedures of conjugal formation have been undertaken — it is assumed — a legally valid union indisputably exists and any ambiguity concerning its status is removed.[2] And, secondly, as Fortes (1962, p. 2) has expressed it, "it is marriage which generates affinal relationship and not vice versa".[3] The functional logic underlying this statement is itself significant:

> In formal terms, marriage is the bridge between the kinship side and the affinal side of the dichotomy that is *of necessity* built into the total genealogically defined domain of social relations which we find in *every* social system. It is a necessary corollary of the incest law, as Levi-Strauss has so cogently demonstrated (1949). In other words, there would be no point to marriage ceremonies and legal instruments if the pre-marital status of the spouses in relation to each other and to their relevant kin were already affinal in character (op. cit.; my italics).

---

[1] Since other contributors, e.g. Barnes and Turton, have noted the terminological problems associated with description of marriage transfers, it would be superfluous to do so again here. I use marriage "payment" and "prestation" interchangeably to convey the broad (and relatively ill-defined) class of material and symbolic exchanges which occur within the context of the conjugal process. Following more-or-less established usage (see, e.g. Goody, 1973), "bridewealth" refers to those prestations which are passed from a man and/or his kin to the kin of his mate.

[2] It is widely accepted that African marriage usually constitutes a process rather than an event, and that, in some societies, the status of a particular union may be equivocal during part of that process (see, e.g. Kuper, loc. cit.; Murray, 1976, p. 194). Nevertheless, to my knowledge at least, this observation has not been seen to challenge the more general assumption.

[3] Here Fortes is stating one — indeed, the most common (cf. Kuper, loc. cit., p. 466) — form of a linear view of the relationship between marriage and affinity, according to which the former is seen as causally prior to the latter. An alternative approach, expressed by Dumont (1957, p. 24) among others, reverses this priority: affinity, and the rules governing it, are seen to generate conjugality. While these opposed positions are grounded both in contrasting ethnographies and in differing views of the analytical relationship between marriage and structure (cf. e.g. Schneider, 1965), neither questions whether it is legitimate to take for granted that the connection between conjugality and affinity is a linear one.

These assertions might appear to have a sound empirical basis in cross-cultural terms. Nonetheless, I shall demonstrate that neither makes much sense of marriage arrangements among the Barolong boo Ratshidi (Tshidi), a consideration which is fundamental to the analysis of their bridewealth exchanges.

In respect of the first, it is true that the Tshidi do stress the formalities associated with the conjugal process in classifying and conceptualising heterosexual relationships. From this point of view, the jural approach would seem to reflect — if not to exhaust — indigenous perceptions. Indeed, available descriptions of Sotho-Tswana marriage emphasize these formalities almost exclusively, having invariably been presented within the established frame of reference alluded to above. Yet it is often difficult to ascertain whether a couple are in fact married — or, more generally, to determine the status of their bond. Furthermore, in spite of the stated distinction between conjugality and concubinage, it is impossible to tell them apart in many ordinary situations. Nor can all this be ascribed to the happy opposition between the "ideal" and the "real". For the ambiguities surrounding the creation and categorisation of heterosexual relationships are not regarded as anomalous, unfortunate or transient departures from the former. On the contrary, they are given explicit cultural recognition: the status of everyday unions is viewed, in the natural order of things, to be potentially equivocal and negotiable; and, it is important to stress, such recognition is most clearly expressed in the jural context *par excellence*, the customary courts. Here cases are regularly heard involving competitive efforts to construe more or less enduring bonds in terms of the repertoire of norms embodied in *mekgwa le melao ya Setswana* ("Tswana law and custom"). What is more, the dispute settlement agencies themselves operate with a markedly flexible and pragmatic notion of conjugal legitimacy. This, of course, would be largely precluded if the formation of marriage involved the unequivocal conferment of legal status and the elimination of ambiguity.[1]

Secondly, and closely related to these considerations, the relationship between marriage and affinity among the Tshidi cannot be reduced to a simple linear one; rather, they are bound up in a complex

[1] This is cogently demonstrated for the Kgatla (Tswana) by Roberts (1977). In noting the flexibility of indigenous norms associated with the creation of valid unions, Roberts, a lawyer, stresses the limited applicability of the concepts of western jurisprudence for analysing conjugal relations in this society.

dialectical process, of which the passage of bridewealth is an integral
aspect. Now it is arguable that the orthodox linear view (see p. 162,
f.n. 3), according to which marriage generates affinity, is derived
primarily from those African societies which share well elaborated
exogamic proscriptions. For it is these which appear to celebrate most
obviously the opposition between "the kinship side and the affinal side
of the dichotomy" to which Fortes refers (see, also 1969, p. 235 f.).
This dichotomy, however, is certainly not "of necessity" found in
"every social system". The Tshidi, who practise all forms of cousin
marriage (and previously allowed unions between half-siblings), do not
conform to the paradigm. As I have argued elsewhere[1] and shall return
to below, FBD marriage mediates the relationship between agnation
and affinity in such a way that it renders distorting any assumptions
founded upon a supposed dichotomy between these categories. It is
precisely this — as Barth (1973), Peters (1977; Chapter 5) and others
have shown — that makes it difficult to apply generalisations based on
African segmentary lineage systems to the analysis of Arab social
structures and affinal arrangements.[2] Under Tshidi conditions, as in
the Arab context (Murphy and Kasdan, 1959, 1967), one immediate
implication of patrilateral parallel cousin marriage is the absence of
structurally defined alliances based on ordered and nesting segmentary
oppositions. And, because ties of agnation, matrilaterality and affinity
constitute an interwoven myriad of overlapping relations which can
rarely be neatly segregated, the onus is always on the individual to
create and manage an effective social network (cf. Murphy, 1971,
p. 142 f., 220 for comparison with the Tuareg).

The Tshidi social universe, then, is intensely individualistic and
competitive, and marriage is a highly valued resource within it. As a
corollary, the potential negotiation of affinity and, *ipso facto*, of the conjugal bond, is a pervasive feature of the politics of everyday life.[3] In
these circumstances, the definition of marriage represents a problem of
meaning and its management; of the construction and control of social

[1] With Jean Comaroff (forthcoming).

[2] It is interesting here to refer back to Fortes's invocation of Levi-Strauss (1949), in which he
suggests that the dichotomy between kinship and affinity is a necessary corollary of incest rules.
As Barth implies (1973), there is good reason why "alliance theory" — like "lineage theory" — is
relatively silent on those systems characterised by FBD marriage; in such systems, the relationship
between marriage proscriptions, incest rules and the definition of structural units and their boundaries is distinctly problematic. (See also Leach, 1961, p. 27 for relevant criticism of Fortes's
views on incest rules).

[3] Of course, Fortes (ibid.) has himself called for analyses of the transactions associated with marriage, possibly in terms of game theory (see also Strathern, Chapter 2). It is clear, however, that this
is envisaged as an adjunct to jural analysis, since it is assumed *a priori* that the "game" will be played
according to fixed rules and agreed constraints which "emanate from the politico-jural domain".
The contrast between this view and the one suggested by the Tshidi data will become evident below.

reality. And bridewealth, in turn, is to be approached in such terms. Since the present essay is devoted to illuminating this most of it describes the cultural logic upon which Tshidi conjugal arrangements are predicated. Marriage payments are only considered towards the end, for it is central to my argument that their meaning remains impenetrable until the nature of marriage itself is reconsidered. I stress, too, that I am concerned here with the *lived-in* universe of the Tshidi, not with the constitutive principles which underlie their system or its ideological forms. The latter are detailed elsewhere (Comaroff and Roberts, forthcoming); it is specifically upon the manifest quality of social experience that this analysis concentrates.

II

In purely formal terms, Tshidi classify unions in terms of a continuum delineated by their duration and jural state.[1] At one extreme are those fleeting relationships in which cohabitation occurs intermittently over a brief period, with neither party making any further committment to the other. If the arrangement becomes an established liaison, it may be regarded as concubinage (*bonyatsi*).[2] In cases where a man and a woman reside together more permanently, but do not initiate any procedural formalities, they may be described as "living together" (*ba dula mmogo*). Once official negotiations are set in motion, however, the union is in the course of becoming a marriage (*nyalo*). And, at the other pole of the continuum, are those relationships which have passed through all the stages of the conjugal process, including the transfer of bridewealth (cf. Matthews, 1940).

Despite the existence of this continuum and the apparent precision with which it is ordered, everyday terminological usage does not distinguish clearly between the different forms of mating — it seems, rather, to obscure such distinctions. Thus, for example, in speaking of his *mosadi* ("woman"), a man may be referring to a wife, a concubine, or a partner in a transient affair. Similarly, *go nyala* (m), usually translated as "to marry", may be loosely used to label the creation of either an approved conjugal tie or a casual liaison. The Tshidi ascribe sharply contrasting material and jural implications to these respective types of linkage. But, in the context of everyday utterance, such contrasts

---

[1] Some of these background data on Tshidi marriage are also discussed — albeit with different purpose — in Comaroff and Comaroff (forthcoming).
[2] The vernacular terms entered in parentheses are the standard translations. However, I discuss these terms separately below.

remain latent. This lack of expressive clarity itself has a particular
semantic cogency: reminiscent of the Sorites paradox,[1] the very power
of these terms lies in their ambiguity, their capacity to obfuscate rather
than specify exclusive categories or statuses. I shall return to this later.
For the present it is enough merely to note the parallel existence of a
well ordered classificatory scheme and a set of inexact verbal forms to
describe the distinctions contained therein; and to stress that this is
closely linked to the fact that the standing of many unions is, in
practice, potentially open to competitive negotiation. Indeed, the
continuum itself encodes the range of possible constructions which an
individual may seek to impose upon a specific bond. In order to
demonstrate this, it is first necessary to consider the process whereby a
legitimate union is ostensibly established.

In theory, this process has five major elements which may, but
seldom do, occur in sequence as a relationship matures. It may begin
with a series of negotiations (*patlo*) between the kin of the prospective
husband and wife, which is concluded by the transfer of a gift
(*mokwele*), usually a sheep, from wife-takers to wife-givers. *Patlo*
deliberations are undertaken by those individuals who comprise the
effective ego-centred kindreds of the respective parents (cf. Kuper, loc.
cit., pp. 468, 479), not by agnatic units, and the passage of *mokwele* is
held to signify the committment of both partners and their kin to the
union. It also entitled the couple formally to cohabit at night in the
woman's homestead (*go ralala*). In the past, this stage continued for
several years, often developing into uxorilocal residence as children
were born. While Tshidi rarely observe *go ralala* formalities any
longer, the practice of temporary uxorilocality still occurs.

In the next stage of the process, the wife should be removed to a new
conjugal homestead, established by her spouse in his ward, and should
be allocated the wherewithal to care for her house. Among modern
Tshidi, this is typically effected with little ceremonial, although some
suggest that, formerly, it was preceded by meetings and accompanied
by feasting. Finally, bridewealth (*bogadi*) should be presented to the
woman's guardian at this point or sometime thereafter. It usually
comprises two to six head of cattle, may include small stock or cash,
and is not differentiated into uxorial and genetricial components
(cf. Parkin, Chapter 7). It is generally mobilised by the man himself,

---

[1] I am grateful to David Webster for alerting me to the writings of Crispin Wright (1976) on the
Sorites paradox and the semantics of ambiguous terms.

but his father and mother's brother may contribute. Where necessary, he may also raise part of the *bogadi* from that presented for his (cattle-linked) sister. Similarly, patterns of distribution are not elaborate: the wife's father will receive the animals and earmark them for her linked brother; if the former is dead, they will be integrated directly into the brother's herd, since these beasts should be used to look after her, especially in the event of divorce or widowhood.

Two features of Tshidi bridewealth arrangements must be stressed here. First, its amount and timing are never negotiated, both being entirely within the discretion of the husband and, where they are involved, his close kin. In fact, it is unseemly for the parties even to discuss these matters. And, secondly, it need not be presented at, or soon after, the establishment of a conjugal relationship (Matthews, 1940). Quite the reverse: most men delay the presentation at least until their children begin to marry. Again in formal terms, Tshidi associate *bogadi* with the legitimacy of unions: it unquestionably makes a valid marriage; and, theoretically, uxorial and genetricial rights are, in the usual African pattern, connected with the transfer. However, Tshidi themselves observe that such rules are mediated by the tendency to defer payment. I shall explore this observation further in a moment.

The final element in the creation of a legitimate union — public recognition — differs from the others in that it is not marked by a particular event. To some extent, of course, it is implicit in those others — e.g. *patlo* — as well as in the length of time which the relationship has endured. But this is not always so, since disagreements could, and do, arise out of competing interests. Unlike some Southern Bantu speaking peoples, the Tshidi have no elaborate *rites de passage* to express public acknowledgement of a new union, and few have church weddings. Moreover, while the transfer of *bogadi* usually occasions feasting and ritual, this frequently occurs late in the development cycle and serves, in practice, to define the conjugal union as an *outcome* of the relationship over time (see below). Nevertheless, the Tshidi courts, in deciding a marital dispute, set greatest store by the way in which the bond is regarded by kin and local groupings. This may be partly attributable to the fact that, given the tendency to defer *bogadi*, those formal incidents which may be held to signify recognition are often easily open to reconstruction.

Before expanding upon this, the major elements of the process may be summarised thus: (i) *patlo* negotiations; (ii) the transfer of *mok-wele*, possibly initiating the *go ralala* period; (iii) co-residence, ideally beginning uxorilocally, followed by the establishment of a permanent patrivirilocal household in which the couple assume conventional conjugal roles: (iv) the presentation of *bogadi*; and (v) public recognition. None of these elements, however, with the qualified exception of the passage of bridewealth, can actually define or legitimise a union beyond all doubt. Thus, for example *patlo* and *mokwele* are desirable, but not essential incidents. In the South African Tshidi capital of Mafikeng, they occur relatively infrequently: in 60 per cent of the domestic disputes in which a marriage was judged to exist (1969-70), one litigant argued unopposed that neither had taken place. But, more significantly, neither *patlo* nor *mokwele* is treated indigenously as having the capacity to create a marriage. Conversely, their absence does not prevent the parties or the courts from establishing the validity of one. Moreover, those concerned sometimes dispute whether *patlo* negotiations were ever expedited, or were successful; or whether a sheep passed between them was *mokwele* or a quite separate transaction. On the other hand, I have heard men, both in court and outside, agree that a cursory chat before a funeral or a public meeting had in fact been a *patlo* discussion; and that a funerary gift or a bottle of brandy consumed together was *mokwele*.

Similarly, co-residence is neither a necessary nor a sufficient feature of a legitimate union (cf. Murray, 1976, p. 194). Hence couples separated for lengthy periods, especially by the exigencies of migrant labour, may still be regarded as married. Furthermore, where a man and woman cohabit but live apart, a valid marriage may be construed as being in the process of formation: in a Mafikeng ward court, in 1970, a woman claimed this successfully on the ground that her father and "in-laws" had agreed to initiate the appropriate proceedings; her consent to sexual intercourse, she suggested, had been conditional upon this. At the same time, conjugal status is never conferred by virtue of co-residence alone: a couple may "just be living together". Even where a new marital household has apparently been created, the respective kin may later debate whether this had been done with their recognition. Nevertheless, the assumption of conventional conjugal roles clearly affects the manner in which a relationship is perceived by others.

In point of fact, as I have already implied, Tshidi agree that only two of the elements are of any real significance in defining a union: public recognition, especially on the part of kin and neighbours, and the passage of bridewealth.[1] It will be clear, however, that the former is seldom invoked unless a crisis arises, and even then may be divided. In other words, it is usually only a factor in deciding what a union *was* — and, in this respect, it is certainly an important one. But it cannot, of itself, represent a jural criterion in determining the nature of an ongoing bond. Everyday utterance, of course, does not clarify this either. Indeed, the absence of formal bridewealth negotiations, *rites de passage* and other expressive contexts[2] appears to suggest that the Tshidi actually avoid imposing public definition upon relationships, unless they are under threat of termination.

But what of bridewealth? As the Tshidi themselves suggest, its passage is the one non-negotiable incident in the conjugal process. And it is true that, once it is agreed to have happened, a union is certainly a marriage. Of course, the status of animals transferred between two men need not always be the subject of consensus: it may be argued that they were actually *mafisa* (loan cattle) or a voluntary *marebana* payment (compensation for seduction), rather than *bogadi*. But such disagreements seem rare; I know of only two cases. More significant in this respect is the tendency to defer the presentation. For, although non-payment does not necessarily mean that a couple will be regarded as living in concubinage, the definition of their bond and the rights entailed in it may be open to dispute until the transfer finally takes place. While this has not occurred — which could be for much of the duration of the union — it is possible both to assert or to deny its legitimacy. Positive claims invoke the (tacit) promise of eventual payment and other circumstantial evidence (see below); counter-claims exploit the definitional ambiguities inherent in conjugal formation and eschew the bridewealth debt and the affinal tie.

---

[1] Professor Schapera informs me that, in the Native Advisory Council (Bechuanaland Protectorate) in the 1940s, Tshidi members stressed this in discussions on marriage customs. It is hardly necessary to point out that Schapera's own writings on *bogadi* (e.g. 1938, 1940) provide an important source of comparative ethnography for the present account.

[2] One obvious context in which the creation of new statuses may be expressed is kinship terminology. However, since the pattern of close kin marriage generates a complex overlap of relational categories, the establishment of an affinal link often cannot be marked off exclusively in this way. In addition, the terms for affines (*bagwe*/*bagwagadi*) are used freely in address and reference in respect of a wide range of people — a fact which Tshidi explain by saying "it is because we all marry each other all the time". Thus, for example, in the ward case mentioned above, the woman called her "husband's" people *bagwe* before cohabitation occurred, since previous unions had linked their respective agnates.

Thus, among the Tshidi, for whom the status of a union is *potentially* negotiable for much of its career, the formal elements of the marriage process are not reducible to a jural device for the legitimisation of marriage. On the contrary, the cultural logic of this process — along with the indigenous proclivity, expedited by everyday linguistic usage, to avoid imposing public definition on ongoing relationships[1] — would appear to emphasize the perpetuation of ambiguity rather than its elimination. Now it is patent that, if justified, such a conclusion would indeed make the Tshidi case an embarassing one for the jural approach. This, in turn, raises the issue of the generation and transfer of marital rights. It is fundamental to the orthodoxy outlined earlier that the essence of African marriage lies in the processual exchange of these rights, their passage often being matched against the reciprocal movement of the appropriate prestation (Evans-Pritchard, 1951, p. 97; Kuper, 1970, pp. 476-7). If the Tshidi really do stress the perpetuation of ambiguity, however, this generalisation clearly could not apply to them; more generally, we would expect their perception of conjugality and its associated liabilities to be less straightforward or legalistic. A few examples confirm that this is in fact so.

Hence, for instance, when specifically questioned, Tshidi link *mokwele* to rights of sexual access. Yet this prestation is frequently not made; and, where it is, cohabitation usually precedes it. Moreover, a woman's father cannot sue in the event of such "illicit" relations unless a pregnancy results (Comaroff and Roberts, 1977). To complicate matters, impregnation may prompt a transfer, which opens room for subsequent debate over whether it was *mokwele* or (voluntarily paid) compensation. Even where *mokwele* is agreed to have passed, the proto-husband cannot actually expect recompense where the woman has intercourse with a lover; but then again, nor can her father if she is not impregnated. Informants sometimes suggest that rights to such

---

[1] This is not to say that Tshidi do not, or cannot, classify any ongoing relationships. Thus, for example, a small number are viewed as unlikely ever to become marriages; they are seen as being firmly situated at the informal end of the continuum. The emic stereotype of such relationships is provided by transient workers visiting the chiefdom, who often enter casual unions with no intention of sustaining them. Conversely, some bonds are indisputably seen as marriages, having lasted a long time. Most, however, occupy the middle ground between the two polarities for much of their duration, and it is upon these which I concentrate here. Ongoing casual relationships, in which the parties preserve only a limited commitment throughout, fall outside the ambit of the present analysis — a reservation which should be born in mind in the context of the general statements made below.

compensation, and to exclusive sexual control, only shift to her mate once that woman is installed in a conjugal household. But he may still be challenged by an "adulterer" to prove the existence of a marriage before any liability is conceded; and, until bridewealth is paid, this may be difficult to do. In short, rights in a woman's sexuality are not transmitted in a neatly prescribed order. The ambiguities surrounding them only disappear finally when *bogadi* changes hands (cf. Schapera, 1938, p. 139), but this may occur only long after she has become sexually inactive.

In the same vein, it is often asserted that bridewealth is necessary to affiliate the progeny of a union to the man's agnatic grouping as his heirs (cf. Schapera, 1938). Nevertheless, prior to its transfer, the co-residence of their mother and her mate implies that guardianship of the children passes effectively to him. He may in fact allocate them property in *inter vivos* devolution and, as they mature, incorporate them into domestic property and productive relations. While the couple live amicably, the children's integration into the man's segment and ward cannot be challenged without eliciting the rebuff that bridewealth will be presented in due course. In addition, if *bogadi* is later received for one of the daughters, it cannot automatically be appropriated by her mother's kin unless her father chooses this moment to offer them this in lieu of his own affinal obligations. The affiliation of children, then, is also not secured in a series of clear steps; it remains implicit at least until the transfer is made, or the parental relationship is threatened. The non-payment of *bogadi*, furthermore, does not invariably occasion a claim to these children by their mother's brothers. For this entails material support and a share in inheritance, a prospect which is not always savoured, particularly in poor families.

Despite the formal association between *bogadi* and affiliation of children, Tshidi courts in Mafikeng specifically do not treat this as an inflexible "rule of law": in 1969-70, two cases, in which bridewealth had not passed, ended with the man gaining control over the children.[1] During the same period, the court dismissed a claim by a litigant that

---

[1] The reasoning behind the decision was broadly the same in each case. Both relationships had broken down irrevocably; but the respective husbands had behaved properly throughout and made provision for their dependents. While it was not clear which of the formal incidents had occurred, the court accepted the husbands' versions that most had. It had no grounds, moreover, to doubt that they had intended to pay *bogadi*. Since the women were at fault, the chief upheld the plea that a marriage had existed in each instance, and that the children should be affiliated to their fathers' groupings.

he had paid *bogadi*. Despite his production of witnesses, the chief accepted the woman's father's plea that these had been *marebana* offered in private settlement. He observed that the man had not behaved as a husband, and that the relationship failed to conform to customary conjugal expectations (see below); a marriage, therefore, did not exist and the animals could not have been *bogadi*.

In the light of the Tshidi conceptualisation of the conjugal process, it is hardly surprising that right and prestation are not linked in a straightforward exchange relationship. Yet Tshidi do not differ from those African peoples who assert that an enduring union gives to a husband both uxorial and genetricial rights over his mate — and, to her, the legitimate expectation of material, social and judicial support. However, these entitlements are thought to be created as an intrinsic feature of the maturation of the relationship itself. Their mutual allocation is held to flow directly from the commitment of the relevant parties to each other, and hence to the union, not simply from its status. The Tshidi perspective may be summarised thus: the substance of a bond cannot be determined in advance of interaction by the mere passage of prestations or whatever; rather, the content of such interaction, over time, gives form to the relationship and the reciprocal expectations and entitlements which it will involve. Thus, while a union endures, the latter become manifest in the natural order of things. Only when it is threatened does the question of jural status and liability arise (see below). In other words, conjugality here is seen more as a state of becoming than a state of being. Consequently, most bonds are regarded as *potential* marriages as long as they persist without threat (see p. 170, f.n. 1). This goes some way in explaining why their status is never spontaneously subjected to classification; it would patently be antithetical to the emic conception of conjugal development.[1]

These various features — the irreducibility of the conjugal process to simple jural formulation, the ongoing negotiability of its component elements, the avoidance of definition and concomitant stress on terminological ambiguity, and the envisaged creation and exchange of rights as an intrinsic feature of the maturation of unions — would all

[1] Tshidi sometimes point out that this orientation corresponds neatly to their everyday world. For, as time passes, the elements of the marriage process generally emerge as a pragmatic condition of the development of the bond. For example, when children are born, the couple will require land and a homestead; as the necessary arrangements are made, some negotiations between kin are likely to occur and tacit recognition for the bond is usually expressed in some form.

appear to fit closely together. But they also raise a number of important questions: when does the definition of a bond become a matter of explicit concern? How can it be determined when it does? Why, indeed, does the process consist in a series of formal incidents when their jural significance is so limited? And, most fundamentally, why should there be such an emphasis on the perpetuation of ambiguity?

The answer to the first question lies in the severance of relationships. While a union is not threatened, there may be no perceived need for spontaneous definition. But the issue of status does become critical the moment one of the parties seeks to terminate it prior to its natural end. For the division of its product — children and accumulated material wealth — must then be organised. Such distributions follow a clear normative pattern today: where a marriage is agreed to have existed, the children are generally awarded to the husband, while a substantial share of the conjugal property is allocated to the wife. This award, which should reflect her contribution to the joint household, is also intended as a contribution to the care of any young children who remain with her until they return later to their father. If the union is designated as an informal one, however, the offspring join their mother's agnatic unit. The material dispensation is correspondingly smaller, being specifically to compensate for pregnancies and provide limited child support; it does not involve the division of a joint holding. The allocation of assets at the dissolution of a union, then, hinges directly upon the classification of its status. Where the interests of the couple converge, i.e. one wishes to retain the children while the other prefers to keep or gain property, the bond may dissolve by mutual consent, possibly accompanied by discussions between the relevant kin. Significantly, in these circumstances its definition is not considered; for here the devolution of its product is agreed. But where interests diverge, and assets cannot be amicably divided, the case will come to court as a formal divorce proceeding. In such disputes, debate invariably turns upon whether or not a formal marriage existed.

Two related points are worth making here. First, the distinction between situations of convergent and divergent interest demonstrates that, in contrast to English law, the way in which a Tshidi union is created does not necessarily decide the manner of its dissolution. Moreover, the mode of severance does not affect the remarriageability of the partners. This suggests, secondly, that marriage, in its legal aspect, is less a jural state than a jural potentiality: it provides a means for designating relationships, at their end, in order to organise the distribution of their product. Indeed, this is where the jurality of Tshidi marriage lies. It does not configure the form or substance of a relationship in advance, but represents a normative medium through which liability may be negotiated when conflicts of interest arise. This is itself a corollary of the indigenous notion that conjugality is a state of becoming.

This raises the question of why the conjugal process consists of a series of formal incidents where these have such limited jural moment. When individuals debate the status of unions — which, of course, happens largely in dispute settlement contexts — they never assume that legitimacy hinges upon any single incident/s, or that their occurrence is easily proven. Nevertheless, the elements of the process *are* utilised — but in a specific fashion, namely, as the components of a *gestalt* in terms of which *composite* images of the union may be drawn and evaluated. The closer a bond is made to conform to the total paradigm — by the careful construction of evidence of its recognition, of co-residence, of the assumption of conjugal roles, and so on — the likelier it is to be defined as a marriage; although counter-suits will naturally assert the opposite. Outcomes depend also on the court's estimation of fault: the rightful or wrongful actions of the respective parties are held to reflect the veracity of their constructions.[1] The elements themselves, then, comprise the normative repertoire through which the complexities of ongoing interaction may be reduced, debated and, when necessary, ordered with reference to the continuum of unions outlined above. It is in this sense that the continuum comprises a range of potential constructions which may be placed on most bonds.

This may indicate, further, why it is that, while Tshidi entertain a common conception of the formal conjugal process, everyday unions are not readily classified or easily defined. The former represents a cultural statement of normative code; the latter refers to the management of existing relations. I shall return to present case material which both illustrates this and, more broadly, explores the pragmatic logic of Tshidi marriage-type relationships and their negotiation. First, however, there remains the critical problem of

---

[1] I stress that Tshidi courts seem not to assume that the incidents of the conjugal process can ever be "objectively" proven. The late Chief Kebalepile Montshiwa emphasized this to me when he explained that they could not, for this reason, be used to discriminate the status of unions.

accounting for the pervasive stress on ambiguity itself. In order to do this it is necessary to extend the analytical focus to embrace some of the principles upon which Tshidi social and political arrangements are predicated.

III

Tshidi describe their society largely with reference to a hierarchy of politico-administrative groupings, in which all offices are embedded.[1] At the lowest level, each individual belongs to a household; two or more households with agnatically related heads form a local agnatic segment; a ward, in turn, typically comprises a few such segments, some of which are usually related. A number of wards — again, some with agnatically related heads — make up a section. And, finally, these sections together constitute the chiefdom. While they are not lineages, units at all but the highest levels have agnatic cores and are conceptualised in terms of a patrilineal ideology. This is sustained by the prevalent stress upon agnatic recruitment and inheritance, and patrivirilocal marriage.

The descent principle, which cuts across the politico-residential hierarchy, is expressed in much the same way among royalty and commoners. Agnatic groupings are not ordered in terms of a pervasive segmentary model, but by relative — and negotiable — genealogical distance from the individual currently recognised as its senior member (cf. Kuper, 1975a, p. 70). These do not occupy contiguous areas, rarely engage in common activities, are not sharply bounded, and, in the case of commoner ones, lack a strong corporate identity. Within them, however, local segments, composed of some close co-resident agnates (and possibly a few other kin), may emerge, albeit transiently, as small factions or as units in wider factional alliances.[2] But they are also characterised by intense internal competition for resources and rank. The Tshidi themselves see the lower order household as the main productive and property holding unit; yet here, too, the shared interest which binds its members is not enduring. For when the sons reach adulthood, rivalries over status and inheritance are expected to arise,

[1] Since descriptions of the structural arrangements of Tswana communities abound (e.g. Schapera, 1935, 1938; Kuper, 1975a), I restrict discussion here to those features which are directly significant in comprehending Tshidi marriage patterns.

[2] As this characterisation suggests, where agnation is not coupled with co-residence or any common action, it gradually lapses.

and often do. In fact, despite generalised ideological statements to the contrary, the explicit emic view is that agnation actually entails conflict. Thus, while related households may join forces for specific purposes, this is interpreted as an expression of temporarily coincident interest, not lasting aggregation. Indeed, most common action, at all levels, is comprehended in these terms.

As this suggests, the Tshidi entertain an emphatically individualistic conception of everyday social, political and economic enterprise. Not only is the social environment thought to be pervaded by intrigue and rivalry (cf. Schapera, 1963a, pp. 161, 169), but success within it is attributed directly to personal acumen in the management of resources and relationships. This orientation is expressed in the kinship order. Notwithstanding descent group affiliations, the effective reservoire of kin ties for any individual is provided by his kindred (*losika*). The *losika* is conceptualised in two ways. In formal terms, it is represented as a bilateral stock, which informants explain by invoking the phrase "we all marry each other"; and, as Kuper (1975a, p. 72) notes, it would actually have this composition if all unions were between kin. Yet, in the behavioural context, the *losika* is described as an ego-centred field. These perspectives are closely connected: cousin marriages serve to concentrate kinship linkages within the kindred and cause them to overlap; but, precisely because they do, the individual must necessarily relate to it as an ego-centred field.

For classificatory purposes, the *losika* is divisible into three categories: agnates (*ba ga etsho*), matrilateral kin (*ba ga etsho mogolo*) and affines (*bagwe/bagwagadi*), each being associated with generalised expectations. Thus close agnation is held to connote rivalry, matrilaterality to be supportive and privileged, and affinity to be easy and egalitarian. But, as I have stated, close kin unions cause these categories to overlap: a person will often describe his relationship to another by detailing a multiplicity of links of all three categories. It follows that such "multiple" bonds entail contradictory normative expectations which, from the actor's standpoint, cannot be sustained in behavioural terms. A multiple relationship, always potentially ambivalent, demands reduction, negotiation and management by those involved in it. This, in turn, reinforces the individuation of the kinship universe and, along with it, the ideology that underpins indigenous perceptions of conjugality and affinity.[1]

[1] As I noted earlier, this interconnection between agnatic principles of recruitment, their mediation

Leaving aside its domestic aspect, marriage is valued, here as elsewhere, for the kinds of relationships which may be organised around it. For, as already noted, Tshidi stress the supportive nature of affinal (and matrilateral) bonds — in sharp contrast to the bitter rivalries associated with agnatic ones. In addition to their easygoing and cooperative quality,[1] they are a potential source of substantial material exchanges, solidarity against agnatic opponents and alliance in wider political arenas. Typically, success and influence are attributed largely to the benefits gained through them. Indeed, Tshidi hold that affinal (and matrilateral) ties *must* — and do — have such a mutually beneficial character.[2] But this raises an obvious problem. For it appears to assume that men generally comply with the expectations associated with affinity. Yet informants are quick to observe that this cannot be taken for granted; individuals linked by a union frequently do not act towards each other in a manner appropriate to affines. The resolution of this paradox, as we shall see, lies partly in the dialectical relationship between marriage and affinity.

More immediately, however, the high political value placed upon marriage is clearly a corollary of structural arrangements — specifically, those underlying the absence of ordered segmentary alliances and bounded relational categories — which place the onus for social management squarely on the individual. Not only is this reflected in the individualistic ideology of the Tshidi; it is also expressed in their stress upon affinity as a critical sphere of investment, a major (potential) counter in the effort to control an inherently unstable, confused and possibly hostile universe. Consequently, apart from those who enter liaisons on grounds of affect alone (see below), Tshidi typically choose partners expressly by virtue of the person/s to whom they may thus gain privileged access, a decision greatly influenced by the wealth, power and personality of those concerned. Of

---

[1] For a more detailed description of these expectations, see Cohen and Comaroff (1976) and Comaroff and Comaroff (forthcoming).

[2] The complexities of multiple relationships do not affect this conception. Where agnatic and affinal or matrilateral ties coincide, the latter are held to take behavioural precedence; affinity always transforms a bond into one of alliance. Elsewhere (Comaroff and Comaroff, forthcoming) we have sought to explain the subtle logic of this emic proposition, which appears to contradict others concerning the nature of social relations (cf. Schapera, 1957, 1963b; Kuper, 1975a, b).

---

by close kin marriage, a stress on ego-centred modes of political alliance, and an ideology of individualism, has been described — with varying degrees of analytical clarity — in the Middle Eastern ethnographic literature.

course, these choices are mediated by circumstantial factors such as the
network of linkages in which an individual finds himself and his envisaged
goals — broadly, whether it is a bond of equality, patronage or clientage
which he seeks. Whatever the logic of specific decisions,[1] the essential
point here is that marriage and affinity entail acknowledged social
resources which people may attempt to exploit to a particular kind of
advantage: and, like most investments, they involve both risks and
returns. These, moreover, refer not only to the selection of spouses, but
also to the management of those relationships that emerge in the process.
For the formation of a union does not automatically ensure a successful
alliance (Barth, 1959, p. 40; Cohen and Comaroff, 1976); it simply
creates a context in which one might be negotiated. In practice, relations
between prospective affines vary widely. Sometimes the parties do actually
become committed to a mutually beneficial alliance. In other instances
they may try to "eat" each other, with the eventual result that either or
both eschew the bond, or that it persists as a markedly unequal one, often
to the growing dissatisfaction of the subordinate partner. Once more,
such particularities are not of direct concern at this juncture. What is,
though, is the implication that, in this competitive social environment,
the control of affinal linkages is as crucial as their creation and, for many,
much more problematic (*vide* the cases below). Now, while this cannot
itself explain the stress on ambiguity in Tshidi conjugal arrangements, it
certainly does prepare the ground. But there remains a missing analytical
link: this, I propose, is to be found in the relatively recent elimination of
plural marriage from a cultural context in which property and power
relations were — and still are — organised largely in terms of it.

It is self-evident that, with sufficient resources, a polygynist may
create a ramifying network of (potential) alliances as his career
progresses, thereby lessening his dependence on any one of them.
As important in this context, however, this also afforded him a
means of actually contriving the success of those alliances: because
the rules regulating wifely rank were decidedly vague (Comaroff,
1973; 1978), he could play off the agnates of his spouses with the
(often implicit) promise to recognise their respective sisters' sons as his
heir and successor. This is highly valued by Tshidi, and, where it
involved access to authority and/or wealth, might yield substantial
benefit. In addition, wifely status was readily negotiable. This derived

---

[1] This too is considered more fully in Comaroff and Comaroff (forthcoming).

from the fact that, formally, a woman could be affiliated to a conjugal household in several capacities: as a wife; as her *mmelegi*, usually a yZ, who accompanied her to help in domestic and nursing activities; as a *seantlo*, again a real or classificatory yZ, proffered as a child-bearer where the wife was barren; as a soror for a deceased spouse; as a widow or wife taken by a man, as levir, on behalf of his dead brother; and as a partner in a casual union. But, given the deferral of bridewealth, the practice of sororal polygyny and the tendency for a *mmelegi* to produce children by the household head, the status of any woman — like that of her modern counterpart — might be less than clear for much of the development cycle. This, as I have argued elsewhere,[1] also provided a polygynist considerable scope in manipulating his affinal alliances and, more generally, his social field.

It must be emphasized here that the management of marriage-type relationships has long been a ubiquitous feature of Tshidi politics at all levels (Comaroff, 1978). This is closely connected to the fact that all offices and statuses devolve ostensibly according to agnatic ranking principles which are predicated ultimately upon the ordering of houses within (polygynous) households.[2] Hence, if ascriptive reckonings are to be subverted, the protagonists *must* contest either the relative standing of these houses and, therefore, either the conjugal status or the wifely rank of the women who produced them.

Plural marriage, then, was not merely a requisite for career-minded men. At the ideological level, *qua* polygyny, it was also an essential component of the folk model in terms of which power relations were negotiated. But these two levels, the political and ideological, are inseparable in fact: because conjugal rank and status provided the established idiom of contestation, their manipulation was a necessary feature of ongoing competitive processes. The management of marriage, in other words, was an endemic feature of the prevailing political mode, not an anomalous or occasional side-effect of individual ambition.

Under these conditions, the elimination of plural marriage would be expected to have significant consequences. For Tshidi themselves, probably the most perceptible has been an increase in the perceived

[1]With S. A. Roberts (1977).
[2]This is such a familiar pattern in African contexts, and particularly in those with the house-property complex, that it is unnecessary to linger upon it here. I use the present tense since, as I shall show, this idiom continues to apply today despite the virtual elimination of plural marriage.

scarcity value of conjugality and affinity. The accumulation of individuated networks of alliance remains as important as ever — after all, the conditions which underlie this have not altered — yet a primary means of achieving it is closed to monogamists. It is not surprising, therefore, that there has been a growth in the incidence of serial monogamy, the establishment of a series of unions one at a time. Thus, for example, in two adjoining Mafikeng wards (pop. 373), one royal and one commoner, just two males over forty had entered only one union; 68 per cent had entered three or more.

This reflects an emergent strategy which is seen to allow an individual room to negotiate affinal relations to some advantage where plural marriage is not an available option. But it requires that he avoid either committing himself to a union until sure of its value, or perpetuating an unsuccessful one. For the cost of formal dissolution may be high and the longer a bond endures the more difficult it may be to terminate it out of court. Thus, typically, a man will enter a liaison as early as he can,[1] promising marriage if he must, and will explore its implications: while it appears to represent an adequate prospect, potentiating a worthwhile affinal alliance and/or emotional satisfaction, he may sustain his involvement. But, as is frequently the case, where he finds it unsatisfactory or believes he can do better, he will seek to withdraw at a judicious moment and construe it as an informal liaison. In this way, an individual may enter one, two or perhaps three relationships before making a more lasting committment.

This strategy, however, would obviously be precluded if every union were allowed to be formally designated at origin. Hence, in employing it, Tshidi have come to invoke the ambiguities implicit in their marital arrangements. But there has been an important change of focus: whereas before, competition over rank and status involved the manipulation of these ambiguities within the context of ongoing conjugal relations, it is now the conjugal bond itself that is the primary object of negotiation. Of course, as a pragmatic response to changing circumstance, serial monogamy represents a transformation within the paradigm of an established ideology, an ideology in terms of which the management of marriage is a fundamental element of political action.

---

[1] While it is impossible to discuss it here, this is also a means whereby men seek to pre-empt parental efforts to arrange their unions. The elimination of plural marriage has also led to the assumption of initiative in conjugal matters by the younger generation.

In this sense, polygyny persists in spite of the disappearance of (contemporaneous) plural marriage — which may explain why, for the Tshidi, the transformation does not constitute a radical departure from continuing practice.

In summary, then, while Tshidi conjugal arrangements have always offered scope for strategic negotiation, the stress on ambiguity in respect of the definition of unions, as it is manifest today, is a corollary of the emergence of serial monogamy as a feature of social regularity.[1] Its particular cultural expressions — some of which pre-date the transformation, others which do not — have already been spelled out: the avoidance of public classification and the semantic imprecision of relevant everyday terms; the definitional inconclusiveness of the incidents comprising the conjugal process; the conception of marriage as a jural potentiality in its legal sense and as a state of becoming — the outcome of a relationship over time — in its social dimension.

The following cases serve both to exemplify and draw together the various strands of my descriptive analysis.

> While in his early twenties, Kabo, a royal, brought Paulina, a commoner, to live at his cattlepost. Informal *patlo* negotiations were initiated but never completed; and no children were born to the union. Paulina, however, was allocated an arable field. Her wealthy father, Silas, had been on good terms with Kabo, and, when the liaison was established, they entered a cooperative farming enterprise together. At first, Kabo remained at the cattlepost with Paulina, visiting the capital rarely, although he had a (derelict) house in Kgosing, the chiefly ward. After some time, however, he began to participate in public affairs, leaving his mate and staying for ever longer periods in Kgosing, where he rebuilt his homestead. Soon he began to court Mmaseremo, his FFFBSSD. While no formal negotiations occurred on this occasion either, the couple occupied Kabo's house and produced three sons in rapid succession.

> Kabo let the bond with Paulina lapse. He and Silas discussed the matter, but little further was done about it. Kabo claimed, retrospectively, that there had been no marriage; the question of formal divorce did not arise, since there were few assets to disagree about. Silas, moreover, had little to gain from a dispute: he was profitting from the farming venture, which Kabo purposely sustained for another two years. For her part, Paulina soon entered another union, going off to live with her new partner — with whom her father also entered an agricul-

---

[1] It is impossible to discuss here the causes underlying the emergence of serial monogamy, save to note: (i) that it cannot be assumed to have occurred in an organised or systematically purposeful fashion; and (ii) that its roots probably lay also in exogenous factors, such as the transformation of domestic life generated by migrant labour and changes in female predicaments. As regards the latter, I take Singer's point (1973) that analyses of bridewealth arrangements have been excessively male-oriented. Regrettably, this essay does not escape the accusation; but, since it is addressed to other issues, the female perspective on Tshidi marriage payments must await separate treatment.

tural project. Kabo, too, encouraged this union. He had benefitted from the liaison and its amicable termination allowed him now to concentrate his marriage strategy in another direction.

In time, Kabo became a trusted adviser of the chief, his classificatory FBS. Mmaseremo's father, Keme, was also a powerful royal adviser and ward headman. He and Kabo became close allies; the former had no personal designs on the chiefship, but persuaded the latter to think of himself as a future incumbent. The union itself was successful for many years. Despite the absence of *patlo*, *mokwele* and *bogadi*, Kabo and Mmaseremo lived as husband and wife, and nobody questioned the status of their bond.

During the following eighteen years, Kabo gradually became a very influential public figure, and, when the chief died (childless), a faction supporting his succession quickly emerged. During the interregnum, however, relations between Kabo and Keme degenerated. Kabo began to cohabit with a junior royal, Tuelo, whose brothers had become his close allies and leading supporters. Keme discouraged this alliance, holding that Kabo's reputation would suffer when it became known that he had recruited inexperienced advisers. Kabo, in turn, accused Keme of senility (he certainly was very old and often ill). At first, Kabo sought to maintain both sets of alliances but, as Keme became more critical, decided that the support of Tuelo's agnates was more consequential.

Kabo wished to bring matters to a head: he transferred bridewealth for Mmaseremo and then indicated that he wanted to divorce her. The transfer was intended unequivocally to assert control over their three children; apart from the value placed upon a chief having sons, the youths were approaching marriageable age. But Mmaseremo, advised by her father, responded that she did not wish to be divorced. Keme then explained to Kabo the dangers of his strategy. The case would have to go to the local Commissioner, since there was no reigning chief, and he would not grant a divorce. For Mmaseremo had behaved impeccably and she would publicly forgive Kabo's "adultery". Thus he risked appearing either a fool or a miscreant. And his chances of becoming chief would suffer.

Kabo discussed this with some of his allies, including Tuelo's brothers. The consensus of advice was to leave the matter, at least until the succession was decided. Three months later, Kabo was designated as chief amidst murmurings about the trouble between him and his affines.

In contrast, the second case emanates from the everyday world of commoners, who had no direct interest in the affairs of the chiefdom or its constituent political arenas.

On leaving school, Modisa began to cohabit secretly with Motlalepula, a girl from a neighbouring ward, at her homestead. Later, when his married brother moved to his cattlepost, the couple occupied his vacant compound. Disagreement emerged afterwards as to whether *patlo* negotiations occurred. The two fathers and their respective kin certainly knew each other well, however, and discussed the union, to which nobody expressed objection.

The couple soon produced a son and Motlalepula settled happily in the ward.

Her father, James, enjoyed amicable and cooperative relations with Modisa, and once mediated successfully when he and his father quarrelled. After two years, however, Modisa went to work in Johannesburg. While he was away, Motlalepula slept with another man and had a daughter by him — much, it seems, to James's regret. Nevertheless, when Modisa returned, he took no action; some say he forgave Motlalepula. At this stage, too, he was devoting his energies to creating a business partnership with his distant agnate and friend, William. James was approached to join them, but refused, claiming that he lacked the means. Modisa later said that he had been irritated by this "excuse", as he had really needed James's help.

The business flourished, but Modisa's relations with Motlalepula and James deteriorated during this period. He now avoided cooperating with James, invoking his business committments, and tended increasingly to mention Motlalepula's unfaithfulness. She responded by asserting that he neglected "their" children and was cohabiting with another woman. At some point, Modisa decided to dissolve the union, and told William. Then, taking him as a witness, he complained to James that, while slandering his name, Motlalepula was again being unfaithful. He should therefore take her home now. James reacted angrily and immediately approached Modisa's father to intercede. The latter, however, supported his son, claiming that Motlalepula was merely Modisa's concubine (*nyatsi*); if he chose to leave her, and contributed to the cost of raising their child, little could be done. With relations degenerating rapidly, the case was reported to the ward headman.

At the hearing, Motlalepula claimed to be married to Modisa, who had neglected her. He should now be ordered to behave appropriately or to divorce her. (She did not state a preference for either alternative). In recounting the history of the union, she alleged that *patlo* negotiations and a *mokwele* transfer had occurred, and a conjugal home been created, which implied paternal and agnatic recognition. Modisa's forgiveness of her "adultery", his acceptance of her child, and the fact that they had indisputably lived as husband and wife were also stressed. Modisa, however, replied that Motlalepula had been his concubine. He challenged her, first, to identify those who had actually participated in *patlo* proceedings. Secondly, the so-called *mokwele*, a blanket, had been an unsolicited gift to her parents brought from the city. Thirdly, they had used his brother's compound, and never set up house independently. Finally, he had not sued Motlalepula's lover, as a husband would do, precisely because he was *not* her husband; and he had succoured the child out of sheer compassion. The headman was duly convinced and decided that Motlalepula was at fault; her other liaison had sparked off the conflict. He also agreed that no marriage existed. Modisa was ordered to pay two beasts in respect of the first child, and the couple were told to part.

Modisa soon set up house, again in his brother's homestead, with Anna, the woman with whom he had been accused of cohabiting. Her father, Mono, was a relatively wealthy farmer whom Modisa had long known and liked. Indeed, when asked whether his decision to court Anna was related to this, he answered: "yes . . . Mind you, she was a pretty girl. But I knew her father better." Modisa persuaded him to join the business and, with the additional capital, it grew markedly. Mono also loaned Modisa some *mafisa* cattle. Modisa's kin liked

Anna and believed that the union would last. She was given an arable field and also worked in the business. After two sons were born, the fathers consulted, and, claimed Modisa, *mokwele* changed hands.

When Mono fell sick, he asked Modisa to manage his herd, having no sons of his own. But he later accused Modisa of deliberate mismanagement. (Some informants explained this sudden transformation by asserting that Mono had been unbalanced by his illness.) At the same time, Anna complained about Modisa's behaviour towards her. According to him, however, her father was "poisoning" her, and she finally left him. But no legal proceedings followed. This seems attributable to Mono's desire to retain his grandsons; he lacked male heirs, and did not need the property that a divorce might bring Anna. Modisa, moreover, was afraid to pursue matters. He believed that Mono would readily turn to mystical evil and bribery if provoked any further. He thus returned Mono's stock and business capital, in spite of having to borrow heavily. He now wished to sever all contact with Anna and her father.

Although he cohabited with two women during the following year, Modisa lived with neither. He often joked that he was waiting for William's younger half-sister, Nonyane. This was a serious intention, however, and he later established a household for her. They have lived amicably since, except for one brief period, when she claimed that he had beaten and neglected her. William tried to intercede, as Modisa was upset by the allegation, which he denied vigorously. Indeed, he ascribed the incident to the influence of Nonyane's embittered friend, Laura, who had been deserted by her mate.

But Nonyane complained to the headman, who, on William's plea, heard the matter informally. In discussion, both Modisa and William stressed that the couple were married — although they later confessed (to me) the absence of *patlo*, *mokwele* or *bogadi*. At the time, in fact, it was not clear what determined the status of this union beyond the assertions of two men who saw themselves as affines. Nevertheless, the headman lectured Nonyane on *wifely* behaviour and the avoidance of bad company. Thus reprimanded, she returned to Modisa, and the incident seems quickly to have been forgotten as they produced a son and a daughter. Their union has continued to mature into a marriage. Furthermore, the partnership between Modisa and William has persisted, despite occasional set-backs, and they remain firm allies.

These examples emphasize that the individual ambitions and particular circumstances underlying the management of marriage may vary widely. Indeed, the contrasts of scale and purpose which marked the two careers might appear to justify a search for systematic covariation between socio-political categories, patterns of conjugal strategy and their respective causal-motivational bases. But this involves the danger of reifying precisely those categories which Tshidi strive to manipulate, as an expression of personal goals, in the course of conjugal management. A commoner competing for a ward headmanship, a migrant trying to maintain rural and urban households simultaneously, a businessman seeking greater success, or an individual who merely desires a satisfactory emotional relationship, may all invoke the ambiguities associated with the conjugal process in pursuing their private ends. Hence, notwithstanding their differing situations, Kabo and Modisa tried in much the same way to negotiate a series of bonds, and the equivocalities surrounding their status, so as to maximise affinal connections. In short, the sociological factors which motivate serial monogamy — and the concomitant tendency to manipulate heterosexual unions — may vary across the component sectors of Tshidi society; but the manipulation itself is ordered by a uniform logic.[1]

The cases, however, have further substantive implications. While both Kabo and Modisa contrived to withdraw from unions whose relative prospects came to appear unattractive, each lost control over his conjugal (and affinal) predicament at least once. Thus Kabo was out-manoeuvred into perpetuating his marriage with Mmaseremo by Keme, who thereby ensured his own continued political centrality.[2] Similarly, had Mono so wished, he could easily have sustained the bond between Anna and Modisa and his alliance with the latter. Modisa had certainly made a strong commitment to both, and Anna had seemed happy in her situation until her father subverted it. The initiative for negotiating conjugal relations, therefore, does not rest exclusively with wife-takers. Such activities occur in the context of the intersecting careers of the various parties involved in them; they are one element in a more embracing set of ongoing relations. Consequently, the constraints which circumscribe conjugal and affinal management derive primarily from the micro-processes of everyday life — and not simply from pre-scriptions which emanate from the politico-jural domain. The jural component of Tshidi marital arrangements, to re-iterate, exists as a potentiality; it resides in a classificatory scheme, of which "marriage" is just one class, that may be used when necessary to negotiate, debate and evaluate the status of a union.[3] The emergent designation, as I

---

[1] I am grateful to Pnina Werbner and Martin Southwold for compelling me to clarify the point that similar forms of conjugal management may have differing causal-motivational bases within a single society.

[2] After the succession, Keme convinced Kabo that, since the union could not be dissolved without great cost, he might as well make the best of things and revive their old alliance by recognising his father-in-law as his principal adviser. As a result, the influence of Tuelo's brothers diminished.

[3] The classificatory continuum is not seen to represent a hierarchy of moral worth, according to which unions approaching the "marriage" polarity are valued higher than others. Nor is it per-ceived as a metaphorical statement of what "ought" and "ought not" to be the state of everyday heterosexual relationships.

have indicated, encodes, *ex post facto*, the liabilities entailed in it.

This leads directly back to the two (jural) assumptions with which I began. It is clear by now that, outside of the classificatory scheme, Tshidi do not distinguish sharply between approved and disapproved unions; and that the establishment of a valid marriage is not a mechanistic jural process consisting of a number of definitive formal incidents. The two biographies provide sufficient demonstration of the inapplicability of this aspect of western jural precept to Tshidi practice.

As the cases also imply, however, the cultural and practical emphasis upon the negotiability of heterosexual bonds only makes sense in relation to a particular indigenous view of affinity. Just as there may be close interdependence between the genesis of a union and the anticipation of a worthwhile affinal link, so successful alliance and conjugality are seen by Tshidi to be *entailed* in one another: while a specific alliance yields the returns normally expected of affinity, the union concerned will be sustained and allowed to mature into a marriage.[1] (In fact, this occasionally occurs even where a couple have parted, for the fiction of conjugality may still rationalise an alliance).[2] Conversely, if that alliance is terminated by one or both parties, the union, *qua* marriage, is generally brought to an end as well. Sometimes the man and woman actually separate, as did Modisa and Anna; but, even where they do not, the former allies may withdraw their recognition from the bond, which thereby becomes construable only as a causal one. Of course, the partners themselves may persuade their respective kin to invest in an affinal link; and, here too, the interdependence of marriage and affinity is stressed. It is in this sense, therefore, that they are connected in a dialectical rather than a linear fashion. Neither is necessarily prior to, or can exist apart from, the other: the management of a conjugal-type relationship, its emergent definition and the negotiation of affinal alliance are reciprocally contitutive elements of a single process.

This, in turn, resolves the paradox noted earlier. While Tshidi hold

[1] Significantly, the perpetuation of the union between Kabo and Mmaseremo was explained to me in much these terms: both the union and the alliance continued only because Kabo came to realise (for whatever reason) that their relative value was the highest available to him at the time.

[2] There is a celebrated case of two Tshidi royals who asserted stridently that they were brothers-in-law, even though the couple concerned had long separated. This situation was usually explained by them as being temporary: the "wife" had to return to her natal home to help out in unfortunate circumstances. The men, moreover, sustained the fiction despite the fact that the woman had entered another liaison, a fact which was generally known.

that the content of affinal bonds always conforms to expectation, they also assert the impossibility of assuming that men's behaviour will accord with the relevant stated norms. Now these formulations, I suggest, are a culturally coded way of describing the dialectical connection between marriage and affinity. The mere fact of being brought into a relationship through the creation of a union will not, in the emic view, make men act as affines. In the same way as the substance of a social tie cannot be shaped by its jural designation alone, individuals do not, in Tshidi theory, behave as in-laws (or anything else for that matter) simply out of an urge to conform with normative expectations. Alliance is a matter of pragmatic action. Where it does develop and endure, the parties concerned are affines *a fortiori*, for the continued recognition of affinity axiomatically connotes the perpetuation of alliance. By contrast, the termination of alliance negates affinity. The latter thus implies a "successful" alliance. The closure of this prescriptive logic means that Tshidi must be correct: affinal bonds measure up to expectation since, where they do not, they are not likely to be — or to remain — affinal. And the indigenous observation of the frequency with which alliances are aborted is less a remark about social deviance than a recognition that men rarely commit themselves to relationships, or to act "as affines", until sure of their investment.

The two ontological assumptions, then, patently do not comprehend conjugal arrangements in this society. Consequently, the meaning of Tshidi marriage payments is not to be sought, in conformity with orthodox explanations, in the legitimisation of unions and their offspring, the formal recognition of new linked social statuses, or the mechanistic transfer of rights and liabilities.

V

Modern Tshidi ideas concerning the form and content of *bogadi* are not elaborate. Attempts to provoke exegeses on the semantics of the term meet with virtually no response, and little symbolic attention is devoted to the colour, sex, species, type or number[1] of animals involved. It is true that preferences in these matters may be elicited —

---

[1] There is one exception to this. Tshidi object strongly to *bogadi* being composed of seven animals, as this number has undesirable mystical connotations. It is avoided in other contexts as well.

e.g. for an even number of beasts; for the inclusion among them of at least one cow and its calf; for the exclusion of any male ones which have yet to be castrated; for cattle and sheep as against goats; and, in some cases, for money. But the insistence on these desirabilia varies in strength and substance between individuals — they are certainly not enjoined rules and are seldom even discussed. Overall, then, Tshidi appear to regard bridewealth in a most matter-of-fact fashion: in summary, it is an undifferentiated prestation, the composition and timing of which fall within the discretion of the giver; its mobilisation and distribution, similarly, are not hedged about by normative constraints or ritual prescriptions; it is not paid by instalment; and its presentation may or may not be accompanied by feasting and display.

Of course, Tshidi do associate bridewealth with uxorial and genetricial rights (see above). But the association is of a specific order: while the transfer is normally a sufficient condition for the recognition of these rights, it is never a necessary one for their creation — as it seems to be, for example, in the (paradigmatic) case of the Gusii (Mayer, 1950), and, indeed, must be wherever the prestation is portrayed as a jural requirement of a valid marriage. This underlines the problematic nature of the Tshidi pattern. If *bogadi* is to be explained, as is usual, with reference to the legitimisation of a union, it is difficult to understand why its passage is so long delayed, particularly when a promise of intent is neither made nor expected[1] and payment is not by instalment. On the other hand, if we seek to comprehend the norm of deferred transfer in terms of the cultural emphasis upon the avoidance of status definition, it becomes equally unclear why there should be any bridewealth arrangements at all.

I have demonstrated that the negotiation of conjugality and affinity is endemic to individual career management, and that the avoidance of status definition is an essential element of strategic activity in Tshidi politics at all levels. However, just as those relationships which are terminated prematurely demand (explicit or implicit) classification, so every bond must eventually be defined and located within the extant agnatic and territorial orders. Were the ambiguities never resolved,

---

[1] Where jural moment is attached to the *promise* of bridewealth — and, particularly, where such a promise is formally or symbolically tendered before the consummation of the marriage — the deferral of payment would make little difference in this respect. On the contrary, as many writers have pointed out, the perpetuation of debt may be a significant aspect of affinal relationship. In the Tshidi case, however, a statement of intent is never made; and, if a union is disputed, the debt is readily eschewed.

these orders — and the politico-administrative structure which they underpin — could not exist in their present form; for they are founded upon the ranking of co-resident houses and their descendants and, hence, on the status of the unions that produced them. More to the *explanatory* point, however, *the political logic of sustaining ambiguity lies in its ultimate removal.*

In order to illuminate this it is necessary to return to the dualistic conception of the social universe entertained by the Tshidi. On the one hand, they invariably assert that all statuses and groupings are articulated within the politico-administrative hierarchy; on the other, they share a vigorously ego-oriented perception of action, interaction and aggregation. From the etic perspective, these observations might appear to refer to principles of distinctly different levels, but they are held indigenously to be interdependent. For the hierarchy is seen as the context of all political and economic activity, the primary point of which is ultimately to gain influence over one or more of the offices and units embedded within it; this provides the established route to control over the allocation of land, the flow of public communication, property relations, the legal agencies and, perhaps, guardianships over persons and their property. At the same time, the hierarchy itself is thought to be generated and perpetuated by these very competitive processes. As a result of them, agnatic groupings divide and are reconstituted as higher order ones.[1] Structural elaboration, therefore, is construed as both a cause and an effect of individualistic enterprise. This may be circular, but it underscores a fundamental emic assumption: that, while everyday strategic action involves the constant and often covert manipulation of resources and social linkages, this action must be referred to relations of rank, status and power within the hierarchy if it is to gain public meaning and/or wider political currency.

Now this applies directly to the management of marriage. The avoidance of status definition is seen, quite explicitly, to facilitate the achievement of an advantageous conjugal and affinal predicament. But this implies the removal of ambiguity once such a state of affairs

---

[1] Thus, in the course of its development cycle, the household fragments in the wake of sibling rivalries and grows into a local agnatic segment. This grouping, however, is also the locus of agnatic competition over seniority and control, so that, as it develops, it will divide into related segments, which together comprise a ward. The fission and fusion of higher order units is seen to follow the same pattern. In each case, ecological and other external constraints ensure that the fragmenting units remain territorially and administratively contiguous.

has been contrived or no further effort is to be made to improve upon it. Individuals differ in their decisions as to when to precipitate this: some do so comparatively early in life and occasionally regret it afterwards; others treat the matter situationally, as Kabo did when he paid *bogadi* in respect of Mmaseremo in order to pre-empt the dissolution of the bond; and the majority wait until late in their careers before doing anything at all. The common denominator, however, is clear. The removal of ambiguity occurs at the point at which the parties are willing to close their options of potential negotiation; the juncture, that is, at which they perceive their conjugal arrangements to have run their course as political or social investments. This may be because they have failed to achieve any substantial alliance and are resigned to the fact or because they no longer have reason to doubt the utility of an existing one. But it may equally express other circumstantial and personal considerations. In any event, when this managerial denoue-ment has been reached, the union may be "fixed" in genealogical and structural space.[1]

This, nevertheless, does not explain why men do not simply leave their options open until they die. As I have noted, there are a number of circumstantial reasons which may persuade individuals to assert in public the status of a particular alliance and/or union. But even for the majority, who never find such cause, there is another practical consideration which affects almost every Tshidi: the final definition of the parental bond is a prerequisite for the initiation of the independent political careers of its progeny. For, if the latter are to engage in the manipulation of rank and relations, it follows that the status and structural location of their houses — and, therefore, of the union of their father and mother — provides a necessary base-line. For it encodes their own starting point in the social field. A man cannot begin to compete for position, or define alliances and oppositions, if some set of ordered linkages does not exist in the first place. This may explain why men so frequently transfer *bogadi* when their daughters are about to enter unions.[2] They tend to have reached middle-age by

[1] This does not mean that its status cannot later be disputed as descendants seek to change the pattern of genealogies. But such disputes generally involve the post-mortem *re*-definition of the union. As this suggests, it can only occur once that union has already been defined and genealogi-cally "fixed".

[2] It also explains why, on occasion, a son will tender *bogadi* in respect of his parents' union. Under these circumstances, the transfer is made either on behalf of a deceased father, or in the name of one who has failed to expedite matters for an unduly long time and no apparent reason. The intent is the same, however; to initiate an independent career.

then, so that their own conjugal careers are usually well set on their course; more specifically, though, this is also the point at which their sons are usually entering the political arena not only as proto-husbands, but also in the capacity of potential brothers-in-law. As one Tshidi informant, a commoner, suggested when reflecting upon his marital biography:

> I am a man of the world and I had three women. I just left the first and she took the daughter. I paid *mokwele* then and we lived together. But there was no *bogadi*. When her father took me to the *kgotla* (court) I said that we were not married; she was just a concubine. Her father said we were married, but the chief listened to me and I only got a fine for seduction. The second woman died after we had a son, also before I paid *bogadi*. And the third woman is still with me. But the time has come now for me to pay *bogadi* for both. All my children are becoming men of the world too. I have had a career. I can rest and they must now know where they come from, where they belong. Its the turn of the next generation. So I must pay *bogadi*. Then there will be a feast and I will kill a beast. Everyone will know my two houses and that I am a respected old man whose children come from this ward.

I have throughout referred to marriage as, among other things, the outcome of a relationship over time. It is the passage of bridewealth which marks this. For it finally resolves the question of status and locates the union and its offspring within the structural hierarchy. This is not the same as saying that it legitimises the children. The concept of legitimacy is not particularly important to modern Tshidi; for the absence of *bogadi* does not render children illegitimate, it merely locates them elsewhere in the structure of relations. To say that a union is, finally, a marriage — i.e. that it is a union "with bogadi" (*nyalo ka bogadi*) — is to close the option of its management and to place it in a wider context of formal relations and statuses (see p. 190, f.n. 1). The qualification *ka bogadi*, moreover, removes the linguistic vagueness implicit in the term *nyalo*.

It is important to stress that I am not suggesting that every union is the object of perpetual rivalry until such time as bridewealth is transferred. As I have noted repeatedly, many relationships are sustained without being competitively negotiated; and, certainly, the longer they last the less prone they become to redefinition. Moreover, it is clear that, where bonds are not negotiated, the conventional expectations associated with conjugality are given expression as a measure of the commitment of the partners. What I am suggesting, however, is that the logic of Tshidi marriage arrangements resides in their potential

ambiguity and the room they allow for construing everyday relationships. The meaning of bridewealth, in turn, derives from this. Its
deferral serves to perpetuate that ambiguity, just as its passage finally
resolves it — a resolution which, extrapolating emic concepts, articulates the complex universe of individual career management within
the ordered world of structured relations. In the terms of the observer,
it marks the convergence between political and formal alliance.

VI

The theoretical implications of the Tshidi ethnography for the
orthodox "jural approach" are as far-reaching as they are obvious.
Nevertheless, there are three possible ways in which they might
conceivably be denied: first, by asserting that this case is so singular as
to have limited general or comparative analytical significance;
secondly, by arguing that *bogadi* is not really bridewealth at all; and,
thirdly, by invoking that old panacea for challenged paradigms, social
change. None of these potential lines of argument, however, are particularly convincing.

Recent literature has begun increasingly to illuminate systems in
which the ambiguities surrounding conjugal and bridewealth
arrangements are simply too marked to be ignored, and too pervasive
to be set aside as transient or anomalous. The Southern African
context alone has produced three such studies. Thus Murray (1976,
1977) shows that, among the Sotho, the transfer of rights does not
occur in a jurally prescribed or mechanically ordered fashion, and the
status of unions also remains inconclusive for lengthy periods. While
not wishing to obscure the fact that there are important differences
between the Tshidi and Sotho, two of Murray's statements are significant for the similarities which they suggest:

> Conventional [jural] criteria for the definition of marriage are difficult to apply
> (1976, p. 104).

And,

> I do not wish to imply that the courts in Lesotho resolve disputes over the validity
> of marriage by referring to a *fixed jural principle* of this sort [i.e. the transfer of
> bridewealth]. For the problem of determining the validity of a particular union
> arises *retrospectively, in circumstances of conjugal dissociation* (1977, p. 86;
> my italics).

Roberts (1977) and Webster (forthcoming) report in similar vein of the Kgatla of Botswana and the Chopi of Mocambique respectively.

These ethnographies are not of consequence merely because they focus upon ambiguity and its control. There are, after all, other studies which reveal some of the same things, albeit less explicitly. What *is* especially interesting about them, though, is the fact that, in the case of these three societies, other accounts have been written from more orthodox perspectives. Most of these, however, have given the impression, wittingly or otherwise, that the conjugal process operates in an orderly and prescribed manner; the negotiability of heterosexual unions is simply not confronted. Clearly, here, it was methodological orientation, not ethnographic fact, which previously deprived us of analyses of the exercise and control of ambiguity and, hence, of the management of meaning in the conjugal context. And, as the Tshidi data implies, this must have a thoroughgoing effect upon the way in which the fundamentals of social and cultural order are to be understood and construed by the observer (cf. also Chapter 1).

It would be equally unsatisfactory to explain away the Tshidi case (not to mention the others) by arguing that *bogadi* does not in fact fall within the category generally described as "bridewealth". For this is tantamount to closing that category in a totally arbitrary fashion in order to include only those instances which might be accounted for by a stipulated methodological approach. This, of course, would reverse established procedure: explanatory paradigms are properly created in order to comprehend existing ranges of phenomena; the latter cannot simply be delineated on the *a priori* assumption of, and in such a way as to reinforce, the validity of the former. It is salutary, furthermore, that, when *bogadi* among Tswana is construed, in terms of the jural approach, as a token of validity and right, the propriety of its translation as "bridewealth" goes unquestioned.

Finally, while it may be true that modern Tshidi conjugal arrangements have emerged as a corollary of a series of political, economic and social transformations, this does not remove the need to explain their contemporary logic. Apart from all else, there is some evidence that similar kinds of conjugal management were occurring more than fifty years ago. But, of greater theoretical consequence, an ongoing system indisputably exists and, hence, requires descriptive analysis; the explanatory power of *any* paradigm lies in its ability to cope with this fact.

Rather than seeking ways to eschew the methodological significance of the Tshidi case, however, it would be more instructive to pursue its positive implications. This necessitates conceding that the *nature* — and, *ipso facto*, the jural nature — of heterosexual unions requires to be treated as problematic. In a literal sense, it also means that there can be no "jural approach", if this is taken narrowly to be predicated upon "the *dictum* that marriage *is* a bundle of rights" (Kuper, 1970, p. 466; my italics). For any such dictum forecloses the very object of study. This is not to deny that, in some societies, marriage may be a bundle of rights, or that its jurality may be unequivocally emphasized. But this simply reinforces the need to seek explanations for the patent variations in the constitutive nature of marriage and its associated prestations: why does the jural form of marriage (as well as its content) vary so markedly between societies? Why is it that, in some, marriage is a state of being and, in others, a state of becoming? How are we to account for the contrasting ways in which conjugal rights are held to be created? These are just a few of the comparative questions that are raised by the particularities of the Tshidi ethnography.

Bibliography

Barth, F. (1959). "Political Leadership Among Swat Pathans". Athlone Press, London.
Barth, F. (1973). Descent and marriage reconsidered. *In* "The Character of Kinship" (Ed. J. Goody). Cambridge University Press, London.
Cohen, A. P. and Comaroff, J. L. (1976). The management of meaning: on the phenomenology of political transactions. *In* "Transaction and Meaning" (Ed. B. Kapferer). A.S.A. Essays in Social Anthropology No. 1. Institute for the Study of Human Issues, Philadelphia.
Comaroff, J. L. (1973). Competition for office and political processes among the Barolong boo Ratshidi. Ph.D. thesis, University of London.
Comaroff, J. L. (1978). Rules and rulers: political processes in a Tswana chiefdom. *Man* (N.S.) 13, 1-20.
Comaroff, J. L. and Comaroff, J. The management of marriage in a Tswana chiefdom. *In* "Essays on African Marriage in Southern Africa" (Eds. E. J. Krige and J. L. Comaroff). Forthcoming.
Comaroff, J. L. and Roberts, S. A. (1977). Marriage and extra-marital sexuality: the dialectics of legal change among the Kgatla. *Journal of African Law*, 21, 1, 97-123.
Comaroff, J. L. and Roberts, S. A. "Rules and Processes: the cultural logic of dispute in an African context". Forthcoming.
Dumont, L. (1957). "Hierarchy and marriage alliance in South Indian kinship". Occasional Papers No. 12, Royal Anthropological Institute, London.
Evans-Pritchard, E. E. (1951). "Kinship and Marriage Among the Nuer". Clarendon Press, Oxford.
Fortes, M. (1962). Introduction. *In* "Marriage in Tribal Societies" (Ed. M. Fortes). Cambridge University Press, London.
Fortes, M. (1969). "Kinship and the Social Order". Routledge & Kegan Paul, London.
Goody, J. (1973). Bridewealth and dowry in Africa and Eurasia. *In* "Bridewealth and Dowry" (Eds. J. Goody and S. J. Tambiah). Cambridge University Press, London.

Kuper, A. (1970). The Kgalagari and the jural consequences of marriage. *Man* (N.S.), **5**, 3, 466-482.

Kuper, A. (1975a). The social structure of the Sotho-speaking peoples of Southern Africa. *Africa*, **45**, 1 and 2, 67-81 and 139-149.

Kuper, A. (1975b). Preferential marriage and polygyny among the Tswana. *In* "Studies in African Social Anthropology" (Eds. M. Fortes and S. Patterson). Academic Press, London.

Leach, E. R. (1955). Polyandry, inheritance and the definition of marriage. *Man*, **55**, 182-186.

Leach, E. R. (1961). "Rethinking Anthropology". Athlone Press, London.

Levi-Strauss, C. (1949). Les structures élémentaires de la parenté. Presses Universitaires de France, Paris.

Matthews, Z. K. (1940). Marriage customs among the Barolong. *Africa*, **13**, 1, 1-24.

Mayer, P. (1950). "Gusii bridewealth law and custom". Rhodes-Livingstone Papers No. 18.

Mitchell, J. C. (1963). Marriage, matriliny and social structure among the Yao of Southern Nyasaland. *In* "Family and Marriage" (Ed. J. Mogey). Brill, Leiden.

Murphy, R. F. (1971). "The Dialectics of Social Life". Basic Books, New York.

Murphy, R. F. and Kasdan, L. (1959). The structure of parallel cousin marriage. *American Anthropologist*, **61**, 17-29.

Murphy, R. F. and Kasdan, L. (1967). Agnation and endogamy: some further considerations. *Southwestern Journal of Anthropology*, **23**, 1-14.

Murray, C. (1976). Marital strategy in Lesotho; the redistribution of migrant earnings. *African Studies*, **35**, 2, 99-121.

Murray, C. (1977). High bridewealth, migrant labour and the position of women in Lesotho. *Journal of African Law*, **21**, 1, 79-96.

Needham, R. (1971). Remarks on the analysis of kinship and marriage. *In* "Rethinking Kinship and Marriage" (Ed. R. Needham). A.S.A. monographs No. 11. Tavistock, London.

Peters, E. L. (1977). Aspects of affinity in a Lebanese Maronite village. *In* "Mediterranean Family Structures" (Ed. J. Peristiany). Cambridge University Press, London.

Roberts, S. A. (1977). The Kgatla marriage: concepts of validity. *In* "Law and the Family in Africa" (Ed. S. A. Roberts). Mouton, The Hague.

Schapera, I. (1935). The social structure of the Tswana ward. *Bantu Studies*, **9**, 203-224.

Schapera, I. (1938). "A Handbook of Tswana Law and Custom". Oxford University Press for the International African Institute, London.

Schapera, I. (1940). "Married Life in an African Tribe". Faber, London.

Schapera, I. (1957). Marriage of near kin among the Tswana. *Africa*, **27**, 139-159.

Schapera, I. (1963a). Kinship and politics in Tswana history. *Journal of the Royal Anthropological Institute*, **93**, 2, 159-173.

Schapera, I. (1963b). Agnatic marriage in Tswana royal families. *In* "Studies in Kinship and Marriage" (Ed. I. Schapera). Occasional Papers No. 16, Royal Anthropological Institute, London.

Schneider, D. M. (1965). Some muddles in the models: or, how the system really works. *In* "The Relevance of Models for Social Anthropology" (Ed. M. Banton). A.S.A. Monographs No. 1. Tavistock, London.

Singer, A. (1973). Marriage payments and the exchange of people. *Man* (N.S.), **8**, 1, 80-92.

Webster, D. Divorce and ephemeral alliance among the Chopi. *In* "Essays on African Marriage in Southern Africa" (Eds. E. J. Krige and J. L. Comaroff). Forthcoming.

Wright, C. (1976). On the sorites paradox. *In* "Truth and Meaning: Essays in Semantics" (Eds. G. Evans and J. McDowell). Clarendon Press, Oxford.

Acknowledgements

Fieldwork among the Barolong boo Ratshidi (Tshidi) of the South Africa-Botswana borderland was conducted in 1969-70 and 1974-5. I am particularly indebted to Simon Roberts and Jean Comaroff, who have been closely involved in the development of many of the ideas expressed here, and wish also to acknowledge the helpful comment made on earlier drafts by Richard Werbner, David Webster, Martin Southwold and Nicholas Mahoney.

7 Kind Bridewealth and Hard Cash: Eventing a Structure

DAVID PARKIN

Let me begin with a commonplace statement: marriage payments in a culture constitute a system of exchange and, as such, provide channels of communication. Their dual nature — that they say things (i.e. are symbolic) as well as having a political and economic character — was clearly recognized by Radcliffe-Brown (1950, p. 54), who suggested that, among some African peoples, "the use of cattle in marriage payments has a significance which a transfer of other goods would not have". Thus, for example, these cattle may have a special, almost mystical, quality which mediates relations between the living and dead.

The most recent example of this symbolic, and therefore ideologically autonomous, aspect of marriage payments is provided by Sansom (1976). He shows how the Pedi of South Africa try to joke off wealth differences in their society through the terms they use to describe bridewealth. They are quite happy to talk about these differences privately to each other but, in public, place newly-weds on an equal footing by referring to the prestations which secured their marriages as consisting only of animals of a restricted range and proportion, thus "hiding" the wide variations in their cash value.

Of course, the Pedi are not really fooled by such etiquette in honour of egalitarianism. But, as we well know, politeness formulas, even when recognized as such, can mollify, if not eliminate, the otherwise exacerbating expression of wealth differences. Sansom has demonstrated that the Pedi can do with words what the Ndembu have been described as doing with both non-verbal as well as verbal symbols: i.e. reconcile divisions while allowing them to continue. While subscribing myself to a view of custom as sometimes masking the development of inequality by communicating the opposite (Parkin, 1972), I think that there is also a broader and more fundamental sense in which we can analyze the message-carrying potential of marriage payments.

In order to introduce this it is necessary to return briefly to the debate between Gluckman (1950) on the one hand and Leach (1961, pp. 114-123) and Fallers (1957) on the other regarding the relationship between the rights in women acquired through marriage payments and the frequency of divorce. As this debate is well known, I do not need to provide details; the two sides of the argument may be stated as propositions.

> Gluckman posits this formula: Strong fa.right:weak fa.right :: rare:frequent divorce :: high:low bridewealth.

> Leach and Fallers put theirs thus: Weak B-Z tie:strong B-Z tie :: rare:frequent divorce :: indeterminate value of bridewealth.

We know that both are partial truths, but this is not what concerns me. For I think that the dispute has concentrated too narrowly on the question of whether or not the frequency of divorce varies with (a) the value of bridewealth, and (b) the strength of either agnatic/uterine or affinal ties. I would rather emphasize the simple fact that together these formulas contrast the roles of men as fathers, brothers and husbands with those of women as mothers, sisters and wives, and ask what it is that the marriage payments "say" about these opposed male and female roles (cf. Rivière, 1971). In other words, does the marriage payment in a particular culture clearly differentiate these contrasting roles available to men and women, and what particular priority does it order among them? Or does it abridge the roles, serving thereby to blur their potential distinctiveness? Can we even talk loosely of a "grammar" of different marriage payments in neighbouring but superficially distinct cultures, a grammar which governs the extent to which the roles are emically distinct?

In this chapter I want to suggest that, by examining the semantics as well as economic composition of marriage payments, it becomes possible to reduce a range of marriage, family and even inheritance patterns dispersed throughout an area to some common logical features. I do not dispute the view that institutional variation might have arisen at least partially as a response to changing economic forces, but also suggest that the restricted ranges within which such institutional variations seem to occur represent different transformations of a particular paradigm of concepts.

The area with which I shall be concerned is that of coastal eastern Kenya, and includes some peoples who regard themselves as broadly similar to, and yet slightly distinct from, each other and who are in fact culturally and linguistically very close. They are nowadays called the Mijikenda, the most numerous group of which is the Giriama. I also draw comparisons and contrasts with an unrelated people in western Kenya, the Luo, among whom I have also worked. I begin by introducing the Luo and Giriama.

The Luo are Nilotic speakers who are distant cultural cousins of the Nuer and, in Gluckman's terms, are similar to the Zulu. They have a nesting system of segmentary patrilineages. By contrast, the Giriama have dispersed patrilineages which are not linked genealogically in terms of a segmentary hierarchy. Their lineages undergo a process of what Fox has called "drift" rather than "perpetual" segmentation (1967, pp. 128-130). There are overarching clans and sub-clans but no genealogical links between these and lower order lineages. These lineages can be visualized as parallel to each other, rather than arranged in a segmentary pyramid. As regards Gluckman's hypothesis regarding the low divorce of the Zulu, however, the Giriama share with the Luo some common characteristics. Both have a low divorce rate, a polygynous house-property complex, valuable bridewealth, and what Gluckman calls a system of marked "father right". But there are also some differences: e.g. the Giriama have widow inheritance rather than the levirate, and do not have woman-to-woman marriage.

So what is there of contrast to draw from a comparison of Giriama with Luo? The striking difference lies in the way these two peoples divide up their marriage payments — terminologically, conceptually, and organizationally. This contrast is of fundamental importance beneath the surface similarities. Thus the Luo make no formal terminological distinction between uxorial (i.e. sexual and domestic) and childbirth payments when they calculate, negotiate and hand over bridewealth. There are many other ways in which some cattle were, and to a much lesser extent are, earmarked for different agnates and non-agnates of the bride (Evans-Pritchard, 1965, pp. 238-40). The

mainly cash payments of many modern Luo, especially those working
in town, have reduced still further these allocations, though a few
remain. But none of the different terms for earmarked cattle or cash,
nor any of the alternative terms for bridewealth itself (e.g. *dhok* or
pesa keny; *nywombo*; the verb *-nywuomo*; and, according to Evans-
Pritchard, 1965, p. 238, *miloha*), distinguishes a special childbirth
payment from within the total amount received.

This is not to say that Luo do not conceptualize some distinction of
this kind. For, if a wife is divorced, the husband keeps the children and
recovers his bridewealth (from 10 to 15 cattle, mostly heifers, or the
cash equivalent) less a customarily agreed deduction for the children;
three cattle for a son and two for a daughter, or the monetary equivalent. But there is no such verbal distinction, either of an animal or of
an amount of cash, that differentiates his genetricial from uxorial
rights at the time of the marriage. In other words, the lexicon of Luo
marriage payments tends to abridge these rights, distinguishing them
only on a *post facto* basis when the marriage has been terminated.

Among the Giriama quite the opposite applies. The uxorial
payment, denoted by the term which I have elsewhere translated as
bridewealth (*(ma) hunda*; 1972, p. 68), consisted in the early mid-
sixties either of: (a) up to 15 heifers, or fewer and the equivalent in
cash, in pastoralist western Giriamaland; or (b) over Shs 1500/- cash in
the non-cattle coconut palm-belt area of eastern Giriamaland. The
childbirth payment, on the other hand, is normally called "the bull"
(*ndzau*), and it is only this which is regarded as securing genetricial
rights in a wife. In the cattle area, a bullock may actually be transacted. It is worth about a half of a heifer which, in turn, was worth
about Shs 150/- in the mid-sixties. Non-pastoralist Giriama provide
the equivalent of this in palm wine, called *uchi wa munazi* (the
"honey" of the coconut tree). Among both, therefore, the value of the
childbirth payment is only a fraction of that of the uxorial payment.
Let me focus here for a moment on the non-cattle area.

The palm wine making up the childbirth payment, "the bull", is
only presented to the bride's kin after all, or nearly all, of the uxorial
one (*mahunda*) has been presented. The palm wine itself has to be
drunk within 24 hours, and preferably sooner, otherwise it loses its
sweetness and becomes bitter; and so, at this stage, it is only an
inexpensive consumer good validating the marriage. Once the palm
wine has been presented to the bride's kin and consumed, however, the

husband and his agnates up to a remarkably wide range have indisputable genetricial rights in the bride. But there might in fact have been a delay of up to five months during which the husband's father has been making the bulk of the valuable uxorial payment, and during which, normally, the husband and wife have been living together. By refusing to accept the palm wine, i.e. the childbirth payment, until most or all of the uxorial payment is transferred, the bride's father can exert pressure on her husband's father to ensure that it is actually paid in full. Thus, in effect, it is only by means of the uxorial as well as the childbirth payment that the husband gets genetricial rights.

This delaying tactic on the part of the bride's father preserves the named and much talked-about distinction between the two kinds of transfer. Paradoxically, though the childbirth payment is itself of negligible economic value, it is the bride's father's trump card, and as such should ensure that he receives the valuable uxorial one. If the husband's father (or the husband himself for a second wife and in other exceptional circumstances) does not make the latter within the agreed period, and so gets no chance to present his palm wine, he is likely to lose his bride and even any future child should she be pregnant. For, during the waiting period before full completion of payment, there are other suitors ready to step in and take the girl. Nor is the father at all adverse to incorporating his daughter's child, especially if she proves to be a girl, to be raised as a member of his own family. Husbands, or more normally their fathers or guardians for first marriages, have therefore to raise the cash quickly, if necessary by selling their land and trees, their main source of livelihood. Let me emphasize, however, that Giriama husbands do usually make the uxorial payment on time, and obtain genetricial as well as uxorial rights when they present the "bull". Thereafter, the couple is unlikely to separate or divorce.

When we look back over time, we find that the two kinds of payment exist in a dynamic relationship with each other. Many years before palms replaced cattle in eastern Giriamaland, the childbirth transfer was presented to the girl's family early on in a more protracted period of uxorial payment. Even until 1956, and certainly when these payments were, respectively, 14 heifers or the equivalent in goats (10 goats = 1 heifer) and a bull or liquor, the childbirth payment would normally be given after about a third to a half of the uxorial one had been made.

In other words, as the years have passed, the childbirth payment has varied as to the timing of its presentation during the wider span of the uxorial transfer: once it was early on, now it is right at the end. The moment of its passage is limited by the temporal range of the uxorial payment, but moves within this range. As this suggests, the distinction between them has persisted, despite changes in the composition of both. Indeed, it seems that, in the course of the changes that each has undergone, they have been in a kind of dialectic relationship.

Somewhat arbitrarily, then, we can distinguish two eras in eastern Giriamaland: an earlier period, when exchanges were mainly in livestock, with the childbirth one (consisting of either a bullock or of millet beer) made early on in a protracted uxorial payment; and the present time, in which they comprise mostly cash, with the "bull" (consisting of palm wine and/or cash) being presented at the end of a much shorter process of uxorial transfers. In other words, the shift from livestock to cash has corresponded, first, with a shortening of the temporal span of uxorial payments and, secondly, with an inversion of the moment of childbirth payments within that span, from near the beginning to near its completion. This may be summarized as follows:

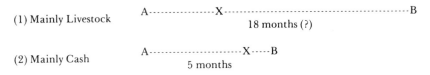

(1) Mainly Livestock   A---------------X-----------------------------------B
                                        18 months (?)

(2) Mainly Cash   A--------------------X-----B
                                5 months

A — Point at which uxorial payment is initiated
B — Point at which uxorial payment is completed
··· — Temporal span over which uxorial payments are made
X — Point at which childbirth payment is made

Note: The same key is used in the diagrams below.

At this point, it should simply be noted that, in the cattle zone of western Giriamaland, the uxorial payment continues today to consist mainly of livestock and the childbirth payment also occurs earlier rather than later in the period of uxorial payment (as represented in (1) above). The shift I have depicted is therefore represented ecologically in the current era as well as historically.

In order to examine further this dynamic interrelationship of the two kinds of named and timed payments, let me now turn to a few of the other Mijikenda peoples who neighbour the Giriama, who speak a variety of the same language and have very similar customs. These other groupings are the Chonyi, Jibana, and the non-cattle Rabai. I shall refer to them collectively as the "Chonyi" for simplicity, since in terms of my present analysis, they show essential similarities. Among the Chonyi, the uxorial payment (also called *mahunda*) is even higher than among the Giriama, ranging between Shs 2000/- and 3000/-. It is *exclusively* cash, allegedly because these people "are frightened of cattle", and is presented almost *immediately* once the groom, his father, the bride and her father agree to the marriage. This immediate transfer includes also, of course, payment of the palm wine (here termed *uchi witsi*, "fresh honey (wine)") for the genetricial rights, which has the same monetary value as among the Giriama. The distinction between the uxorial and childbirth payments is certainly conceptualized by the Chonyi and, at the marriage ceremony where the latter is distributed, may be explicitly talked about. But it is clearly not a distinction with which people normally need be actively concerned: neither the husband nor his father-in-law ever have cause to worry about it, since their marriage exchanges, and the bargain they seek each to effect, are completed on the spot. Hence we may characterize the relationship between uxorial and childbirth payments thus:

$$\text{(3) Exclusively Cash} \qquad \frac{\text{A/B}}{\text{immediate}} \; X$$

What is to explain this difference in the relative timing of payments between the eastern non-cattle Giriama, who use mainly cash, and the Chonyi who also use it? That is to say, why do these Giriama make childbirth payments at the end of the period of uxorial payment when, among the Chonyi, both are transferred together without delay?

This contrast corresponds with another difference between the two groups in respect of the distinction made between uxorial and childbirth payments. At divorce, the Giriama[1] preserve this distinction by (a) returning *both* payments to the husband only if the marriage has

---

[1] As do the Kambe, Kauma, and Ribe, three other Mijikenda sub-groups.

not produced children, but (b) returning only the more valuable uxorial payment if the wife did produce children, in whom the husband retains full rights. By means of this distinction, the Giriama emphasize quite unambiguously the role of a wife as either a producer or non-producer of her husband's children. In contrast, the Chonyi return both the uxorial and childbirth payments at divorce, regardless of whether or not the wife produced children. This implies that her role is ambiguous: it is as if there is a tacit uncertainty as to where the woman's children belong. For the reimbursement of the childbirth payment to the husband, even when his wife has produced children, questions whether he had really paid for them. Legally, the children do belong to him, and courts rule accordingly. But, alongside this formal legal definition, the implicit uncertainty regarding filiation among the Chonyi gives rise to yet another factor contrasting them with the Giriama.

While it seems that, due to a high rate of polygyny, there is a scarcity of marriageable women among the Giriama, this scarcity is even greater among the Chonyi. Although they also practise polygyny, this is due additionally to the fact that some of their women emigrate to Mombasa, where they brew beer and may engage in something akin to prostitution. In the course of this, they pay back their own bridewealth and so become independent women of assumed Muslim Swahili status, perhaps formally marrying "Swahili" men. This tendency is much less common among the Giriama, but there are some cases, a development which Giriama men blame on Chonyi influence.

Because marriageable women are so scarce among the Chonyi, rights in them have to be paid for quickly; that is, genetricial and uxorial rights together. The competition for wives is so great that the practice has developed whereby men "bid" for wives already married to others who have made both uxorial and childbirth payments for them. In some cases, such women have been married long enough to have had children but are unhappy in the marriage. A suitor may bid for another man's wife by approaching both the woman and her father, offering her the promise of a richer and more comfortable life and him a higher uxorial payment, as well as the standard childbirth one of palm wine. If the wife accepts the suitor, and her father the higher offer, the latter returns the original uxorial and childbirth payments, *without* any deductions, to the (former) husband. The woman's children stay with that husband if they are old enough, or return to him eventually where they are too young to leave the mother immediately. Complications leading to disputes can occur if she switches husbands early on in a marriage and is subsequently found to be pregnant by the first, who may, when the child is born, claim in a government court that the child is his.

If a woman does eventually liberate herself by becoming "Swahili" and returning to the husband the marriage payments made for her, she never formally regains her children. But she usually arranges, as people say, "to meet them secretly on pathways", an open admission by men as well as women of the *de facto* uncertainty of filiation rights.

The non-cattle Giriama blame the Chonyi for having introduced similar cases among themselves of wife-bidding and wife-manumission through her return of the respective payments. In fact, such imitation has to be seen also in the context of a convergence to a common ecology, i.e. of palm trees, which encourages the use of cash rather than cattle. Corresponding to this is an apparently decreasing rate of intermarriage between the western cattle and eastern non-cattle Giriama, and increasing intermarriage between the latter and the Chonyi. Thus, both over time and over contrasting ecological zones, we have a progression:

A	B	C
modern cattle Giriama/pre-palm belt cattle Giriama	modern non-cattle Giriama	non-cattle Chonyi
Infrequent separation and divorce	Infrequent separation and divorce but moving towards (C)	Frequent separation and divorce

A, B, and C, therefore, represent stages of a progression towards the increased use of cash in marriage payments corresponding with an increase in separation and divorce.

From this it might be inferred that a switch in marriage payments from mainly livestock to mainly cash is likely to bring about a significant increase in the separation and divorce rates. But, if we turn back to the early example of the Luo, we find an immediate exception to this generalization. Their divorce and separation rates are still low even though, nowadays, their marriage payments are predominantly

cash.[1] The shift from the use of valuable amounts of livestock to the
monetary equivalent does not, therefore, alone account for a corresponding shift from low to high divorce/separation. What other factor
may be involved? I suggest that a second variable is the named
distinction, or lack of it, between the uxorial and the childbirth
payments. The Luo, it will be remembered, make no such distinction
when they make their marriage payment. The others — i.e. cattle and
non-cattle Giriama and the non-cattle Chonyi — all do.

In summary, then, I suggest that there are two main variables which
determine the question of whether wives stay with husbands: one is the
presence or absence of a named distinction between uxorial and childbirth payments; the other lies in the material content, cash or livestock, of these payments. In dealing with the latter variable first, I
shall examine the special qualities that characterize livestock and cash
respectively.

1. *Livestock versus cash*

The distinctive feature of the mainly livestock marriage payments of
the Giriama in the cattle zone is that they are likely to involve a wide
range of agnates as contributors of animals. Individual homesteads
within a descent group vary at any one time in their possession of
livestock. One year they have plenty to spare, while in another, they
may have incurred a loss through a series of contingencies, e.g. sickness, funerals, the settlement of past debts and marriage payments in
respect of younger agnates. But fellow agnates, and sometimes non-
agnates, are quite prepared to lend each other animals during times of
need. For, unlike cash, which is seen as something which can be
consumed but cannot renew itself, a small number of livestock, it is
thought, can be carefully husbanded to increase themselves many
times. Fluctuations in family stockholding fortunes are an accepted
feature of everyday life.

However, in the non-cattle zone, agnates among both Giriama and
Chonyi try to avoid lending each other cash. As they say, "If my
brother does not return it, then how can I get it back? It is difficult to
sue my own brother in court, for elders will say that this is a private
family matter." In other words, the idea that livestock constitute self-

---

[1] Here I refer to a sample of relatively well paid Luo working in Nairobi whom I studied and
among whom the use of cash may be particularly pronounced.

renewable capital enables a man whose herd is temporarily depleted to obtain a loan from a fellow agnate. But, in contrast, the prevailing notion that cash is for consumption rather than for investment, and so is unlikely to be returned, obliges the man who needs it in order to make a marriage payment to approach non-agnates.

The greater element of trust and reliability attaching to the use of livestock in transactions is apparent in the early childbirth payment within the relatively protracted period of uxorial transfers among the cattle Giriama.[1] The latter might echo here the sentiment expressed to me by a Luo who, in reminiscing perhaps of a past in which marriage payments mainly comprised livestock, said of his ideal preference for cattle, "you can see cattle in the (bride's father's) homestead. You know they are there and that they will eventually return to you (i.e. in the event of divorce). But cash is a private thing which you cannot see and cannot know if they (the bride's family) have spent it" (Parkin, 1978, p. 110) Nowadays such payments are increasingly of cash. For the most prosperous Luo men work in towns for wages and, since they are likely to marry the most and most desirable wives, it is they who have determined the use of urban wages in marriage payments. Earned cash is not converted into cattle, unless the bride's father so insists, except for a minority proportion which is used to buy and transact what are regarded as an essential livestock minimum of a couple of heifers and a bullock or goat. Some Luo claim also that the shift among them from the predominant use of cattle to cash has also been accompanied by a shortening of the period of the bulk of the payment. But this was difficult to substantiate. Nevertheless, the loan and distribution of livestock to relatives characteristic of many cattle-based economies does tend to encourage long, drawn-out bridewealth payments whose duration may well become shortened by the use of cash accumulated privately by single families and individuals.

Both the Luo and the Giriama, then, distinguish livestock in marriage payments as a more open, public medium of exchange, and one which visibly lends itself to trust and reliability. By contrast, cash is

---

[1] Recent fieldwork since the paper was written enables me to update certain figures here: the Giriama uxorial cash payment has now doubled to Shs 3000/- since the mid-sixties; a heifer increased in value to Shs 400/- from Shs 150/-; and Digo *harusi* payments have increased to at least Shs 3000/- from Shs 1200/-. Chonyi uxorial payments have not increased at the same rate but are at least Shs 3000/-, as among the Giriama of the palm belt. Other changes have occurred, such as the greater use of cash in the Giriama and Duruma cattle zone, which I shall document in due course. Here let me thank George Mkangi, Tom Spear, and members of a recent seminar at the Nairobi Institute of African Studies, for their comments.

a privatizing medium. This contrast is of course common in ethnographic description as, for example, in Bohannan's analysis of Tiv
exchange spheres (1959), in which the use of money eventually emerges
at the bottom of a scale of moral evaluations of exchange.

It is relevant here to note Simmel's characterization of cash use
(1964, p. 335):

> Ever since traffic in economic values has been carried on by means of money
> alone, an otherwise unattainable secrecy has become possible. Three character-
> istics of the monetary form of value are relevant here: its compressibility, which
> permits one to make somebody rich by slipping a cheque in his hand without
> anybody's noticing it; its abstractness and qualitylessness, through which trans-
> actions, acquisitions, and changes in ownership can be rendered hidden and
> unrecognizable in a way impossible where values are owned only in the form of
> extensive, unambiguously tangible objects; and, finally, its effect-at-a-distance,
> which allows its investment in very remote and ever-changing values, and thus
> its complete withdrawal from the eyes of the immediate environment.

The three characteristics of money can be classed as its privatizing
quality, its capacity for carrying secret messages and its ability to affect
issues at a distance without the personal involvement of those who
transact it. The views of Simmel and of the Luo, Giriama, and Chonyi
here roughly converge. It is easy to see how, in the light of these
characteristics, the Giriama and Chonyi clearly link the use of cash in
marriage payments with the capacity of wives to escape the public,
traditional restraints of their and their husband's male agnates and, by
"secretly" going off to the nearby town of Mombasa, to purchase their
freedom at a distance by returning their uxorial payments in the form
of earned cash.

Among the Luo this does not happen, however. There are towns to
which a Luo woman may escape if she so wishes. And, by earning
money and returning the bridewealth transacted for her, less
deductions for any children to which her husband is entitled, it should
be technically possible for her to obtain a similar freedom. But this is
where the contrast lies: for Luo women there is no equivalent of the
coastal Muslim Swahili "culture" which, for all the preachings of
orthodox Islam, in fact facilitates informal modes of cohabitation in
which women, once freed from the customary restraints of their erst-
while Giriama and Chonyi ethnic membership, may control any
children they produce. There is, in other words, no established process
by which a Luo woman can, through cash earnings, switch ethnic
membership. But what prevents an enterprising individual from re-

turning her own bridewealth and setting up on her own? Having done this, could she not decide with whom she should live and whether she should have full rights in any children she subsequently produces? I know of no case of this having happened. The main reason may be as follows. According to Luo customary law, bridewealth can only be returned less deductions for children produced in the marriage. Therefore, should a woman ever be able to make such a return, she would still be obliged to make the appropriate deductions for any children she has had, in whom she foregoes all rights. The childbirth deductions are valuable and made automatically under the supervision of elders and a court. So, if she has produced four or five children, she would have virtually no bridewealth at all to return. This would seal the husband's claim to the children as being beyond question.

We can merely speculate that a sufficiently large number of individual Luo women would have to set themselves up independently for them to develop self-awareness as an identifiable collectivity able effectively to oppose and reformulate the customary law; only then is some cultural recognition likely to follow. But this has by no means yet happened and we should probably have to wait a long time for it to do so.

Therefore, while there are clearly many historical reasons for this contrast between the Luo and non-Luo, underlying it is the presence or absence of the named distinction between the uxorial and childbirth payments. This distinction, which is made at marriage by the non-Luo (i.e. Giriama and Chonyi), predisposes people to think of the two rights as separable and, hence, as potentially negotiable; its formal absence among the Luo, except at divorce, guarantees that the husband's right to his wife's children are non-negotiable. This, in turn, leads us to a discussion of the second variable affecting conjugal and jural stability.

2. *The distinctiveness of uxorial and childbirth payments*

In concentrating specifically upon the Mijikenda, I shall seek to demonstrate (a) some of the different ways in which a basic distinction between uxorial and childbirth payments may be expressed in different combinations; and (b) how these different combinations can variously represent the status of women and notions of conjugality and filiation.

In their emic comparisons of each others' marriage patterns, the neighbouring Giriama and Chonyi are well aware of the way in which the distinction between the two types of payment can be employed, through the use of cash, to control the rate of convertability of women's status from daughters and sisters to other men's wives. Cash, in other words, is *seen* to have been the medium by which the two kinds of named rights can be separated. Giriama fathers who insist on delayed transfer of the almost worthless childbirth payment in order to secure the valuable uxorial payment, play on this separability of the two rights. By contrast, Chonyi fathers, who accept offers for both rights in one immediate transaction after another as prospective husbands outbid each other, minimize their separability. Chonyi and Giriama women who thereafter escape (as people say) and become "Swahili", also exploit the potential separability. They return the childbirth as well as the valuable uxorial payment, even when they nominally forego rights in their children; and, under the cover of the implicit uncertainty as to whom the children really belong, they create independent matri-focal families in which these children gradually assume full rights, especially as they get older. It is this named and culturally recognized distinction between the two payments which, I believe, facilitates the variations among neighbouring cultures of notions of rights in children through the varying statuses of women.

We can see how the cultural separability of the two rights and payments operates to even greater effect by widening the area of comparison to yet two other neighbouring Mijikenda peoples, also speaking a mutually intelligible dialect and having similar customs. These are the non-Muslim Duruma and the Muslim Digo, both of Kwale province. I shall deal first with the non-Muslim Duruma.

The Duruma have two distinct forms of marriage: a valuable "cattle" one and a much cheaper "cash" one, distinguished in the vernacular thus. A cattle marriage secures childbirth as well as uxorial rights in a wife, and a man will seek to ensure that his first union is of this type. If he does not possess and cannot afford to buy the cattle — for they are scarce and their ownership is confined to a relatively few families — then a cheaper cash marriage must suffice. A man's second wife, however, may be married in this way.

The cattle marriage is said by Duruma to be "for a wife whose children inherit from their father". The marriage payment is valuable and consists of 15 heifers for the bride's father or agnatic representative; Shs 500/- for the wife's mother's brother; and a bullock which is slaughtered, and some palm wine, both of which are specifically for the bride's father at the wedding ceremony towards the end of the payment of cattle. It is interesting that, though the bull and palm wine given to the bride's father are formally and historically equivalent to the childbirth payment known as the "bull" among the Giriama and Chonyi, it is not normally distinguished as such in a Duruma cattle marriage. It is the status of the marriage payment as a whole, and not this constituent part of it, that determines the patrifiliation of children born in it. Its contrast is with the cash marriage which, to cite Duruma again, is "for a wife whose children inherit from their mother's brother". In other words, Duruma cash marriage involves only an uxorial payment. This is very low, consisting of only Shs 40/-, ten goats (the customary equivalent of one heifer), four hoes, one gourd of honey, and thirty large gourds of palm wine. It may be noted that, while the marriage is called a cash one, money does not make up most of the payment. Wives married to one man in these contrasting ways may be found living within a single homestead with their children, some "owned" by their mother's husband and others by their mother's brother.

In other words, the contrast made among the Giriama and, less explicitly, among the Chonyi, between the uxorial and childbirth payments within a *single* marriage transaction are terminologically and conceptually reformulated among the Duruma as a contrast between *two* entirely separate kinds of marriage: the expensive cattle one, predicating patriliny through the acquisition of genetricial rights; and the cheaper cash one, predicating matriliny through the denial of genetricial rights to the wife's husband and their retention by her brother. As might be expected, the cattle and cash forms of marriage are each associated with low and high conjugal separation rates.

Duruma cattle marriage, by abridging uxorial and childbirth payments into one undifferentiated whole, here comes close to the Luo form which, though now largely cash, still lacks the distinction between the two payments, as it did when it was exclusively cattle. We can thus characterize Duruma cattle marriage as:

(4) Mainly Livestock   uxorial/childbirth
        (valuable)   payments combined
                                             A------------------B
                                               Up to 1 year

            * childbirth payments deducted automatically and
        without option from the palm wine component of the
            recovered marriage payments on divorce only

This is a variant on contemporary Luo marriage, which may be summarized as:

(5) Mainly Cash   uxorial/childbirth
        (valuable)   payments combined
                                             A------------------B
                                               up to 1 year

            * childbirth payments deducted automatically and
        without option from recovered marriage payments on
            divorce only

Both Duruma and Luo patterns are associated with a low rate of divorce and separation. In this respect, they both contrast with the second type of Duruma marriage, which reads as follows:

(6) Mixture of Cash/   A/B
      Livestock/Wine/   ---
          Goods   immediate
      (non-valuable)

        * uxorial payment only

While (4) and (5) are both associated with low divorce, (6) is associated with frequent separation, though not normally with any return of payment.

Among the immediately adjoining Muslim Digo, the pattern is even more complex. Not only do they have two separate marriage forms, but they preserve within each a named distinction between the childbirth payment and the uxorial payment, *both* mainly consisting of cash, as I interpret Gomm's recent study (1972):

(7) Mainly Cash + Dowry	combined uxorial/childbirth payment early during cohabitation (?)	— valuable
	childbirth payments deducted by agreement from recovered marriage payments on divorce	— low value
(8) Mainly Cash	early uxorial payment	— low value
	childbirth payments negotiated separately for each child as born or at divorce	— low value

The more prestigeful, and more expensive form of marriage is called *harusi*, (No. 7), a Swahili rather than Digo term, and it is modelled on the local Arab-Swahili variant of codified Islamic marriage. There are long betrothals, over half of which are with patrilateral cross-cousins (i.e. FZD-MBS), though only a minority of betrothals actually last until a formal marriage is established.

The contrasting and much cheaper type (No. 8) approximates in terminology to customary marriage among the non-Muslim Mijikenda peoples. It is called *uhala* (from the verb *ku-hala*, "to take") and connotes marriage by elopement, though not nowadays involving capture. (The Giriama also distinguish marriages by either elopement or arrangement.) Among the Digo, the elopement usually disrupts a previous *harusi* betrothal. But it is institutionalized elopement. The couple disappear for only a few days and then communicate their whereabouts and their wish to settle the marriage payment due to the girl's parents through a trusted go-between.

The expensive Islamic marriage, *harusi*, in fact incurs costs for both bride's and groom's kin. The groom pays up to Shs 1200/- to the bride's father, who has, however, to re-imburse a third to a half of it, the *mahari*, in wedding expenses and dowry goods for his daughter. So he does not stand to gain much from this money (called *mahunda*) received for a daughter. Similarly, though his expenses on the cheaper *uhala* marriage are negligible, so also is the money (also called *mahunda*) received for a daughter.

Gomm (1972, p. 97) cites Prins (1952, p. 68) as suggesting that the *uhala* elopement marriage was once an alternative to a high status customary form of marriage by arrangement. This high status form seems, then, to have been supplanted by the current Muslim *harusi* marriage, which is certainly nowadays the high status one. We may speculate that this earlier non-Islamic dual marriage system corresponds to that found today among the neighbouring Duruma. This leaves the question of the extent of the correspondence between the *modern* Digo dual marriage system and its Duruma counterpart. In other words, how far can Digo marriage also be seen as a variant of a common underlying pattern, in spite of being influenced by Islam?

The cheap *uhala* elopement marriage among Digo draws a clear distinction between the small *mahunda*, or uxorial payment, and a quite separate childbirth payment (*malezi*), payable as each child arrives or at least some time thereafter. (*Malezi* comes from the verb *kulea*, "to rear".) But if a husband delays too long in making childbirth payments his children come under the control of his wife's brothers, i.e. the child's matrilineal kin. In this case, marriage payments eventually received for a daughter would go to the girl's matrilineal kin and not her own father. Such childbirth payments are subject to much negotiation and may in fact be paid by a genitor who is not the wife's husband, and even by ordinary adopters. In other words, the separation between uxorial and childbirth payments could hardly be more explicit than in Digo *uhala* marriage and, not surprisingly, articulates a distinction between groups based on patri- and matri-filiation. The point is that the negotiable nature of the individual childbirth payments (i.e. negotiated individually for each child and not for them collectively), enables *paters* and *genitors* or adopters to acquire their children: but it also allows individual children to be retained by their matrikin if neither the *pater*, *genitor*, nor an adopter makes the necessary transfer. The most important corporate groups among the Digo were in fact once recruited matrilineally. Nowadays an interesting mix has developed in which homesteads comprise an agnatic core, while some old and valuable estates of tree crops are transferred matrilaterally and marriage preferences and prohibitions turn on the use of matriliny (Gomm, 1972, pp. 96-7).

The high status *harusi* marriage payment, on the other hand, technically transfers both uxorial and genetricial rights to the husband. But, in practice, in the event of divorce involving the return of the marriage payment (the *mahunda*), the husband pays individual childbirth payments (again called *malezi*) to his wife's brothers and her mother's brothers to make sure of retaining his paternal rights over the children produced in the terminated marriage. When the Luo return bridewealth for a marriage which has ended in divorce, they make deductions for any children produced. The Luo view that the *pater's* right to his divorced wife's children is beyond question is anticipated in these deductions. No such assumptions are made when a Digo *harusi* marriage breaks up: the husband is effectively given a choice as to whether he pays and keeps the children (Gomm, 1972, pp. 92-100).

Finally, the highly negotiable nature of childbirth payments (*malezi*) among the Digo, and its clearly conceptualized separability from the uxorial payment (*mahunda*), corresponds with what we may call the self-negotiable status of a relatively large number of Digo women who set up matrifocal family units independently in Mombasa, and who do so through beer-brewing, sometimes through prostitution and, on occasion, by building and letting small houses. Under these circumstances, the rights of a woman's brothers to her children on whose behalf childbirth payments have not been presented, effectively passes to the mother herself. This, of course, becomes tantamount to a system of mother-right.

The Digo present the most complicated case of all those I have discussed. The two marriage types are nevertheless partial reformulations of the wider Mijikenda distinction between uxorial and childbirth payments. It is likely, as I mentioned before, that the Digo did once have a non-Islamic dual marriage system generally like that of the Duruma. Whatever the situation some time ago, the present day Digo distinction between childbirth and uxorial payments applies to both the high status Muslim and low status non-Muslim marriage forms: it cuts across them, and tells us something of Digo social stratification. This, Gomm points out, is covertly based on a former distinction between free-born and slaves, and *may* be assuming a new meaning consistent with contemporary political and economic divisions.

The conversion of part of the uxorial payment (*mahunda*) into indirect dowry (*mahari*) (Goody, 1973, p. 20) in the high status Digo Muslim marriage is the critical link between what we may crudely call the non-Muslim Mijikenda paradigm of separable uxorial and childbirth payments on the one hand, and the Arab-Swahili system of marriage and property on the other hand. Through the creation of a dowry out of and in addition to the uxorial payment, the "original" Mijikenda two-fold distinction becomes a three-fold one, and comprises a negotiable childbirth payment of cash, an uxorial cash payment of highly varying value, and a wife's dowry in goods paid for with some of the uxorial cash payment.

There is no reason to suppose that the dowry in marriage payments by itself generates favourable conditions for women to set up matri-focal family units. But, in combination with the negotiable and therefore potentially ambiguous nature of childbirth payments as among the Digo, dowry does seem to provide the potential means by which a woman can effectively retain control over her own powers of reproduction. That is to say, a Digo divorcee of a Muslim (*harusi*) marriage does at least retain her dowry (Gomm, 1972, p. 112, f.5); this she can use to set up an independent matrifocal family of her own, over which her brothers may come to have only nominal control. This three-fold distinction between named uxorial, childbirth, and dowry payments would seem, then, to constitute a paradigmatic shift in the generation of marriage and family types among the Mijikenda peoples of eastern Kenya. The shift involves a change from (a) viri-local marriages in which a wife's children become affiliated either to their *pater* or *genitor*, an adopter, or to their mother's brothers; to (b) matrifocal families without formal marriage in which children are directly affiliated to the mother independently of her brothers or a previous husband or lover.

To summarise this section, the Luo, Giriama, Chonyi, Duruma, and Digo marriage payments all presuppose an underlying distinction between uxorial and genetricial rights. In all except the Luo and, to a lesser extent, the Duruma cattle transfers, in which it has become terminologically abridged, the distinction between the two kinds of payment is culturally explicit and named. As such, it allows for a range of co-varying relationships between the two kinds of payment, and for corresponding variations of marriage and family type.

Conclusion

Let me now bring together the two variables of the changing com-position and the terminological features of marriage payments and suggest the following three-part hypothesis.

1. Where the two kinds of payment, uxorial and childbirth, are ter-minologically and culturally fused as one, as among the Luo, we may expect it to be valuable and to be associated with patrifiliation and infrequent divorce. We may also anticipate that its conversion from

livestock to cash will have little effect on the rates of patrifiliation and of divorce.

2. Where the two kinds of payment are terminologically and culturally distinguished, then, following their conversion from livestock to mainly cash, we may expect them to co-vary in their relationship to each other in such a way that they generate a wide range of different marriage tendencies. Some of those I have noted involve:

(a) patrifiliation, low divorce and non-valuable childbirth payments made at the end of a valuable uxorial transfer, as among the palm-belt Giriama (No. 2): (b) patrifiliation, high divorce, and high and low value uxorial and childbirth payments respectively, paid together immediately the marriage is agreed upon, as among the Chonyi (No. 3); (c) a dual system of marriage, as among the Duruma, involving on the one hand, patrifiliation, low divorce and valuable combined uxorial and childbirth payments (No. 4) and, on the other, matrilineal filiation, high divorce and low value uxorial payments alone (No. 6); and (d) ambifiliation (i.e. to *pater*, *genitor*, mother's brother or adopter) by negotiation, high divorce, a low uxorial payment and low childbirth payments for individual children, either as they are born or sometimes afterwards, as among the Digo (No. 8).

3. Where inalienable dowry payments of goods or cash co-exist with culturally distinguished uxorial and childbirth cash payments, it may be possible for a wife effectively to convert her dowry into exclusive rights in her own children, even to the extent of setting up her own independent matrifocal family, as among some Digo divorcees (Nos. 7-8).

Apart from the Luo, I have confined myself to a single general culture area of peoples speaking mutually intelligible speech varieties or dialects and sharing closely similar customs. What I have summarized here are obviously not exhaustive of the range of co-varying relationships of uxorial and childbirth payments, with or without dowry. For instance, nowadays among the Kikuyu the uxorial mainly cash payment called the *ruracio* varies considerably in value from a few hundred to over a thousand shillings, sometimes with a few goats, and may be paid early on in the "marriage" or over a period of years. The childbirth payment, by contrast, always involves slaughtering what is called the *ngurario* ram, together with expenses of varying amounts, for an accompanying ceremonial feast. But, from data I have of Kikuyu living in or near Nairobi, the timing of this *ngurario*

event varies considerably but has, in some cases, been so long delayed
that children born to a marriage have reached ten years of age. Since
conjugal separation appears to be on the increase among the Kikuyu,
this means that many separating wives can legitimately take their
children with them. Also, Kikuyu brothers are not generally concerned
to exert rights over their sister's children, the girls among whom cannot
guarantee valuable bridewealth and the boys among whom will only
add to the problems of land pressure. So divorced Kikuyu women whose
husbands have not slaughtered the *ngurario* ram can keep their
children and set up matrifocal families quite independently, the
opportunities for which do exist in a town like Nairobi (Nelson, 1977).
By contrast, no such process has developed among the Luo in Nairobi.
When a man marries a wife, he transacts a payment that makes no
distinction between uxorial and childbirth rights and so covers both of
them. In the event of divorce, then, which is rare after the birth of a
child, a Luo woman loses both children and husband.

I illustrate this contrast to suggest that, whatever local variations
within a culture area there may be, as among the Mijikenda, the
named distinction between uxorial and childbirth payments does facilitate the transformation of marriage and family types. There is here a
fundamental rule of culture: where uxorial and childbirth rights are
semantically distinguished in transactions, they may also be thought of
as separately negotiable and manipulable. At an observational level,
this is expressed as the potential ability of the bride's father to determine the duration and timing of the payments relative to each other,
rather than simply their value.

The distinction is not of course confined to Kenya, as a few examples
from "African Systems of Kinship and Marriage" (1950) will indicate.
The Nyamwezi have a dual marriage system comparable to that of the
Duruma (Radcliffe-Brown, 1950, p. 51), which is based on a similar
separation of uxorial from childbirth payments; the Swazi identify the
lobola, the childbirth payment, and the *emabeka*, the uxorial payment
(H. Kuper, 1950, pp. 88-9), and Hilda Kuper implies that neighbouring Bantu peoples of the Swazi articulate similar categories to varying
effect; while, among the Yakö of West Africa, we can infer a similar
distinction (Forde, 1950, p. 325). Finally, outside Africa, the Melpa of
New Guinea differentiate clearly between the two payments
(M. Strathern, 1972, p. 97), and there is the hint by Radcliffe-Brown
(1950, p. 51) that the dual marriage system of Sumatra and other parts

of the Malay Archipelago also draw on this distinction.

One could go on extending the examples, but these would only have value if they were placed within a more comprehensive analytical framework. As a general conclusion, however, it does seem relevant to suggest that the interrelationships of such phenomena as divorce and the degree of conjugal stability, "father-right" as against "mother-right", the degree of strength of brother-sister ties or of affinal alliances, and the high or low value of bridewealth, turn on the problem of whether or not uxorial and childbirth payments are distinguished in a particular culture, and whether this distinction is employed in the negotiation of marriage arrangements. If we start with this cultural contrast and trace out its manifestations and their transformations across neighbouring and sometimes cognate cultures, it may be easier to assess the relative weight of these factors.

In many ways this is not so very different from Gluckman's original hypothesis, which implied a distinction between uxorial and childbirth payments. But I have not concentrated on marriage payments as variable cultural interpretations of the relative value of women as producers of children, as producers of labour, or, as in some societies, as non-productive indices of men's prestige, though I certainly regard these as being of critical importance. Rather, I have focused here on the *inherent* logical capacity of marriage payments to provide conceptual and terminological distinctions and, therefore, yardsticks by which opposed parties to the transaction can shift the balance of power between them within broad outlines of customarily acceptable behaviour; this, as I have shown, is especially likely to occur when cash replaces livestock in sectors of the economy.

I would generally hypothesize, then, that the *absence* of the terminological distinction between uxorial and childbirth payments, as among the Luo, culturally presupposes a total and unambiguous transfer to a woman's husband's group of her roles as mother and wife, and the negation of her roles as daughter and sister in her natal group. The *presence* of the distinction culturally presupposes the separate negotiability of these roles. Where this negotiability is expressed mainly in cash, it further presupposes a greater propensity for separation and divorce and, in turn, has radical implications for future changes in the status of women. This hypothesis refers to logical possibilities. It is reminiscent of the kind of model that Leach had in mind when he introduced his topological metaphor of the rubber sheet which can be stretched in different ways to produce a range of mathematically possible variations (Leach, 1961, p. 7). Aptly, therefore, it subsumes Gluckman's empirically derived insights on the subject.

Bibliography

Bohannan, P. (1959). The impact of money on an African subsistence economy. *Journal of Economic History*, **19**, 4, 491-503.

Evans-Pritchard, E. E. (1965). "The Position of Women in Primitive Society". Faber, London.

Fallers, L. (1957). Some determinants of marriage stability in Busoga. *Africa*, **27**, 106-123.

Forde, D. (1950). Double descent among the Yakö. *In* "African Systems of Kinship and Marriage" (Eds. A. R. Radcliffe-Brown and D. Forde). International African Institute, London.

Fox, R. (1967). "Kinship and Marriage". Penguin, Harmondsworth.

Gluckman, M. (1959). Kinship and marriage among the Lozi of Northern Rhodesia and the Zulu of Natal. *In* "African Systems of Kinship and Marriage" (Eds. A. R. Radcliffe-Brown and D. Forde). International African Institute, London.

Gomm, R. (1972). Harlots and bachelors; marital instability among the coastal Digo of Kenya. *Man* (N.S.), **7**, 4, 95-113.

Goody, J. and Tambiah, S. J. (1973). "Bridewealth and Dowry". Cambridge Papers in Social Anthropology No. 7. Cambridge University Press, London.

Kuper, H. (1950). Kinship among the Swazi. *In* "African Systems of Kinship and Marriage" (Eds. A. R. Radcliffe-Brown and D. Forde). International African Institute, London.

Leach, E. R. (1961). "Rethinking Anthropology". Athlone Press, London.

Nelson, N. (1977). Dependence and independence: female household heads in Mathare Valley, a squatter community in Nairobi, Kenya. D.Phil. dissertation presented to the University of London (unpublished).

Parkin, D. J. (1972). "Palms, Wine and Witnesses". Chandler, San Francisco.

Parkin, D. J. (1978). "The Cultural Definition of Political Response". Academic Press, London and New York.

Prins, A. H. J. (1952). "The Coastal Tribes of the North-Eastern Bantu". International African Institute, London.

Radcliffe-Brown, A. R. (1950). Introduction. *In* "African Systems of Kinship and Marriage" (Eds. A. R. Radcliffe-Brown and D. Forde). International African Institute, London.

Radcliffe-Brown, A. R. and Forde, D. (Eds). (1950). "African Systems of Kinship and Marriage". International African Institute, London.

Riviere, P. (1971). Marriage: a reassessment. *In* "Rethinking Kinship and Marriage" (Ed. R. Needham). Tavistock, London.

Sansom, B. (1976). A signal transaction and its currency. *In* "Transaction and Meaning" (Ed. B. Kapferer). I.S.H.I., Philadelphia.

Simmel, G. (1964). "The Sociology of George Simmel" (translated and edited by K. H. Wolff). The Free Press, Glencoe.

Strathern, M. (1972). "Women in Between". Seminar Press, London and New York.

8 Dowry and Wedding Celebrations in Yugoslav Macedonia

D. B. RHEUBOTTOM

I

In this chapter I shall examine a series of prestations which take place during wedding celebrations in Skopska Crna Gora, a rural area in Yugoslav Macedonia. Of course, the exchange of gifts and other items during a wedding is only a small part of what might be considered as marriage payments. But since weddings are such signal occasions in Skopska Crna Gora, and since they so fundamentally alter social relationships, it seems useful to isolate this limited set of exchanges in order to see what it reveals, or conceals, about those relationships.

One segment of wedding festivities includes the presentation of a dowry. While it is part of the trappings of our Western heritage, I think it fair to state that anthropological understanding of dowry is decidedly less advanced than that of bridewealth. It is important, therefore, to consider this particular payment in some detail; but it cannot be discussed apart from other prestations. For, as I intend to demonstrate, it is not a single transfer, but a collection of different kinds of things which convey different meanings. These meanings only become manifest when dowry is examined in the broader setting of the various wedding prestations.

Skopska Crna Gora is a small region of eleven nucleated villages. It is located just north of the city of Skopje, the capital of the Peoples'

Republic of Macedonia, and it is shaped like an arc of a circle.[1] If we locate Skopje at the centre of this arc, then a ring of mountains forms its circumference. Most of the villages are located at the base of these mountains and their fields point down, like radii towards Skopje, about twenty kilometers away. The inhabitants of this region, or Crna Gorci as I shall call them, are Eastern (Macedonian) Orthodox and speak a dialect that lies somewhere between Serbo-Croatian and Macedonian. Kučevište is the largest of the villages with about 300 households and 1,900 members. Brodec is the smallest, having less than 30 households and 130 members (*Popis Stanovništva*, 1961).

Each village contains a number of exogamous patrilineal clans and generally genealogical links cannot be traced between all members of a clan. Clan identity is expressed through a common surname, a shared patron saint, and certain other customs and usages. Where genealogical links cannot be traced, Crna Gorci are likely to say that they are "distant" agnates and use multiples of five degrees of cousinship to express this distance. Thus, distant agnates are reckoned to be tenth, fifteenth, or twentieth cousins. "Close" agnates, on the other hand, are thought to be within the range of fifth cousins. Since genealogies are relatively shallow, the positions of the most distant remembered ancestors are juggled as generations pass to preserve the fiction of close agnation and the fifth cousin span.

With very few exceptions, all clansmen live within a single village. Clans are internally segmented into maximal, major, minor, and minimal lineages. Each level of segmentation is marked by distinctive attributes (Rheubottom, 1971). But the clan has little contemporary significance in local political and economic affairs. Indeed, its members engage in common action almost exclusively in the context of weddings.

Most villagers live within walled compounds. Gates and guard dogs keep unwanted visitors outside, and the dwelling itself faces away from public thoroughfares; this spatial arrangement ensures considerable privacy and security. The household is strongly corporate and its members regard the outside world with considerable distrust (Rheubottom, 1976a, b). Some members now work in Skopje for wages, although virtually every household depends upon agriculture for its

---

[1] Skopska Crna Gora ("Skopje's Black Mountain") should not be confused with the Republic of Montenegro which is also known as Crna Gora.

livelihood. A number also supplement their agricultural pursuits with shepherding and large-scale viticulture.

II

I begin this account with a short description of wedding festivities which emphasize those features which will bulk large in the analysis of wedding payments.

According to older informants, marriages used to be arranged. On occasion the bride and groom would meet for the first time in front of the church altar on their wedding day. Nowadays there is a period of court-ship and the choice of spouse is left largely to the young people involved. But others are still very much concerned. Crna Gorci believe that, if a maiden[1] has a known suitor, no other youth will take an interest in her. They explain that no youth could accept a bride who had been linked to another: that would clearly demonstrate the inferiority of the second suitor. Therefore, a spurned maiden has great difficulty in finding a husband. If she marries at all, it is to a poor widower or to a man with a serious mental or physical handicap. Moreover, her brothers or close kinsmen should take revenge. Because of this, courtship must appear as a sequence of disinterested encounters, all of which are quite fortuitous.

When a serious interest develops, a matchmaker, usually a person who is related to both sides, makes discreet inquiries at the maiden's house-hold about the interests of its members in the match and, secondly, about the extent of her dowry. This dowry has three components: the trousseau of clothing and linen, a sum of money "for the pocket" as Crna Gorci say, and some furniture. But in the preliminary stage representatives of the bride's household merely indicate about how much they are prepared to spend on these items. If these preliminary discussions prove satisfactory to both sides, then an engagement party is arranged during which the date of the wedding and remaining details will be worked out.

Wedding festivities are very costly. The households of both bride and groom incur major expenditures which require years of careful planning and husbandry. Indeed, most households have an explicit long-range strategy of work and saving that may cover a decade or more and several different weddings. In 1966 an average village

[1] The term "maiden" is a literal translation of the native term *devojka*.

wedding cost the bride's household 600,000 dinars (£200). Of this, about half was allocated for the gift of pocket money while the other half covered the trousseau, furniture, and the expense of feasting a number of guests. These were the costs of an average wedding. A poor household would try to keep the total expenses to about 400,000 dinars while a wealthy one might spend one million or more. The outlay of the groom's household is about half as much as the bride's; this includes the cost of feasting plus a considerable amount for gifts.

To place these expenses in context, a wagon and team of oxen cost 400,000 dinars in 1966. It cost about one million dinars to build a small, one-storey village house. A house-site with an average house and garden cost ten million, while fields varied in price between one and four million dinars. In comparison, an unskilled labourer working for wages earned about 360,000 per annum and a university lecturer about 800,000. Thus, while wedding expenses represent only a small fraction of the working capital of a peasant household, cash needs for a wedding are far in excess of likely annual cash income.

Because of the need for detailed and long-range planning, the bride's household knows exactly how much they can afford to spend when the matchmaker makes his inquiries. There is little flexibility in this overall sum. Individual items in the budget can be adjusted some-what, but there is a relatively clear upper limit on the total. Ordinarily a household does not sell land or livestock to finance a wedding, although a unit with sheep will expand their herd and then sell part of the flock as the occasion draws near.[1]

On the day of the engagement party a small group of the groom's kin and his ritual sponsor (*kum*) arrive at the bride's house for a meal. They bring a number of gifts for the bride on a pan used for making festive bread and these include such items as slips, brassières, and nylon stockings. The presentation and acceptance of these items indicates that both sides are publically committed to the match and it marks the formal beginning of the wedding sequence.

The engagement feast (*zagovorka*; "the speaking for") is an impor-tant transition in the relationship between the two groups of kin. During the feast, kinsmen of the prospective bride and groom address

---

[1] To avoid cumbersome sentences, I speak of households as doing things, holding beliefs, and so on. In fact, of course, only the members can act. For the same reason, I freely substitute the words "family", "home", "house", and similar terms for "household" when the meaning is clear.

one another as "affine" (*svaća*) and the couple are spoken of as "bride" (*navesta*) and "groom" (*mladoženja*). The bride also addresses and refers to the groom's kin by their appropriate kin terms (cf. Petrović, 1907, p. 356).

During the meal, a basket of handmade items is brought in and passed among the groom's kin. These items include a series of traditional gifts for the groom and his mother, such as socks, an apron, embroidered vests, and so on. As the basket is passed around, each guest puts some money into it. The amount varies with the genealogical distance between the giver and groom. After the basket has made its rounds, the bride enters, offers each guest a drink of brandy, and is given a sum of money in return. The money is concealed in the palm and is passed to the bride as she kisses the hand. The sums given again reflect kinship distance; in fact, all money gifts throughout the wedding reflect kinship distance. As the meal draws to a close, the remaining wedding details are arranged and a date is set. The wedding is usually only a few weeks away so as to reduce the likelihood of postponement or interference.

The groom's agnates speak of the wedding as "our wedding" and the bride as "our bride". Everyday conversations in the village tend to imply that weddings are the result of a massive and highly organized effort on the part of a single clan, an impression which both clansmen and outsiders reinforce. This is misleading, however. Agnates do serve the wedding feast and they do assemble on other occasions to create the image of great solidarity, but their contribution to the labour or finance of the wedding is negligible. Nor are they consulted over the selection of the bride or the making of marriage arrangements. All of these matters are left to the households directly concerned.

But, on the day before the church ceremony, they gather at the groom's house and then set off in a great procession to fetch the bride. This procession is led by musicians and a youth carrying the national flag. Mounted and armed men come next and are followed by other men, women, and girls. They take a circuitous route to the bride's home so that the entire village will have the opportunity to see and hear them go by. As they proceed, they boast to onlookers about what fine people they are, and how they are going to "take" their bride. On arrival at the bride's home, they find the gates are locked and the bride and her kinsmen are barricaded inside. There follows a brief skirmish between a representative from each side before they are allowed in.

After they have eaten, amidst loud complaints amongst themselves about the quality of food and hospitality, they demand their bride and her trousseau and then return in triumphant procession to the groom's house.

The following morning, the morning of the church ceremony, they again gather at the groom's house.[1] But this time only the males form into a procession to fetch the three officiants needed in the church service — the groom's ritual sponsor (*kum*), a senior affine of some standing in the community (*stari svat*), and a young unmarried man who will lead the bride and champion her interests (*dever*). This procession is led by a senior agnate who carries a large flask of brandy. When all the officiants have been collected and returned to the groom's house, yet another procession then forms to go to the church for the wedding service.

Significantly, the bride's kinsmen are not present on this day. They do not go to the church for the service and do not attend the feast or participate in the dancing. The wedding day is a festive occasion only for the groom's agnates and invited guests. It is also significant, as I shall explain later, that guests bring presents to the wedding feast. Each guest is the designated representative of an invited household and this person delivers a gift which has been purchased with household funds. These gifts, in turn, are merged into the common store of possessions held by the groom's household. The bride and groom have no special claim to any of them despite the fact that they were given on the occasion of their wedding. When the household eventually divides, the gifts will be distributed in the same manner as other common possessions.

At the beginning of the wedding feast, the bride greets each guest and offers them a drink of brandy. They, in turn, place a small sum of money in her palm. Sometime later, an apple is brought in on a plate and passed around, each guest pushing a coin into the apple before it is passed on: this money is said to be for the groom. And, finally, before the feast ends, the bride enters and goes around to kiss the hand of each guest. They again hand her a sum of money, almost furtively, and she, in turn, gives each a gift of clothing. While the dancing may continue for several hours, this concludes the wedding feast.

Here, in short compass, we have most of the elements which will

---

[1] Sometimes, in the wedding celebrations of very poor households, all of the festivities occur on the day of the church service. This eliminates some of the expenses of feasting.

figure in the present analysis. The engagement begins the wedding festivities; these have a distinct beginning and end. The beginning, as I have indicated, is marked by the presentation of undergarments for the bride. The end occurs the morning after the church ceremony when the groom's mother takes sweetened brandy to the households of wedding guests to celebrate the successful deflowering of the virgin bride. Today villagers joke that all brides are virgins by definition, even if a chicken has to be slaughtered to fabricate the evidence. But in theory a non-virgin could be returned to her house in disgrace seated backwards on a donkey.

Before entering into more detailed analysis, it may help to summarize the wedding prestations. The bride's household gives the bride three different types of items: a trousseau of clothing and linen; some furniture and (perhaps) kitchen appliances; and a gift of money. The trousseau accompanies her when she leaves her natal home. Her family usually buys the furniture sometime after the wedding and it is delivered quietly to her new home. The cash sum may be given at any time, although it is my understanding that the payment is usually made after the wedding. Sometimes it is transferred in a series of instalments which stretch over several years, notwithstanding that Crna Gorci believe it should occur at the time of the wedding. And whatever the facts may be in any particular case, the parties concerned give the impression that the money has already been paid. These three types of items constitute the dowry. While there is no single term which covers all three, Crna Gorci see them as being inseparable, and an integral, if relatively recent, part of all weddings. In addition to the dowry, several other presentations take place during the festivities. Gifts of clothing are made to the bride, the groom and his mother, and to the several guests who attend the feast. The guests, in turn, bring gifts to the groom's household. These usually take the form of pots and pans although they may include pictures and other decorative items. Finally, the guests give small sums of cash to the bride and groom on several occasions.

III

Let us begin the analysis by considering the trousseau. It includes clothing, bed linen, towels, blankets, some hand-woven bedspreads, and perhaps a hand-woven rug as well. A number of these are em-

broidered by the bride. Most, however, are purchased at shops in
Skopje and have been accumulated over a period of years. While the
quantity of items included in the trousseau is variable, as is the quality
and workmanship, there is relatively little variation in the trousseaus
given by the same household.

The size and quality of the trousseau is taken as an indication of the
wealth and prestige of the bride's household. Since material goods are
put on view for all to examine, it represents a public display of
standing; indeed, those present are careful to evaluate the evidence.
Old women in the village are particularly keen critics of these goods
and, upon arrival at the bride's home, make straight for them to gauge
their extent and quality. After they finger them and discuss points of
difference, they arrive at a composite estimate of the trousseau's worth.
Members of the bride's family are then questioned and cross-
questioned in order to obtain their own estimate. These two estimates
are compared and the result passes quickly around a village. As the
prices of store-goods are widely known, their value can be settled
immediately. But other objects present special problems; for example,
the quality of materials that have gone into the making must be
determined, as does the question of workmanship on the handcrafted
items. The task of assessment is further complicated by the techniques
used to show the goods at best advantage. They are often set out in a
corner of the room and stacked in piles, with only a portion of them
being visible. Moreover, only a few women can examine them at any
one time. The finest items are prominently placed, while inferior ones
are buried inaccessibly at the bottom; and inexpensive substitutes are
placed beneath more expensive look-alikes. The women, of course,
are aware of all these devices and they may, using one pretext or
another, disassemble much of a pile.

While every household is concerned to provide a good show of the
trousseau it offers each daughter, attempts are not made to inflate the
display in order to outbid others in a quest for prestige; that would be
foolish. The bride's household must keep a close balance between the
amount spent on one wedding and that spent on the next. The family
knows how many weddings they will have to finance in coming years
and they plan activities and expenditures with a view to overall parity.
Wedding expenses are not deducted from the working capital of the
household. As a marriage approaches, the household tries to increase
production of marketable produce and to reduce expenditures. Little

by little, items for the trousseau are purchased and stored away, and the family seeks to build up a cash fund.

If they were to offer an inflated amount at the wedding of one daughter, outsiders would suspect that the bride had a serious short-coming. Given the elaborate precautions to maintain privacy and family secrecy, such a shortcoming might easily be hidden away from outsiders, so a large trousseau would provide *prima facie* grounds for suspicion. On the other hand, if they offered a diminished trousseau for another daughter, her suitor would feel insulted; and, romantic considerations playing a much smaller role than financial ones, he may decide to look elsewhere for a bride. In fact, since market mechanisms are an important factor in marriage prospects, that particular maiden would find it difficult to marry at all. Furthermore, siblings must marry in order of age, a consideration that dissuades most families from taking any risk which could imperil the chance of each one doing so as soon as it becomes appropriate. Almost everyone marries and an unmarried member brings the entire household into disrepute. The same constraints apply to males: because their sisters' trousseaus are taken to measure household standing, the category of girls they will be able to court is directly contingent upon such marriage payments. All, therefore, have an interest in ensuring that equity is maintained from one wedding in the household to the next. Thus, there is relatively little variation in the value of the trousseaus presented on behalf of a single set of sisters, or on the wedding expenses of a group of brothers. And there is a relatively fixed ratio between the amount spent on daughters and that spent on sons.

This concern with equity among the weddings of a household reveals part of the meaning of wedding prestations in Skopska Crna Gora: their importance in preserving the boundaries and internal solidarity in both households. Young couples do not establish homes of their own, but join the groom's household.[1] In their daily affairs these units operate as tightly organized "firms" under the supervision of the head (*domaćin*). And they maintain a unified work force which produces for a common budget. Except in the evening and on designated holidays, the time and labour of all members is at the disposal of the household and the *domaćin*; individual members do not determine how their own

---

[1] In certain circumstances, the couple take up residence with the bride's parents if she has no brothers. For purposes of the wedding, however, they initially join the groom's household and then later move into the bride's.

time is to be allocated. Similarly, the products of this time and labour are also at the disposal of the household. Even if one member earns wages in Skopje, the income goes into the common purse. The wage earner himself has no special claims on it. If, therefore, a member wishes to buy even a packet of cigarettes, he must in theory ask the *domaćin* for the money. Each household has a set of clear and equitable procedures for distributing money and consumable goods so that no component unit of the household can justifiably assert that others are being favoured at its expense.

In large households with complex internal organization, continuing domestic harmony is seen to depend upon the maintenance of a strong, centralized and equitable administration. Private incomes and differential access to resources would immediately lead to friction, and soon to division. To counterbalance these fissiparous potentialities, Crna Gorci have clear principles and procedures regulating work and reward. They say that those who labour for the household have the right to be maintained by it. Conversely, those who are so maintained have the obligation to labour. This labour, of course, not only sustains the household, but also gradually adds to the common holding of working capital. Such assets are divided into a number of different categories and rights over them are established by different principles. But, for my immediate purposes, it is sufficient to note that a maiden is entitled to her dowry as compensation for her contribution to her natal household.

This suggests that dowry may plausibly be regarded as a form of inheritance; as equivalent and complementary to the shares which will eventually devolve to the bride's brothers.[1] This type of argument has a certain cogency in respect of societies in countries such as Greece and Italy, where unilineal descent groups are (largely) absent and where young couples establish independent homes. In such cases, the dowry can readily be interpreted as the contribution of the bride's family to the funding of a new home. There is some evidence in the data from Skopska Crna Gora to support this. Peasants say that a bride only needs a token dowry if she has some special occupational skills. In one household I knew well, a man had sent his daughter to Skopje to train to be a dental technician. Being comparatively wealthy himself, he anticipated that she would marry favourably. But, as he boasted to me, he would need to offer only a small dowry since she had important job

[1] This argument has been made by a number of authors (cf. Goody, 1973).

skills and would make a considerable contribution to her new household. From this, it would appear that dowry is intended to fund the bride's new home. Nevertheless, this explanation makes little logical sense in the Crna Goran context. Why, in a patrilineal, virilocal society would the wife-givers endow the groom with rights over the bride's labour, her sexuality, her reproductive capacity, and then give the couple a substantial amount of clothing, cash and furniture as well?

The apparent absurdity of the question itself suggests the answer. The bride's family does *not* endow the groom or his household: they endow the bride. But they do not endow her in order to balance the amount her brothers will receive as their inheritance. This is patently demonstrated in those cases where a man dies leaving several unmarried children. If his estate is distributed before all his offspring are married, then it is divided into as many shares as there are sons, plus an additional share which will be used to support any unmarried sibling, male or female. Thus, if a man has four children, two married sons and an unmarried son and daughter, then his estate would be divided into five parts: three form the inheritance of the sons (the two married ones and the bachelor), while the other two are intended for the weddings and upkeep of the two unwed siblings. Such shares cannot be considered as the equivalent of an inheritance, however. Their purpose is to provide for the unmarried siblings but only until they marry. It should also cover the appropriate wedding expenses. But the share itself is given to the married son who looks after his younger siblings and makes the wedding arrangements. After these expenses have been met, the remainder is kept by the former.

Dowry and inheritance resemble one another neither in timing, value, nor the manner in which they are allocated. In fact, Crna Gorci never speak of the former as equivalent of, or a substitute for, the latter. Rather, they say that the bride is entitled to a trousseau, bridal furniture, and pocket money because she has worked on behalf of the household. As I have already stressed, this is a basic principle of domestic life. This suggests that the dowry might be seen, following the emic view, as compensation for labour, i.e. as a form of delayed wage. Nevertheless, while it may serve as a partial explanation, this (delayed wage) argument cannot be taken too far either. The longer a daughter works for her natal household, the larger her dowry should be. There is a simple explanation for this being so. For the longer she remains unmarried the more time she has to accumulate clothing and goods.

But why should the household furnish her with these, or else with the materials to make them? It is certainly possible to have conventions on the size of the trousseau. Once the conventional number of items had been accumulated, then she could stop work. But Crna Gorci say that the maiden is entitled to accumulate because she continues to contribute to the household's well-being.

Similarly, and as we have already seen, a woman with special occupational skills need have only a token dowry. The reasoning behind this is especially important. The daughter with skills gets a smaller dowry, peasants say, because she has worked less on behalf of the household. They refer here to the time spent in school or in job training and, therefore, not devoted to enhancing the well-being of the household. Furthermore, her training or schooling has entailed costs. There were, for example, the special expenses for clothing, transportation, supplies, and perhaps for food sent to compensate a kinsman who looked after the student or trainee. These special expenses are, as it were, deducted from the dowry.

Exactly the same principle applies to a youth at school or in the army. If a field is purchased by the household while such a youth is away, he is not entitled to a share in it when it is eventually divided since he did not work for it. But his sisters are and they receive theirs in their dowry. All this seems to support the "labour theory" of dowry, but this is only half the story.

The preceding comments apply to the entire dowry, not just to the trousseau. But we have been considering it only from the perspective of the bride's natal household. In this respect explanations based upon compensation for labour may account partially for the amount of dowry, but the argument cannot be taken too far. This becomes evident when we examine dowry in the context of its destination: the groom's household.

IV

As I have noted, the trousseau component of the dowry comprises clothing, bed linen, and so on. Over the past several decades there has been a noticeable shift in proportions. Nowadays it contains relatively little clothing and a fair amount of linen, while in the past, it consisted almost exclusively of clothing. Crna Gorci say that, in earlier times, a bride should come to her husband's household completely outfitted for life. As far as clothing is concerned, she should not have to depend upon her conjugal unit for anything. This was seen as a device for reducing areas of friction between the women of the household. This same argument still applies. The modern wife is equipped with those items which serve her private, personal needs in her capacity as "wife". The objects she brings imply the status "married woman" — a woven bread bag, vests and scarves in the form and design that married women, as opposed to maidens, wear. They do not, however, imply the status of "mother". Cradle blankets and the other accoutrements of motherhood are later made by her, or are purchased for her by her new household.

The new bride is an outsider to her husband's household and she carries the stigma of an unwanted interloper. She is addressed as "bride" by those with longer service in the household — and initially this is everyone — or, more rarely, by the feminine form of her husband's Christian name. During the first year she should not make bread and is expected to wait on all the other members of the household. She should be the first one up in the morning to tend the fire and the last to bed at night. If anyone wants a drink, she is peremptorily ordered to leave her meal and fetch the water jug. Furthermore, she is isolated from her own kin and friends. When she ventures outside the homestead, she is accompanied by her mother-in-law or some other senior woman. She can visit her own family only on prescribed, and rare, occasions. The position of the new bride is not an enviable one. Nor does she obtain much comfort from her husband.

To the married adults of the household, and to the unmarried males, the bride threatens household unity. While her presence swells the ranks of the domestic workforce and promises to increase the size of the household with the birth of children, Crna Gorci hold that it is women who create dissension which leads to household division. It is the sexual bond, they suggest, that draws the husband into the web of his wife's misery and which reluctantly convinces him that they must divide. But to one another other members maintain the pretext that their solidarity is unyielding. The young groom is expected to show little interest in his bride. If he speaks to her at all in public, he should be gruff and commanding; and he should indicate no interest in the marital bed (cf. Campbell, 1964, pp. 65-66).

The trousseau, therefore, has a number of symbolic dimensions. It indicates, on the one hand, the exclusion of the bride from her natal household. In giving her compensation for labour and assistance, her family end any claims she may make for shelter and support. If she is widowed or divorced, she cannot expect to be received back. She will be given a warm welcome on her return visits, as will her children, but this is the hospitality due to a privileged outsider. It does not indicate that she has a home-away-from-home. When she does return, she does not revert to the demure and unassuming status of resident daughter, or even to the quiet efficiency of a wife. She becomes assertive, knowing, the master of new and better ways of doing things. In giving the trousseau, the bride's natal household has redefined the boundaries of their membership.

The boundaries of the groom's household have also been redefined. As a bride and wife, the new woman comes outfitted for life. She is among them, but outfitted by others so that she can never be completely of them. I think it is particularly significant that the items included in the public display are not associated with domestic production. The bride does not come endowed with land, livestock, buildings, or tools and not even the implements of the kitchen or nursery. These requisites for an independent domestic unit come from within and rights to them are established only through agnation and labour. Thus, when the groom's kinsmen take the bride and her trousseau back to the groom's home, the goods they carry represent neither an addition nor a threat to their productive capital.

V

In addition to her trousseau, the contemporary bride may also receive a gift of furniture from her natal household. The total amount to be spent is negotiated before the wedding. Usually the bride and groom visit the city with some of the bride's family to select the furniture and to arrange for its later delivery. While the number and quality of pieces vary from one wedding to the next, most gifts of furniture are likely to include a bed and wardrobe, table and chairs, and perhaps some other pieces as well. A very "modern" and well-to-do bride may select an electric stove and refrigerator, especially if she is to make her new home in Skopje.

The inclusion of furniture in the dowry is a very recent innovation. It had not been accepted by some of the poorer and more conservative households during my first period of fieldwork in 1966-67. But three years later gifts of furniture had become an integral part of *all* village weddings. Crna Gorci are keenly aware that it will be used in due course to help outfit an independent household. Perhaps this is why its delivery is arranged to take place after the wedding and with as little ostentation as possible. Certainly little is made of it during wedding festivities, and queries about this part of the dowry are met with evasive answers. In the past the groom's household provided the couple with a bed, and the bride with a wedding chest. When a loom was required, or a cradle, these were given by the head of the groom's household.

Nowadays when the bride has taken up residence in her new home and the bridal furniture has arrived, most of it is set aside in a room that is reserved for special guests and special occasions. Most visitors will never see it. But in that room it is merged and used with other effects. There is nothing which distinguishes the furniture of a particular wedding or of a particular couple. Yet its ownership is clear and when the household eventually divides, it is not included in the common stock of domestic equipment which is to be parcelled out.

But the furtive way in which bridal furniture is brought into the home cannot be explained solely in terms of the public opprobrium attached to division. Crna Gorci are generally reluctant to make a public display of wealth, for this might create envy and lead to vandalism and mystical attacks. It might also lead to requests for loans and assistance. To forestall such an eventuality, most peasants prefer to maintain a facade of uniform poverty. Then, if a request for help is received, they can say that they would like to help but are unable to do so because of their own strained circumstances. Old patched trousers and the deteriorating condition of an outbuilding are all used as evidence of inability, but not unwillingness. And the evidence must be good because Crna Gorci are extremely loath to ask assistance unless they are certain that their request cannot be denied. Any request, therefore, comes at the end of a long series of deliberations and it creates a most delicate situation for all involved. Those refusing a request must have plausible evidence and lots of it.

The bridal furniture is a necessary, but hidden, element in all contemporary weddings. In this respect it contrasts rather sharply with the trousseau. It contrasts in another way as well. While most people never see the bridal furniture, they do learn what it consists of. And since the items are few in number and their prices are easy to discover, village gossip very quickly passes remarkably accurate estimates of the furniture's cash value. The trousseau, in comparison, may include hundreds of different items. Some are purchased, some are made by hand by the bride and her family, some are made to order, and some are purchased and then embellished with hand work. So the trousseau, while it is displayed in "public", is very difficult to evaluate in monetary terms. And because of the number and variety of items, cash value is the only meaningful measure of one trousseau as opposed to another.

VI

The bride is also given a sum of cash as part of her dowry. Crna Gorci say this is money "for the pocket" and it is normally administered by the groom. It is important to note that only the bride, groom, and members of the bride's household know exactly how much is given.

The amount depends upon two things: the status of the groom and the wealth and standing of the bride. Let us begin with the groom. A village youth of good family and average means can demand about 300,000 dinars from the bride's household. But if he has some schooling and a promising career, then he might demand about 500,000. A poor peasant, on the other hand, can only expect 200,000 dinars.

Crna Gorci say that young men are only interested in courting maidens whose households can offer what they are worth. In the local view, therefore, it is money which attracts the youth. They do not expect that a promising young man would court a poor girl hoping that her family could raise the appropriate sum. The amount the girl's family is able to afford is relatively fixed and most villagers are quite shrewd in guessing the amount.

It could happen, of course, that some romantic youth from a prosperous family loses his heart to a poor maid and agrees to accept only a small sum of money. While the maiden's household might relish such a match, the youth is likely to encounter fierce opposition within his own family. His siblings will oppose the match because it would jeopardize their claims to a certain standing and, hence, the possibility of arranging an appropriate attachment for themselves. Considerations of prestige weigh heavily on other members as well. Furthermore, while Crna Gorci recognize yearning of the heart, they believe that community standing, property, capacity for work, and a congenial temperament are much more important in a marriage. As one woman explained, "After they have two children, any couple will find their common interest."

Because of this, a misalliance is strongly opposed within the groom's household. And since the groom must depend upon others for his livelihood, and since others will not support and finance a wedding that they oppose, the groom must acquiesce. Crna Gorci do say, however, that differences in family wealth were much less important in the past. As long as both families enjoyed a good reputation, it made little difference if the groom came from a prosperous household and the bride from a poor one.

In contrast to the groom, a prospective bride finds it somewhat easier to marry down. If she faces implacable opposition at home, she can always run away. The runaway (*begajka*) is quite a local figure. She may, of course, lose her dowry to the ire of her family.[1] To the groom this is a mixed blessing. On the one hand, he foregoes a useful sum and the possibility of some wedding furniture. His wife loses clothing and linen. But there is an enormous amount of prestige to be gained. With a *begajka* in their midst, the groom and his kinsmen can strut and boast for years. They are such princely folk, they claim, that maidens will run away from home to marry them. On one occasion when a *begajka* arrived at a neighbour's house, I was called out to witness the spectacle. A huge throng had assembled. Everyone, including an aged grandmother in the household, was dancing and roaring drunk. The festivities continued all night and by the next day they had managed to hire some musicians. The celebration lasted several days. As onlookers explained, it would take them a year, perhaps two, to save for the wedding, but they would have the additional labour of the bride-to-be to help them.

As a result of her dramatic flight, the maid's natal household becomes the butt of gossip and humour. Little of it is good natured and none of it is said to their face. Since several villages have their quota of *begajkas*, they will know what is being said behind their backs. Therefore, the threat of a runaway maid ensures that most households will listen carefully when a girl voices strong opinions about whom she will marry. They may oppose her intentions, but they do so with great tact. Thus, while youths almost never marry below their station, maidens sometimes do.

[1] The question of right is a difficult one in these circumstances. While the maiden is still entitled to the dowry, she cannot arrange for its delivery until amends have been made.

Money is always kept by the wife in her wedding chest. This is kept locked and the keys hang from her belt. These keys, along with a bread knife which hangs from the same belt, indicate wifely status. No one except the wife, or the husband accompanied by her, ever has access to this chest. Its contents are private and, in large measure, unknown to others. Part of the dowry money will go into this chest to meet the private expenses of husband and wife. But since the groom's household is likely to be short of cash after meeting the various wedding expenses, the couple is wise to dispose of the dowry money before it can be requested as a temporary loan from the household. Formerly, I was told, they would give the money to money lenders to be put out at interest. Some may still do this although it is more likely for them to invest in a small field or in additional furniture. Then, if they are asked for a loan, they can say that their dowry money is all spent.

Since only the bride, groom and the bride's household know exactly how much cash is included in the dowry, the groom is inclined to inflate the amount when boasting to his friends. His revelations are usually received with appreciation, but will later be discussed with great scepticism. This, in turn, creates a real problem for prospective grooms. On the one hand they are led to believe that dowry money is given in smaller sums than is generally reported by husbands, a belief which is supported by village gossip. Therefore, when later negotiating on his own behalf for this money, a suitor might be inclined to seek a relatively modest sum. And this might lead him to ask for less than the bride's household is really prepared to give. Consequently, he could actually receive less than his due and thereby appear foolish to his in-laws. It is impossible to collect satisfactory data on this, but it is my impression that prospective grooms, fearing this possibility, tend initially to ask for inflated amounts and then settle, after some hard bargaining, for slightly less than publicly stated averages.

As I have already explained, members of the bride's household have a clear upper limit on the amount they are willing to spend on a particular wedding. About half of the total is earmarked for the cash gift; the remainder is spent on the trousseau, bridal furniture, and festive expenses. The mechanism which keeps the proportions relatively fixed is the opposing interests of the groom and the bride's family. For his part, the groom is most interested in the cash although he, too, is concerned that the bride's family make a good impression with the trousseau and their part of the festivities. They, on the other hand, want to keep their cash outlay to a minimum, since they require cash for a number of different purposes and it is extremely difficult to obtain. They could, of course, give the groom only a small amount of cash while investing heavily in the feasting and goods on display. But few grooms would agree to this.

Another option would be to give the groom a large amount of cash and then reduce other expenses. But since only they and the groom ever see the cash, other villagers would not believe the story. The bride's family is most concerned with maintaining and enhancing their standing as it affects the marriage choices of other members. Their standing is closely pegged to those items which can be publicly scrutinized.

Competing interests keep the various categories of wedding expense in rough proportion. It is these proportions that outsiders use in gauging the overall wedding investment. I should add that the bride's family can only estimate their investment in a single wedding since it represents the labour and savings of several years of effort.

It is paradoxical that the largest component of the dowry — the cash gift — should be the most difficult for outsiders to evaluate. Even though it is given in a medium whose worth is common knowledge, the actual gift is given in secret and its substance is deliberately mis-represented. The cash value of the bridal furniture is also not easy to judge and it is transferred in such a way that it is not readily access-ible to public scrutiny. The component of the dowry which is, as it were, most visible is the trousseau. But since it contains a large variety of different items, its assessment presents a formidable task. As I now turn to consider other wedding prestations, we shall see that this set of dowry components is paralleled by another.

VII

Several monetary streams flow into the conjugal fund held by the married couple. Having just examined the cash gift in the dowry, I wish to consider, first, those small gifts of money which the wedding guests give to the bride, add to the basket of clothing, or press into the apple for the groom. Each guest gives a bill or coin of small denomin-ation. The exact amount depends upon the tie between donor and recipient. A very close relative, or the ritual sponsor, might contribute one thousand to five thousand dinars, a close relative between five hundred and one thousand, and an ordinary guest about one hundred. The guests know beforehand the exact number of occasions on which they will be obliged to give and they know how much is appropriate. This money, and perhaps a bit extra for tipping the musicians, is given to them by their *domaćin* and it comes out of their common household purse. It is impossible to get accurate figures on how much the bride and groom collect in this way, but I estimate that there are about seven different occasions when money gifts are called for. Rough calculations indicate that a wedding with an "average" number of guests would yield about 120,000 dinars (£40).

This is a small, but important, sum. I find it significant that a gift which marks the distance between the donor and recipient should find its way into the private funds of the bride and groom. It represents the tie to this particular couple and not, let it be noted, between the donating household and the household of the groom. In most cases, of course, these are virtually the same; but where they are not, it is the guest/couple relationship that determines the amount. It is as if the guests, in their capacity as kinsmen, are financing the formation of an embryo of dissolution within the womb of the household. Note further that when the money is intended for the groom, or when it is given solely in the presence of agnates (as during the engagement party), it is given publicly and with a certain amount of display. But when it is given to the bride, it is, or it should be, slipped surreptitiously into her palm. Some informants claimed that this was to protect her sensibilities. Others said, and perhaps this amounts to the same thing, that the mother-in-law should not be shown the private fund that is being established under her roof. In fact, most of these monies pass through the mother-in-law's hands and she takes note if any guest does not meet his obligations. But she probably does not have a very accurate idea of the total amount collected.

Some of this money, like the dowry money, will be invested. But most of it is kept by the couple to cover personal, incidental expenses. When asked for examples, Crna Gorci said it would probably be used to buy special clothing for their children.

In addition to money, wedding guests also bring presents to the festivities. Peasants usually give enamelled cooking pots. Guests from the city are more likely to bring pictures for the wall, small lamps, and other decorative items. None of these items, however, are received by the bridal couple. Usually the groom's mother greets each guest at the door and she takes them. They are given to the groom's household and will be used, and later divided, as ordinary domestic equipment. These gifts are, therefore, gifts to the household as a unit. When pressed for an explanation, informants said that the entire household should receive them because they had all worked to put on the wedding.

Significantly, these gifts have a corporate donor as well as recipient. Both parties acknowledge that the guest is acting as a representative of his domestic unit. The gift will have been purchased out of common funds and its value is an expression of social distance between the two households. Enamel ware makes a useful gift because it is available in a range of different sized objects. It follows that if several guests attend from the same household, only one, the designated representative, brings a gift; but each guest will separately give money to the bridal couple.

One informant told me that the bridal couple do not resent the corporate destination of these gifts. Indeed, the stock of enamel ware received at any single wedding is usually far in excess of the household's requirements and so some of it, perhaps most of it, will be redistributed when the unit sends a representative to other weddings. While I have no direct evidence of this happening, I was told that some households have arrangements with merchants whereby gifts can be returned for cash or credit. I doubt whether this is common practice.

The final type of presentation that I want to consider are the gifts of clothing which are given to their guests by the celebrating household. Towards the end of the wedding feast, the bride comes around to each guest accompanied by her mother-in-law. After she kisses the hand and the guest slips her some money, she places a gift of clothing on the guest's shoulder. Her mother-in-law hands her the appropriate gift. A close male kinsman might receive a white dress-shirt, a more distant one an undershirt, and the most remote a pair of socks. There is a comparable set of items for female guests. Here again, but in contrast to gifts of domestic ware, social distance is measured by the relationship between the couple and the particular guest. The mother-in-law accompanies the bride to ensure that each guest receives the proper gift.

It is particularly important to the groom's household that they have enough gifts for each category of guest. Since it is difficult to predict accurately how many will attend, however, they must buy enough to be safe. Reasonably precise guesses may be made for the more expensive gifts because the number of close kin is relatively small and their presence is almost a certainty. The problem arises in respect of more distant kin and friends. Poor weather and competing fetes will result in a small attendance, whereas more favourable conditions could produce one of several hundred. To save themselves embarrassment, then, many households buy from merchants who will accept the return of unused gifts, but at the cost of a slightly higher purchase price. The outlay for these gifts is the heaviest expense that the groom's household is likely to face.

The clothing itself becomes the personal possession of each recipient guest. Other household members have no right to it even though the guest was a corporate representative. As Crna Gorci explain, all adult members have regular opportunities to attend weddings and some units choose delegates by rota. Since each one receives dozens of invitations every year, all individuals have a chance to attend. Indeed, sometimes they may be short-handed when several different fetes are being held in different villages.

VIII

What do these various prestations mean? In this concluding section I shall separate the various strands of argument into two broad, but related, categories: basic structural conditions and dominant symbolic themes.

Crna Goran weddings are, pre-eminently, occasions when agnatic solidarity is emphasized. While agnation does not have the economic and political significance it once had, it still remains a vital structural feature in village life, for exogamous clans are the units which alienate their own women in order to receive others. Weddings dramatize this transfer. But it is rights in procreative power that are being alienated and appropriated. These transactions do not, as I have argued, involve the transfer of other forms of productive property. Rights to land, dwellings, livestock, and other productive resources are not transferred at weddings.

A clan must give women in order to receive them, for its continuity depends upon others. Indeed, its reputation depends upon this process of giving and receiving. The actual units in these exchanges are households. But since individual households are only relatively durable, and since it is difficult to assess the reputation of several thousand of these, public opinion tends to treat all the constituent units of a single clan as being much alike.

It follows that group boundaries are critically important in these exchanges. As I have noted, ties of clanship are not given by a genealogical framework. Villagers, unless they know one another well, tend to derive clan affiliation from household membership and, to a lesser extent, neighbourhood. Because of this, the differing ties of affinity and kinship (as opposed to agnation) within a household can jeopardize its internal solidarity and allocation of responsibility, and this is especially clear in those units which contain a resident son-in-law (*domazet*) and his family. It is important, if households are to operate as strongly corporate entities, for the loyalty of women and children to be unambiguously fixed: this is brought out during wedding festivities.

The wedding effects the transfer of a woman from one group to another. The boundaries of both, and the process of transfer, is clearly marked in the festivities. Once the bride departs from her natal group with her trousseau, they are no longer obliged to offer her support and protection. The giving of the trousseau symbolizes that she has fulfilled her obligations to her family, and they have fulfilled theirs. Significantly, her kinsmen and her ritual sponsor are called to witness her passage into the custody of another group, but they do *not* observe the rites of her incorporation into that group. That is, as it were, an internal matter for them. Once she leaves, the ties and attachments she makes are no longer of concern.

Much the same can be observed on the groom's side. When they set off to fetch the bride, it is the groom's agnates and his ritual sponsor that make up the procession. They are concerned that their kinsman and the bride's kinsmen have made a proper transfer; and the following day during the church service, the *kum*, *stari svat*, and *dever* will testify to this before the priest.

As the boundaries of her natal group close firmly behind her, and as their involvement in the exchange ends, a complex series of changes is occurring within the groom's group. I shall simplify the discussion by considering, firstly, those which occur within the (undifferentiated) clan and, secondly, those within the groom's immediate household. The interests of the groom's clansmen centre on the procreative powers that are being transacted. I have noted that the entire wedding process features these powers. A gift of undergarments initiates the sequence. These nylons, brassiéres, and slips are not part of ordinary village dress and it is unlikely that, save for these very gifts, most village women own any. The sexual and procreative element is unmistakable.

Similarly, when the groom's kinsmen set out to fetch the bride from her natal home, they impale an orange or apple on the point of the standard which leads the procession. Significantly, it must be a virginal youth of the groom's clan (and preferably from his household) who carries the standard. As the procession winds its way through the village towards the bride's home, the maidens sing songs which make allusions to the deflowering of the bride. Sexuality, as opposed to maternity, is a theme that occurs in other parts of the festivities as well. On the morning of the church service, the young women of the groom's household knead a loaf of bread (see below). The risen dough is carried amidst much hilarity to a young unmarried man of the groom's house who proceeds to slam a pestle into the middle of it. The young man is usually very embarrassed and reluctant to perform this act, but he is chased, cornered, and harassed until he relents. The maidens of the groom's household, and of closely related households, are preoccupied with the bride's deflowering. They make allusions to it in their singing, as I have noted, and after the wedding night they joke with the groom's mother as she sets out to carry sweetened brandy to the wedding guests. As she leaves the household, they throw water on the front of her costume and claim that she is so excited by the successful deflowering that she has urinated on herself. The presence of the *kum* during the celebration is integral to the transfer of procreative power. His blessings are necessary to ensure the continuity of the group. Without them children will die. Procreative power, however, is not the only issue.

Affinity must also be dealt with if clan boundaries are to remain sharp and unambiguous. Affinity depends upon the "fusion" of the roles of daughter, wife, and mother. As a rite of status passage, the wedding separates these several statuses and gives them different emphasis.

As a newcomer to the group, the bride has only shadowy status as a wife and no standing as a mother. She is received and treated much as a daughter. Note that she greets the guests by kissing their hands and offering them brandy: this was the last symbolic act she performed before leaving her natal home. In the course of daily life this small ritual of greeting and homage is left to the daughters of the household. During her first year of marriage, the bride wears clothing which is essentially an augmented version of the maiden's outfit. She dons the distinctive dress of a married woman only later. Similarly, the bride is immediately incorporated into the work parties of the unmarried women and treated as part of her mother-in-law's conjugal family. She will help others, and even make clothing for them, but she is not given wool in her own right as a married woman. Neither is she permitted to bake bread. Significantly, she addresses her father, her husband's father, his *kum*, and his *stari svat* as *"tate"* (father).

If the bride is treated as "daughter", little is made of her new status as wife. As I have noted, the bond between husband and wife is treated as if it did not exist. Indeed, her husband plays only a small part in the entire wedding celebration.[1] Bride and groom are extremely prudish when in the presence of others; but she is permitted, indeed expected, to engage in sexual horseplay with her *dever*. Her relationship with him is much like that between a brother and sister. Her status as wife is presaged by the gift of bread knife and key from the *dever*. Later on her wifely status will be reflected in the chest that is given to her for storing her trousseau and money, and in being addressed in the feminine form of her husband's Christian name. But the couple emerge clearly as a conjugal unit only with the birth of their first child.[2] Indeed, it might be said that the union of husband and wife is more clearly marked in the christening rite than it is during the wedding.

There is one further status involved here, and this brings us to the last of the structural conditions featured in wedding celebrations. The mother-in-law, as I have shown, is a prominent figure in the festivities. The identity between bride and mother-in-law is close, and appropriate. It is through these outsiders that the household and clan grow and flourish. A large household, and a substantial clan, are sources of pride. Crna Gorci believe that both wealth and power derive from numbers of members. And a large household is a testament to a skillful *domaćin* and harmonious relationships. But continuity and growth are only possible through women who come from the outside.

As I have shown, the mother-in-law is one of the two people that the bride makes special garments for, the other being the groom. Her

[1] Among the Bedouin of Cyrenaica, the father of the groom absents himself from the proceedings. Compare the discussion in Peters (1965).
[2] This point has frequently been made with reference to the African literature, but it has not generally been thought to apply to Europe (cf. Radcliffe-Brown, 1950, p. 49).

presence is felt immediately when the new wife returns after the church service. Sticks of firewood are strewn along the way and she picks these up as she moves along. Her mother-in-law bars the door upon her return and she is only given entrée after she kisses the hand of the older woman and presents her with the wood. Later, in every appearance before the guests, she is accompanied by the latter: when she offers brandy to the guests, the mother-in-law holds the bottle; when she is given money by the guests, it passes into the mother-in-law's hands; when she gives each guest a gift, it is the mother-in-law who chooses it and passes it to her. Indeed, she is everywhere guided and directed by the mother-in-law. Even the successful consummation of the marriage is announced by her.

Several symbolic dimensions are involved here. On the one hand, mother and son are closely identified. Crna Gorci claim that this is the strongest human bond and it is the subject of numerous songs and stories. It is because of her sons, they say, that a woman is successful in cajoling her husband into dividing from his brothers and establishing an independent household. Thus, in mediating between the bride and the guests, the mother substitutes for her son. It is perhaps significant in this regard that mother-in-law and daughter-in-law do not appear together in any context where the bride's sexuality is at issue.

The mother-in-law may be said to mediate in another sense. During the feasting when the bride and her husband's mother make their appearances together, the groom's agnates are busy helping in the kitchen and in carrying dishes to the guests. These guests tend to be kinsmen, but not agnates, who are related to the groom through his mother. It could be said, therefore, that the mother-in-law presents the bride to those guests that both she and her son share in common.

But more important, through the developmental cycle in the domestic group, the new bride will one day become the mistress of the household and a mother-in-law herself. The wedding festivities, and the linking of bride with the husband's mother, presage this cycle. But there is a fundamental paradox involved in this. On the one hand the new bride will ensure the continuity of the larger agnatic group as children are born to her. On the other, this continuity is likely to be achieved at the cost of dissolving the household of the mother-in-law. For her part, the mother-in-law is determined to prevent division since it would destroy the esteem she enjoys in the community as well as jeopardizing her material well-being.

In sum, the wedding highlights a number of structural conditions. First among these is the strong corporate nature of the Crna Goran household and the importance of its boundaries vis-à-vis similar units. Secondly, household boundedness and agnatic solidarity are closely linked to the denial of affinity. But this, in turn, can be achieved only by decomposing and segregating the three female roles that affinity depends upon: those of wife, mother, and daughter. And, finally, the continuity and internal elaboration of the lineage depends upon the eventual replacement of the mother-in-law by the bride, and with it the likely dissolution of the original household. As we have seen, these three structural features are marked, respectively, in three sets of gifts given in the wedding celebration.

Thus, household solidarity is clearly celebrated in the wedding presents which guests give to the groom's unit. In-so-far as they are incorporated into the common property of the latter, they highlight the strongly corporate nature of Crna Goran households, as does the fact that the guests are the representatives of invited units. And how better could the dilemma of continuity in division be portrayed than to have the mother-in-law receive these gifts of communally owned and used pots and pans?

Dowry, too, carries a complex structural message. The negation of affinity and the separation of the roles of daughter, wife and mother are reflected in the three components of this dowry. The trousseau stands for the bride as *daughter*, both in her natal homestead and in her new one. It is given amidst much display and indicates household prestige at the same time as it asserts that the daughter has fulfilled her obligations to her natal family; and, with this endowment, she will not be a drain on the resources of her home or a threat to its solidarity.

But the cash represents something quite different. This second component of the dowry goes to the bride as *wife*. She will keep it secreted away in her marriage chest where it will be used by the couple to finance personal expenditures which may, significantly, include children's clothing. It is no wonder, then, that this source of differentiation within the household is given covertly and in unknown quantity.

The third component of the dowry is the bridal furniture. This is the "corner-stone" of a new home. It symbolizes a future that is both threatening and hopeful; threatening to the stability of the house that the new bride joins, yet hopeful to the lineage that will flourish through her productive and reproductive capacities. The bridal bed and the kitchen furniture are associated with the role of *mother*. And these items, as we have seen, come last in the sequence of dowry presentations. The manner in which they are given reflects the ambiguity associated with motherhood. They appear in due course, after the wedding festivities are past, and with little fanfare.

It is striking that these components of the dowry, with their symbolic associations to the different roles of the bride, and the temporal sequence in which they are manifest, should be given by the bride's natal household. It is they who provide the means through which affinity is symbolically negated. And, thus, they enhance the boundedness of the group which the bride leaves, and the one into which she passes.

The final set of gifts are the festive presents given to the bride by the guests, and to the guests by the bride. These are, clearly, tokens of relationship. But since there are few denominations which must cover a wide range of relationships, there can be some room for negotiation over the closeness of a particular tie. In the majority of cases, however, they mark out spheres and categories of attachment for the bride to see and take due note. These festive gifts carry other meanings as well. It is significant in these exchanges that the guests give money and receive clothing. Money, the symbol of affinity, must, however, be transferred furtively whereas clothing, the symbol of kinship, is openly presented, and the legitimate use of this money, as Crna Gorci express it, is to transform it into clothing: to pass, in other words, from affinity to kinship.

Dowry in Skopska Crna Gora, then, has little to do with the devolution of property, as is often suggested in the analyses of such marriage prestations (e.g. Goody, 1973, 1976a, b). But, as I have demonstrated, it has everything to do with relationships, their quality, and their transformation. In this respect, interpretations which dwell on objects of property and their devolution would be fundamentally mistaken and profoundly unsociological. In Skopska Crna Gora, the dowry, and the wedding festivities of which it is a part, are an elaborate commentary on the relationship between agnation and affinity.

Bibliography

Campbell, J. (1964). "Honour, Family and Patronage". Clarendon Press, Oxford.

Denich, B. (1974). Sex and power in the Balkans. *In* "Woman, Culture and Society" (Eds. S. M. Rosaldo and L. Lamphere). Stanford University Press, Stanford.

Goody, J. (1973). Bridewealth and dowry in Africa and Eurasia. *In* "Bridewealth and Dowry" (Eds. J. Goody and S. J. Tambiah). Cambridge University Press, London.

Goody, J. (1976a). "Production and Reproduction". Cambridge University Press, London.

Goody, J. (1976b). Inheritance, property and women: some comparative considerations. *In* "Family and Inheritance" (Eds. J. Goody, J. Thirsk and E. P. Thompson). Cambridge University Press, London.

Halpern, J. and Halpern, B. (1972). "A Serbian Village in Historical Perspective". Holt, Rinehart & Winston, New York.

Hammel, E. (1968). "Alternative Social Structures and Ritual Relations in the Balkans". Prentice-Hall, Englewood Cliffs, New Jersey.

Lodge, O. (1941). "Peasant Life in Jugoslavia". Seeley Service, London.

Peters, E. L. (1965). Aspects of the family among the bedouin of Cyrenaica. *In* "Comparative Family Systems" (Ed. M. Nimkoff). Houghton Mifflin, Boston.

Petrović, A. (1907). Narodni život i običaji u Skopska Crnoj Gori. *Srpski Etnog. Zbornik* (Običaji Naroda Srpskoga) 1, 335-528.

"Popis Stanovništva" (1961). Belgrade.

Radcliffe-Brown, A. R. (1950). Introduction. *In* "African Systems of Kinship and Marriage" (Eds. A. R. Radcliffe-Brown and D. Forde). Oxford University Press, London.

Rheubottom, D. B. (1971). A structural analysis of conflict and cleavage in Macedonian domestic groups. Ph.D. thesis, University of Rochester.

Rheubottom, D. B. (1976a). The saint's feast and Skopska Crna Goran social structure. *Man* (N.S.), 11, 18-34.

Rheubottom, D. B. (1976b). Time and form: contemporary Macedonian households and the Zadruga controversy. *In* "Communal Families in the Balkans" (Ed. R. Byrnes). University of Notre Dame Press, Notre Dame.

Acknowledgements

Fieldwork in Skopska Crna Gora was conducted in 1966-67 and in the autumn of 1970. I am indebted to the Dept. of Anthropology of the University of Rochester and to the University of Houston Faculty Research Support Program for their grants. In 1966-67 I was affiliated to the Economics Faculty of the University of Skopje. I wish to acknowledge the many kindnesses extended to me by the (then) Rector Ksente Bogoev and by Dr. Vlado Taneski. These materials have been discussed in seminars at the University of Manchester and the School of Oriental and African Studies. I am grateful to the participants for their comments and suggestions. Both the form and substance of this chapter have received the detailed attention of Drs. John Comaroff and Richard Werbner. But since I have not always had the wisdom to follow their advice, they cannot be held responsible for extant errors.

Index

A

Adonara, 112, 113
Adoption, 99, 103, 107, 113
Adultery, women accused of, 145
Affiliation of children, 6, 18, 19
Affinal ties, 8, 12, 13, 14, 15, 16, 17, 19, 21, 35, 37, 40, 42, 50, 59, 63, 65, 74, 87, 88, 93, 107, 108
Africa and Eurasia, bridewealth and dowry, 7
African attitudes, 95
African socio-economic situation, 9
African and Indian societies, exchanges at marriage, 63
   Southern conjugal and bridewealth arrangements, 192
African segmentary lineage model, 19, 164
African societies, 8, 13, 16, 49, 50, 52, 55, 59, 63, 68, 164, 197
African systems, 6, 8
Agnates, 7, 71, 73, 74, 75, 76, 77, 98, 102, 107, 109, 128, 135, 138, 149, 152, 153, 155, 159, 164, 222, 240, 248
Agnatic affinal and matrilateral ties, 177
   groupings, 189
   solidarity, 242
   unit, 166, 169, 173, 175, 176, 177

uterine and affinal ties, 198, 201, 206, 207
Agricultural economy, cattle in, 83
Alliance, affinal, 98, 112, 114, 125, 128, 146, 147, 148, 149, 152, 153, 154, 157, 162, 164, 176, 177, *bagwe/ bagwagadi* 169, 171, 178, 180, 186, 187, 198, 244, 247, 248
   asymmetric (*see* Affinal alliance)
   exchanges, 107
   pattern of, 102
   political and formal, 192
   pragmatic action, 187
   prestations, 96
   structurally defined, 164
   terms of, 96
   traditional ties, 103, 107
Allotted herd, 87
Almagor, U., 76, 87, 91
Al-walad li'l' farsh, 145
Amanatun, 109
Amarasi, 107, 109
Amassai, 70
Amb pek rui, 58
Amfoan, 106, 108
Anas of Amanatun, 109
Ancillary values, 49, 59
Animals, 151

Anthropology, 1, 3, 17, 32, 33, 63, 95, 98, 161
"Appointed daughter", position of, 51, 63
Ardener, E. W., 2, 44
Arndt, P., 110, 111, 112, 113, 121
Aroa urukaki or *aroa urukoa mereki*, 61
Arusha, 90, 91
Ashanti, 69
Asia, perspectives on bridewealth, 49
Asian practice of uxorilocal residence, 63
   systems of prestations, 95
Aswa'n, 135
Atoni,
   agnation, shift from, 109
   alliance ties, 107, 108
   area occupied by, 106
   bridewealth, 97
   definition and continuation, 98
   unilineal descent, 118
Aulad'Ali, tribe in Egypt, 137
Australian and Papua New Guinea goods, 52

B

Ba dula mmogo, 165
Ba ga etsho (mogolo), 176
Bagwe/bagwagadi, 176
Baker, P. R., 81, 91
Bamalete, 18
Baraka, 143, 144
Barolong boo Ratshidi (Tshidi), 163
Barnes, J. A., 1, 6, 10, 28, 29, 30, 36, 37, 39, 41, 42, 43, 44, 50, 65
Barnes, R. H., 110, 112, 113, 114, 115, 121
Barotse, 18
Barth, F., 8, 11, 44, 164, 178, 194
Bedouin,
   animals as bridewealth, 144, 151, 159
   bridewealth, 41, 140, 141
   camels, negotiation for, 143
   cousin marriage, 157
   FBD marriage systems, 29
   hulwan, 144
   incest group, limited, 158

kissing of heads, 143
land, 159
mahr, 144
marriage, 133
   prestations, 38, 39
   relationship, patterns of, 35
   transhumant pastoralists, 129
Berreman, G. D., 12, 44
Berthe, L., 97, 101, 102, 103, 104, 106, 121
Betrothals, Muslim-Digo, 213
Bilateral kin, 12, 13, 14, 16
Blau, P., 11, 44
Bogadi (see Bridewealth)
Bohannan, P., 208, 220
Bonyatsi, 165
Bourdieu, P., 29, 44
Brides,
   agnate, close, 71
   capital value represented in, 57
   child bearing, 65
   deflowering, 244
   descendant, agnatic, 74
   dowry, sum of cash, 236
   economic value of, 59
   endowed, 231
   exogamous unilineal systems, 40
   families, 4, 5, 14, 239
   father, 57, 63, 75, 76, 142, 143, 207, 211
   furniture, 231, 234, 235, 236, 237, 239, 247
   genetricial rights, 201
   gifts, 248
   groom, meeting, 223
   groom, celebrations and, 225
   groom, relationship with, 245
   hajara, 156
   household of, 224, 228, 238
   items to receive, 147
   kin, 57, 77, 140, 141, 200, 213
   labour, 231
   mother of, 115, 246
   mother-in-law, replacement of, 247
   negotiations, bride and groom, 138
   outsider to husband's household, 237

Brides (*contd*)
  parents and marriage gifts, 110
  pigs sent with, 65
  prestations, 40
  price, 22
  private funds of, 240
  sexual and procreative capacities, 50, 231
  trousseau, 226, 234, 236, 243
  virgin, 227
Bridewealth,
  affinal tie, 35
  Africa, in, 16
  alienation of rights, and, 5
  Amfoan, 108
  amount of, 71, 75, 81, 90, 91
  analogue of dowry, and, 14
  analysis of, 28
  animal wealth, 159
  arrangements, 20, 22, 26
  Bedouin, 125
  camels, and, 152
  cash, introduction of, 43
  cattle, 71, 75, 81, 90, 91
  conjugal fund aspect, 54
  commercial character of, 15
  compensation to agnates, 7
  conditions, 6
  control over, 23
  currency of, 24
  distribution of, 73, 88
  economic value, 95
  explanation of, 5, 11, 15
  father and, 139
  gifts, return, 111
  goods and valuables, 52, 55
  Indonesia, in, 118
  inter-group affinal ties, 17
  kind and hard cash, 197
  label, as, 10
  legal dimension of, 19
  lineal devolution and, 8
  marriage and, 104, 112, 154
  Melpa and Wiru, among, 49, 65
  Mursi, economics of, 67, 69
  negotiations, 53, 148, 169
  odd-job word, as, 68
  passage of, 18, 42, 164, 168, 191
  payments, 50, 59, 62, 70, 83, 85, 87, 93, 107, 109
  presence or absence of, 97
  prestations and, 4, 96
  property and name, 110
  progeny of union and, 171
  purchase, commercial, 119
  return of, 209, 214, 215
  rights, 151, 156
  sahiba, 144, 145, 146
  stock, 78, 79, 86
  theorising and generalisations, 63
  transactions, 49, 73, 208
  transfers, 12, 162, 165, 182
  Tshidi, features of, 167
  Tswana chiefdom, in, 161
  use of, 51
  uxorial and genetricial rights, 188
  variations in, 155
  wife-givers, and, 37
Brown, L. H., 78, 80, 85, 86, 91
"Bruidschat", 94
Buganda, 23
Buna' (of Eastern Indonesia)
  bridewealth, 97
  children, 106, 118
  corporation, definition and continuance 98
  descent groups, 99, 104
  marriage, 6, 37, 102, 103
  neighbours of the Ema, 101
  two primary forms of union, 37
Butzer, K. W., 79, 91

C

Camels, and Turkana economy, 85
Campbell, J., 233, 249
Capital value and prestation, 49, 50
Cattle wealth,
  and bridewealth, 70, 71, 75
  economic role, 81
Children,
  adoption of, 104
  affiliation of, 97

Children (*contd*)
  affiliation to father's descent group,
    102, 171
  birth and naming, 96
  "bodies", 62
  corporations and, 93
  division of, 100
  divorce and, 101
  initiation of wife into husband's lineage,
    107
  legitimate and illegitimate, 191
  lineage membership, no, 105
  marriage in, 62
  matrilateral, patrilateral links, 97
  mother's lineage and, 103
  mother's patrilineage, 100
  no bridewealth, 109
  patrifiliation, 211
  payment, 118
  prestations and rights, 19
  resultant independence, 114
  rights, 108, 210
  suckled by same woman, 132
  wealth, 59
  wife's lineage, 105
Chonyi,
  bridewealth, 208
  livestock and bridewealth, 207
  marriage, 203, 204, 206, 207, 216, 217
  status, 210
Chopi of Mozambique, 193
Clamagirand, Brigitte, 99, 100, 101, 121
Clients,
  accumulation of, 23
  "client of the goodness", 143
  marriage to daughters of freeborn
    men, 152
Co-habitation, 183, 184
  and mokwele, 170
  and payments, 213
Cohen, A. P. and Comaroff, J. L., 177,
    178, 194
Coquery-Vidrovitch, C., 23, 44
Comaroff, J. L., 18, 36, 41, 178, 179
Comaroff, J. L. and Comaroff, J., 13,
    165, 177, 178

Comaroff, Jean, 18, 44, 164
Comaroff, J. L., and Roberts, S., 11, 18,
    44
Commoners, 102
Common fund, 14
Community, 23
Concubinage,
  distinction between marriage and, 163
  as an established liaison, 165
  and non-payment, 169
  nyatsi, 183
Conjugal bond, 12
  fund, 8, 53-55
  process, 168, 169
  productive unit, 53
Conjugal expectations,
  arrangements as political or social
    investments, 190
  customary, 172
  management, 184
  process, formal, 174
  progress, 174
  roles, 174
  strategy, 184
Consanguinity,
  and Islamic law, 133
  conditions for marriage and, 138
  degrees of, 128
  opposition to affinity, 42
Contract, 18
  contractual definition, 17
Corporate unity, 9, 117, 120
Corporate groups,
  agnates and, 159
  alliances and, 137
  bridewealth, 139
  economy, 157
  selected marriages, 154
Cost-benefit ratio, 4, 6
Crna Goran, 14
Cross-cousin unions, 29, 40
  agnatic group and, 135, 136, 137
  Islamic law and, 133, 134
  likelihood of, 154
  matrilateral, 102
  property and, 12

Cross-cousin unions (*contd*)
  Tshidi and, 12
Cross-cultural comparisons, 2
  diversity, 24
  diversity of marriage payments, 2
  marriage payments and, 33
  marriage transactions, variability, 40
Cunningham, C. E., 97, 106, 107, 108, 118, 121

D

Dahl, G. and Hjort, A., 78, 86, 91
Daribi, 60
Dassanetch, 70, 77, 86, 87
Daughter, maintaining status of, 63
De Heusch, 28, 44
Descent systems,
  alliance, 17
  bridewealth, 93
  corporateness, 9, 12, 94, 116, 120
  descent lines, 74
  groups, 15, 97, 98, 102, 111, 112, 176
  ideology, 12, 17, 25
  matrilineal and patrilineal, 109, 117
  rules, 43, 64, 120
  structure, 6, 104, 111
  theory, 8, 16
Deschler, W. W., 84, 86, 91
Dhok, 200
Digo, muslim, 210, 212, 213, 214, 216, 217
Dis, 148
Disease, 71, 79
Divorce, 86, 100, 101, 103, 111, 113, 115, 133, 183, 198, 199
  uxorial and childbirth payments, 204, 205, 206, 212, 215, 216
Dodos, in Karimojong cluster, 84
Domacin, 229, 230, 240, 245
Douglas, M., 24, 44
Dowry,
  among the Digo, 216
  amount of, 232
  bargain, result of, 12
  bridewealth and, 7, 51, 67, 68

compensation, 230
component of, 53, 232, 239, 247, 248
creation of, 215
culture areas in, 11
dower and, 4
endemic, 8
furniture, 234
in India, 12
in Macedonia, 5
labour and, 232
loss of, 237
marriage and, 41
money, 240
necessary conditions, 9
particular societies in, 15
payments, 217
social characteristics, 13
token, 232
types of items, 227
Dumont, L., 8, 44, 94, 96, 121, 162, 194
Dupré, G. and Rey, R. P., 23, 45
Duruma,
  cattle, 207, 210, 211
  divorce, low rate, 212
  marriage, 212, 214, 216, 217, 218
Dyson-Hudson, N., 81, 91

E

East Africa, 6, 78, 90
East African herding peoples, 67, 68, 69, 70, 76, 89
Eastern Indonesia, 40-42
  hierarchization, 9
  kinship, 98
  marriage exchanges, 93
  two forms of marriage, 6
  unilineal descent, affinal alliance and marriage exchanges, 16
East Sumba society, 95
Ecology, 9
Economy, agricultural, 83
Economy of Mursi bridewealth, 67
Economistic logic, 6
Economistic model, 7
Egalitarianism, 21, 28

Egypt, 137
Elders, 22, 23, 24, 25
Elopement, 213, 214
Ema, 98, 99, 101, 104, 106, 116
Endogamy, 110
Engagement feast (*zagovorka*) 224
Epidemics,
  bovine trypanosomiasis, 71
Epistemological, 3, 32, 43
Epistemology, 1, 2, 15
Evans-Pritchard, E. E., 1, 10, 18, 34, 76,
    78, 79, 81, 94, 95, 126, 127, 128,
    129, 151, 170, 199, 200, 220
Exogamy, 125-129
  group and, 118
  patrilineages and, 114
  proscriptions, 17
  rules of affiliation and, 42

F

Fallers, L. A., 9, 45, 198, 220
Fatiha, 143
FBD unions, 12, 17, 29, 41, 133
  marriage, 164
FBS, 182
Female property rights, 12
Fertility, 146, 150, 204
Firth, R., 116, 121
Fischer, H. Th., 97, 106, 118, 121
Flood cultivation, 79, 80, 81
Forde, D., 116, 121
Fortes, M., 15, 18, 19, 20, 36, 49, 50, 57,
    58, 59, 64, 69, 98, 125, 145, 161,
    162, 164, 194
Fostering, 132
Fox, R., 125, 160, 199, 220
Friedberg, (*see* Berthe, L., 101)
Friedman, J., 25, 45
Funerals, 96
FZD-MBS, 213

G

Game theory, 49
Ganda, 9

Giriama,
  childbirth payment, 207, 210
  elopement or arrangement, 213
  Giriamaland, western, 200, 201, 202
  marriage payments, 208, 211, 216
  Mijikenda, and, 199
  non-cattle, 205, 206
  uxorial payment, 200, 203, 204
Gisu, marriage, 19
Gluckman, M., 18, 45, 89, 91, 126, 160,
    198, 199, 219, 220
Gogo,
  bridewealth payments, 83
  cattle, 78, 84, 85, 87, 88, 91
  livestock, 82
  pastoral society, 82, 83
  stock and bridewealth, 70, 76
Goody, J., 4, 7, 8, 9, 10, 11, 12, 13, 15,
    20, 21, 45, 49, 50, 158, 160, 248, 249
  and Tambiah, S. J., 51, 52, 56, 63, 65,
    160
Goldschmidt, W., 11, 45
Gomm, R., 212, 213, 215, 216, 220
Go nyala, 165
Go ralala, 166, 168
Gray, R. F., 11, 45, 95, 121
Groom,
  affines, 77
  agnates of, 225
  Ashanti, 69
  bargaining, 49
  bridewealth, 70, 82, 83, 111
  clothes, cost of, 148
  delegation, 140
  dower, 4
  groomprice, 6
  groomwealth, 4, 112
  herd, surrender of, 84, 85
  house, 226
  household, 234, 235, 237, 240, 241,
    244
  kin, groom and bride, 77, 83, 224, 226
  marriage, cost of, 213
  meeting with bride, 223
  negotiations, bride and groom, 138,
    142

Groom (*contd*)
  not endowed, 231
  payments, 70, 71, 76
  pigs, provision of, 57, 62
  relationships, 149, 150
  Samburu, 87, 88
  status of, 236
  wedding expenses, 238
Gulliver, P. H., 70, 76, 84, 85, 90, 91

H

Hagen, 63, 65
Hajara, 156
Halla wahida, 140, 154
Haqq, 146
Haqq al-halib, 148
Harris, G., 129, 160
Harusi,
  prestige and, 213, 214, 216
Hegemony, 24
Heterosexual bonds,
  negotiability of, 186
Heterosexual unions, manipulation of, 185, 193, 194
Hicks, D., 97, 104, 105, 106, 109, 121
Hierarchy,
  Buna and, 101
  dowry and, 7-8
  exchange and, 21
  limited, 7
  lineages and, 23
  politico-residential groupings, 175
  relationship to egalitarianism, 28
  segmentary, 199
  status and marriage, 51
  structural, 191
  variability in nature of, 9
Hindess, B. and Hirst, P. Q., 22, 45
Homogeneity, 8
Howell, P. P., 76, 91
Hulwan, 144
Husband,
  agnates, 201
  allocation, 118
  animals, 141

  bridewealth, 71
  death, 133
  definition, 38
  descent group, 6
  household, 233
    wife's status in, 245
  jural rights, 20
  lineage, 112
  marriage alliance, 139
  marriage gift and rights, 110, 111
  mother, 246
  uxorial payment, 204
  wife,
    disgrace, 146
    liberating herself, 205
    "throws her off his back", 147
Hypergamy, 5, 8, 12, 13

I

'Iddat, 133
Indian society, 63
  alliance theorists and, 63
  variations in, 63
Incest law, 162
Indonesia,
  alliance and marriage exchanges, 119
  bridewealth, 95, 97
  hierarchization, 9
  institutions, 117
Inheritance, 11, 14
Insaf 146, 147
Insana, 109
Intermarriage, Chonyi and Giriama, 205
Ipono, 60, 62

J

Jacobs, A. H., 76, 77, 87, 91
Jarvie, I. C., 1, 45
Jibana, 203
Jie,
  actual and real bridewealth, 70, 77, 78, 84
  livestock and bridewealth, 83, 85
Jieland. 84, 85

Jural,
    analysis, 65, 161
    approach, 18, 19, 161, 162, 163, 194
    arrangements, 15, 17
    assumptions, 186
    designation, 187
    force, 20
    instrument, 18
    logic, orthodox approach, 36, 192
    rights, 62
    significance, 173
    state, 165, 174

K

Kachin analysis, 27, 28
Kai luneri, 62
Kamba group, 202
Kandyan Sinhalese and female inheritance, 12
Kafil, 140
Karimojong, 81, 84
Karimui, 60
Kauma group, 203
Kédang (see Prescriptive alliance), 98, 114, 115, 116, 117 120
Kennedy, R., 112, 113, 119, 121
Kenya, 80, 199, 218
Kem kng, 57, 58, 62
Kgatla, of Botswana, 13, 193
Kgotla, 191
Khuri, F., 154, 160
Kikuyu, 217, 218
Kiswa, 147, 148
Kng mbo, 53
Kola kng, 57
Kuimo ngoromen, 53
Kuper, A., 13, 18, 45, 161, 162, 166, 170, 175, 177, 194, 195
Kuper, H., 9, 45, 218, 220

L

La Fontaine, J. S., 19, 45, 129, 160
Lamaholot, 112-114
    land and patrilineal descent, 117
    resemblance to Kedang, 115
Lamphere, L., 15, 45
Langi, 64
"Large price", 100
Laughlin, C. D., 11, 46
Laws,
    Jewish and Islamic, 133
    Tswana, 163
Leach, E. R., 1, 2, 3, 8, 10, 12, 21, 28, 46, 51, 94, 116, 122, 125, 161, 164, 195, 198, 219, 220
Lesotho, 192
Levirate,
    bridewealth and, 179
    corroboration of marriage as, 126
    forms of secondary union, 15
Levi-Strauss, C., 26, 27, 28, 29, 30, 32, 36, 46, 125, 158, 160, 162, 164, 195
Lewis, I. M., 8, 14, 46, 126, 129, 160
Lewotobi, 114
Lineage,
    natal, 69
    theory, 164
Lineality,
    "enterprising" lineages, 29
    hierarchy, 23
    "strength", 11
Linear view, 164
Livestock, 83
Losika, 176
Luo,
    marriage payments, 199, 200, 205-209, 212, 214-217

M

Maasai, 77, 86, 87
MBD, 37
Macedonia, 5, 9, 13, 14, 38, 41, 221, 222
Madan, T., 12
Mae Enga, 64
Mahari, 215
Mahunda, 200, 214, 215
Mafisa, 169, 183
Maine, Sir H., 93, 98, 120

Mair, L. P., 11, 15, 16, 18
Malezi, 214, 215
Mam peng kng, 57
Mar, 127
Marebana, 160, 172
Maring, 55
Marikeri-ke mereko, 60
Marital home, 13
Marobo, 99
Marriage,
  affinity and, 19, 163, 177, 178
  agnatic right of passage, 105
  alienation, 95
  alliances, 101, 108, 116, 129
  Arab-Swahili system, 215
  bride's father, 62
  bridewealth, 54, 63, 90, 125, 141, 155
  "bundle of rights", 18
  children, 61, 93
  conjugal fund, 53
  consanguinity, 137
  corporate groups, 154
  consummation, 246
  Dassenetch, 87
  definition, 105
  descent groups, 104
  division of labour and, 25
  dowry, 41
  exchanges and strategy, 17, 93
  exogamy, 42
  FBD systems, 29
  formalities, 140-151
  forms of, 102, 103
  "game theory", 49
  harusi, 123
  implications of, 51
  intra-descent group, 16
  jural approach, 161
  jural potentiality, 174
  jural view of rights, 64
  kinship, 128, 134
    and affinity, 164
  land rights, 51
  legitimisation, 170
  lineage, 105, 109, 110
  "marriage by purchase", 27, 28, 30

Marxist discussion of prestations, 22
Mursi, 82, 89
Muslim, 215
negotiations, 77, 168, 174
Nuer, 89
patrilateral parallel cousin, 40, 156
payments, 3, 7, 10, 11, 16, 24, 35, 36,
    57, 65, 68, 86, 100, 118, 160, 162,
    165, 197, 198, 205-208
politics, 179
polygynous, 15
prescriptions, 117
prestations, (*see* prestations)
previous marriages, 72
product, division, 173
prohibited, 74, 127
"proper", 20
spinsterhood, 139
status, 152
structural functionalist system and,
    34
systems, 9, 12, 13
ties, 52
Timor, 97
two forms of, 6
within village, 113
Marxist and structuralist approaches, 3,
    21, 31, 34
  anthropology, 33
  perspectives, 22, 23
Matriarchy, 96
Matrilateral, 14, 15, 65, 82, 97, 115, 154,
    164, 176
Matrilineality, 5, 104, 108
  communities, 96
  descent groups, 69
  kin, 214
Matrilocality, 97
Matrimony,
  compensation, 106
  status of woman, 233
Matthews, Z. K., 165, 195
Mau-gatal, 103, 104
Mauss, M., 26, 33, 46, 95
Mayer, P., 188, 195
Meggitt, M. J., 64, 66

Meillassoux, C., 22, 23, 24, 25, 26, 32, 36, 45, 46
Mekgwa le melao ya setswana, 163
Melanesian societies, 64
Melpa,
   "analogue of dowry", 14
   bridewealth, 19, 49, 57, 58, 59, 65
   capital value, 56
   conjugal fund, 53, 54
   ideology of exchange, 38
   payments, differentiation, 218
   prestations, 50
   topo tiki, 61
   uxorilocality, 55, 56
Middelkoop, P., 109, 122
Mijikenda, 203, 210
   bridewealth, 43
   dowry, 40
   marriage and family types, 216
   non-Muslim Mijikenda peoples, 213
   payments, 6
   semantic logic of prestations, 37
   tribes comprising Mijikenda, 199
   uxorial and childbirth payments, 209, 215, 218
Miloha, 200
Mitchell, J. C., 18, 162
Mmelegi, 179
Moka, 56, 58, 60, 63, 65
Mokwele, 166, 168, 170, 182, 183, 184, 191
Molo, 108, 109
Monogamy, ideology of, 180, 181, 185
Mosadi, 165
Monothetic class, 68, 69
Muller, J. C., 21, 46
Murphy, R. F. and Kasdan, L., 164, 195
Murray, C., 19, 46, 162, 168, 192, 195
Mursi, 67
   bridewealth, 69, 70, 71, 73, 74, 75, 82, 83, 84, 87
   economy, 81, 85
   ethnography, 6, 35
   livestock, 88, 89
   patrilineal ideology, 16

prestations, strategic manipulation of, 39
stratification, 9
Mursi-Nuer-Gogo pattern, 90
Muslim Swahili,
   culture, 208
   status, 204

N

Naqatain was suwar, 155
Naqs al-haqq, 155
Nasab, 146, 154
Nash, J., 4, 46
Nasib, 146
Ndembu, 198
Ndzaum, 200
Needham, R., 1, 2, 3, 15, 26, 27, 30, 32, 46, 91, 95, 116, 122, 161, 195
Nelson, N., 218, 220
Ngada, 93, 95, 97, 98, 110, 112
Ngurario ram, 217, 218
Noemuti, 109
Nubility, 7, 42
Nuer,
   bridewealth, 72, 77, 82, 129
   cattle, 78, 79, 82, 83, 84, 85, 87, 88, 91
   corporations, 94, 159
   cultural cousins, 199
   exogamy, 157
   fishing, 81
   groom and wife's kin, 69
   marriage, 89, 126, 127, 158
   stockwealth and bridewealth, 70, 76
   Swazi, and, 9
   territorial arrangements, 42
   village residence, change of, 128
Nuerland, 83, 127, 158
Nyalo, 165
Nyalo ka bogadi, 191
Nyamwezi, 218
Nyatsi, 183
Nywombo, 200

O

"Omaha type" kinship terminology, 71

Onvlee, L., 95, 122
Ouwehand, C., 112, 114, 122
Overarching clans and sub-clans, 199
  schemes, 4

P

Papua New Guinea, 4, 49, 50, 51, 56, 57,
  59, 62, 64
Parallel cousin marriage, 155, 156, 157
Parallel cousins, matrilateral, 155
Parkin, D., 24, 29, 36, 37, 43, 197, 198,
  220
Pastoralism, 78, 84, 86, 158, 200
Patlo, 166, 167, 168, 181, 182, 183,
  184
Patriarchy, 96
Paradigms,
  analysis of bridewealth, 15
  approaches, three major, 35
  dowry, 11, 14
  Guro arrangements, 23
  highest precept of major, 32
  marriage payments, 4
  theoretical, 3
Patrifilial kin, 82
  inheritance, 55
Patrilateral, filiation, 97
Patrilineal systems,
  bridewealth in, 16, 96
  bridewealth cattle, 74
  children and mother, 100
  clans, 94, 114
  corporate households, 5
  descent, 69, 73, 74, 97, 98, 112
  dispersed, 199
  endogamy, 12
  father, 99, 115
  ideologies of, 16, 69, 76, 175
  limited range, 136
  lineages, 104
  scale of gradation, 108
Patrilocal residence, 6, 106
Patrimony, 99
Payment,
  childbirth, 217

dowry, 217
  rights, 18
Patrons and clients, 23, 178
Patriuxorilocal residence, 55
Patrivirilocal marriage, 175
  residence, 55
Pedi, 197,198
Penal presentation, 59
Peng pokla, 57
Penal kng, 53
Pesa keny, 200
Peters, E. L., 2, 35, 40, 42, 125, 153,
  154, 160, 164
Peters, S. M., 160
"People of the Saliva", 71
Petrović, A., 225, 249
Pitt-Rivers, J., 158, 160
Political economy, Melpa and Wiru, 52
Politico-administrative structure (Tshidi),
  189
Polyandry, adelphic, 12
Polygyny, 179, 181, 204
Polythetic class, 2, 68, 69
Pre-capitalist modes of production, 22,
  23
Prestations,
  alienation of, 28, 33
  alliance, 115
  alternative schedules, 104
  between families, 51
  children, 106
  complementary, 6
  complete set of, 110
  cycling from takers to givers, 100
  descent alliance and, 17
  dominant type of, 12
  due to elders, 23
  flows, two-way, 10
  forms of, various, 29, 109, 242
  formula of exchange, 27
  integral elements, 26
  "kind" of, 7
  lineage, husband's, 107
  marriage, 16, 21, 22, 31, 32, 35, 36,
    38, 39, 40, 41, 42, 43, 96, 99, 103,
    105, 111, 112, 120, 239, 248

Prestations, (*contd*)
  mating and, 37
  prime and contingent, 50, 57, 59, 62, 64
  rights, and, 19
  systematic relationship, 24
  sexual access, 170
  total, 95, 96
Primogeniture, 23
Prins, A. H. J., 213, 220
Procreative capacity, woman, 50, 69, 248
Productivity/reproductivity, 5, 6
Property,
  conjugal, division of, 173
  dowry and devolution of, 248
  relations, 7, 8
  retention of, 12
  women, or, 21
  women implicated in, 153

Q

"Quantum of rights" hypothesis, 21, 69
Qadamak, 145

R

Rabai group, 203
Radcliffe-Brown, A. R., 10, 13, 18, 46, 93, 197, 218
Rain cultivation, 79, 80
Rappaport, R., 55, 66
Reciprocal material exchanges, 63
Reproductive capacity, 5, 6
Rheubottom, D. B., 5, 9, 222, 249
Ribe group, 203
Rigby, P., 76, 82, 92
Rights, 18
  filiation, 205
  genetricial, 211
  of sexual access, 170, 171
  uxorial, 212, 218
  uxorial and genetricial, 172, 188, 200
Ritual slaughters, 87
Rivers, W. H. R., 93, 116, 117, 122

Riviere, P. G., 2, 47, 198
Roberts, S. A., 17, 18, 46, 47, 161, 179, 193
Rousseau, J. J., 95, 122

S

Sacrificial alienations, 30
Ṣaḥiba (part of bridewealth), 144, 145, 146, 147
Sahlins, M., 10, 21, 34, 47, 96
Samburu, 70, 77, 86, 87, 88
Sansom, B., 15, 50, 66, 197
Saussure, F. de, 39
  and Mauss, M., 30
Schapera, I., 13, 47, 169, 171, 175, 176, 177
Schneider, D. M., 162, 195
Schulte Nordholt, H. G., 97, 101, 106, 107, 108, 109, 110, 122
Segmentary lineage model, 16
Segmentation, 222
  perpetual and drift, 199
Serotwana (arable field), 13
Sexual capacity, 50
Sexuality, 245, 246
Shart ha kaif sharta umm ha (female contract), 151
Siaq (animals), 140, 141, 142, 146, 147
Siblings, 5, 8, 15, 229, 231
Simmel, G., 208, 220
Singer, A., 15, 47, 181, 196
Skopska Crna Gora, 5, 13, 249
Smanaf (vital force), 109, 110
Socio-cultural constitution, 40
Socio-cultural system, 39, 44
  order, 38
  rules, 16
  variations, 19
Socio-economic equality, 8
  complexes, 8
Socio-political categories, 184
Solor archipelago, 98
Sororal polygyny, 179
  marriage, 132, 144
Sorites paradox, 166

Sorority, 15, 126, 132, 179
Sotho, 19, 192
South Asia, 4, 12, 51
  groomwealth in, 4
  women's property rights, 51
South East Asia, 53, 55, 59
Southern Bantu speaking peoples, 167
Southwestern Ethiopia, 67
Southwold, M., 19
Spencer, P., 76, 86, 88, 92
Spinsterhood, 139
Spiro, M., 4, 5, 6, 7, 10, 47
Straten, L. B. van, 94
Stockwealth and bridewealth, 76
Strathern, A. J., 6, 10, 14, 19, 30, 39, 49,
  58, 59, 60, 65, 66
Strathern, M., 49, 58, 59, 66
Structural differences, 8
  approaches, 30, 31
  arrangements, 15
Structural functionalism, 3
  discourse on marriage, 11
  methodology of, 8, 15, 30, 31
  overarching schemes, 4
  perspectives, 26
Suitors, 223, 238
Suwar al-halib (silver bracelets of the
  milk), 148
Swahili, 204, 205, 210
Swazi (royals), 41

T

Tabadul, 156
Talab, 139
Tallensi, 19
Taluai yorokokai, 61
Tambiah, S. J., 4, 11, 12, 47, 49, 50, 51,
  53
Tanzania, 82, 90
Tardits, C., 28, 30, 47
Taxonomy, 10
Te, 64
Temboki kng, 57
Terray, E., 22, 23, 47
Tetun, 95, 105

Caraubalo Princedom, 104
  Eastern 98, 104, 106
  Eastern and Western, 97, 104
Tha'r, 155
Tingine (or tingini), 61
Tingine kai, 61
Tiv, 208
Tonga, 19
Topo tiki, 60
Transhumance, 79
  Pastoralists, 129
Transmission of material property, 63
"Tribal bulls", 128
Trousseau, 227, 228, 229, 231, 232, 233,
  234, 236, 239, 243
Tshidi, 13, 17, 19, 29, 38, 39, 41, 163
  conjugal arrangements, 178
  ethnography, 192, 193, 194
  marriage and affinity, 163, 164, 165,
    167, 168, 169, 170, 171, 173, 174,
    175, 176, 177
  parental bond, 190
  politics, 179, 180, 181, 184
  society, 185, 186, 188
Tswana, 13, 14, 18, 161, 175, 193
Tuareg, 164
Turkana, 70, 77, 78, 84, 85, 86
Turner, T., 31, 47
Turton, D., 2, 6, 47, 80, 89, 92

U

Ugogo, 83
Uhala, 213, 214
Unilineal affiliation, 42
  alliance, 99
  corporations, 31
  descent groups, 15, 50, 99, 110, 112,
    116, 118, 230
  ideology of, 118
  institutions, 98
  peoples, 93
  principles, 116
  rules, 93, 98
  ties, 40
Utilitarian methodologies, 11

Utilitarian methodologies (*contd*)
  positions, 11
Uxorial childbirth payments, 212, 213,
    215, 217, 219
  payments, 201, 202, 203, 204, 206,
    208, 209, 210, 211, 213, 214, 215,
    216
  residence, 6, 37, 51, 56, 63, 97, 109,
    114
  transfer, 217
Uxorilocal marriage, 56, 97, 108
  sons-in-law, 56

V

van Velsen, J., 19, 47
Vatter, E., 112, 114, 122
Virginity, 142, 227
Virilocal pattern, 101
  residence, 15, 55, 97, 100, 118
  society, 5
Vroklage, B. A. G., 97, 106, 122

W

Wagner, R., 60, 66
Wailolong, 115, 116, 117
Walker, J. M., 18, 47
Wealth, 12
Weber, Max, 98, 122
Webster, D., 193, 195
Weddings, 148, 222, 223
  ceremony, 211, 226
  chest, 238
  feast and festivities, 226, 227, 240, 248
  gifts, 87, 240
Wet nurse, 132
Wife-givers, 71
Wifely status, 238
Wilken, G. A., 96, 97, 122
Wiru,
  "analogue of dowry", 14
  bridewealth, 19, 54, 59-63, 65
  childwealth, 59

conjugal fund, 53, 55
dowry, 40
economy, 60, 64
"game theory", 49
prestations, 38, 50-52, 57
Wittgenstein, L., 15, 47, 68
Wives,
  adultery, 146
  availability, 22
  bidding and manumission, 205, 210
  bridewealth, 62
  children, 144, 150, 179, 200, 204
  cross-cousin unions, 147
  definitions, 38
  givers and takers, 37, 99, 100, 102,
    103, 106
  lineage, 110
  marriage and alliance exchanges, 109,
    119
  marriage gifts, none, 105
  payments, 70, 82, 118
  prestations, 24
  sources of, 27
  uxorial rights and childbirth, 210, 234
  wedding, 148
Women,
  exchange of, 22, 27, 29, 69
  immediate reciprocity, 21
  indirect flow of, 36
  recruitment to segment, 25
  terminology associated with, 38
"Work teams", 24, 25

Y

Yalman, N., 12, 47, 51
Yangi, 62
"Young donkey", 133
Yakö, 218

Z

Zuo a modain, 71, 72, 74, 75
Zulu, the, 199